Media Law in Israel

Media Law in Israel

Ido Baum

This book was originally published as a monograph in the International Encyclopaedia of Laws/Media Law.

General Editor: Roger Blanpain
Associate General Editor: Michele Colucci
Volume Editor: Kurt Deketelaere
Associate Volume Editor: Eva Lievens

Wolters Kluwer
Law & Business

Published by:
Kluwer Law International
PO Box 316
2400 AH Alphen aan den Rijn
The Netherlands
Website: www.kluwerlaw.com

Sold and distributed in North, Central and South America by:
Aspen Publishers, Inc.
7201 McKinney Circle
Frederick, MD 21704
United States of America
Email: customer.service@aspenpublishers.com

Sold and distributed in all other countries by:
Turpin Distribution Services Ltd.
Stratton Business Park
Pegasus Drive, Biggleswade
Bedfordshire SG18 8TQ
United Kingdom
Email: kluwerlaw@turpin-distribution.com

Printed on acid-free paper

ISBN 978-90-411-5179-7

This title is available on www.kluwerlawonline.com

Printed and Bound by CPI Group (UK) Ltd, Croydon, CR0 4YY.

The Author

Dr (jur.) Ido Baum is associate professor of law at the Haim Striks School of Law in the College of Management-Academic Studies (COLM), Israel, where he also holds the position of Director of the Integrated Study Programmes. He teaches and researches in the fields of procedural law, economic analysis of law, media law, securities and corporate governance. Dr Baum is a fellow at the Media and Law Center at Bar Ilan University, Israel.

In 2007 Dr Baum obtained his doctoral degree from the Graduate College Law & Economics at Hamburg University, Germany, *summa cum laude*. He wrote his dissertation on 'Economic Analysis of Professional Testimonial Privileges' and it was subsequently published by Gabler Publishing. Dr Baum was a visiting scholar at Boalt Hall School of law, UC Berkeley, during the spring term 2006 and at the University of Tilburg Law and Economics Center (Tilec) during the spring term 2012. In 2013 he served as a judge in the Monroe Price International Moot Court Competition on Media Law and Policy in Oxford University.

Dr Baum obtained his bachelor and master degrees in law from Tel Aviv University, Israel, and a European Master in law and economics (EMLE), *cum laude*, for which he was also awarded the best thesis prize for his work on 'The Influence of Concentration of Ownership in the Media Business on Information Delivered to Consumer'.

Additionally, Dr Baum has diverse practical legal and media experience. Before joining the Haim Striks School of Law he worked as an attorney for the Claims Resolution Tribunal on Dormant World War II Era Swiss Bank Accounts in Zurich, Switzerland. Prior to embarking on an academic career, he served as the spokesperson of the Israeli Ministry of Justice and as the assistant of the Israeli Attorney General for civil and administrative law affairs. In the latter position he was in charge, *inter alia*, of coordinating the government's regulatory policy on media and telecommunications.

In addition to his academic career, Dr Baum is a prominent journalist and columnist in Israel writing for 'Haaretz-TheMarker', one of the country's most influential newspapers. He is the legal commentator of the newspaper in which he has written countless pieces on legal and economic current affairs. He is often invited to speak in professional media and legal forums as well as on television and radio programmes. During his earlier journalistic career he served as the military

The Author

correspondent of the Israeli Defense Force Radio; editor and anchor of the radio's newscasts; news editor of Haaretz newspaper; and editor at the news corporation of the commercial television Channel 2.

Foreword

I wish to express my gratitude to the legal advisor of the Ministry of Communications Dana Neufeld, and her predecessor Noga Rubinstein, as well as to Michael Birnhack, for their comments on earlier drafts of this monograph. Additional thanks go to the series editor Peggy Valcke and to an anonymous referee for their important observations and guidance. For sharing their thoughts the author also thanks Tamir Afori and Didi Lachman-Messer. Shany Braun provided excellent research assistance in the initial phases of collecting the material for this monograph. The author is grateful for research grants from the Research Foundation of the Haim Striks School of Law.

Last but not least, I thank my loved ones, Romy and Yotam, for their patience and their impatience.

Ido Baum,
May 2013, Tel Aviv

Foreword

Table of Contents

Table of Contents

List of Abbreviations

AG	Attorney General
ARBP	the Administration for Regulating Broadcasts to the Public
BCC	Broadcast Coordination Committee
BCL Rules	The Communications (Telecommunications and Broadcasts) (Broadcast Licensee) Rules 1987 (the 'BCL Rules')
CA	civil appeal
CBF	Commercial Broadcast Franchise
CBL	Cable Broadcast License
CEC	Central Elections Committee
CommAD	The Communications (Telecommunications and Broadcasting) (Advertisements, Public Service Announcements and Sponsorship Announcements in Designated Channels) Rules, 2004
Communications Law	The Communications (Telecommunications and Broadcasts) Law, 1982
Cr. A.	Criminal Appeal
CRF	Commercial Radio Franchise
CRL	Commercial Radio License
CSBC	Cable and Satellite Broadcasting Council
DTT	Digital Terrestrial Television
ETV	Educational Television
GLZ	Galei Zahal, the Army Radio Station

List of Abbreviations

GPO	Government Press Office
HCJ	High Court of Justice
IBA	Israeli Broadcasting Authority
IBA Law	The Broadcasting Authority Law, 1965
IBARadA Rules	The IBA (Radio Advertisements and Announcements) Rules 1993
KTV	Knesset Television Channel
KTV Law	Television Broadcasts from the Knesset Law, 2003
LCA	Leave of Civil Appeal
LCri. A.	Leave of Criminal Appeal
MOC	Ministry of Communications
NIS	New Israeli Shekel (the Israeli currency)
PSA	Public Service Announcement
SAC	Second Authority Council
SAAD Rules	The SATR (Integrating Advertisements in Television Broadcasts) Rules 1992
SAERAD Rules	The SATR (Ethics in Radio Advertisements) Rules 1999
SAEthAD Rules	The SATR (Ethics in Television Advertisements) Rules 1994
SAEthic Rules	The SATR (Ethics in Television and Radio Broadcasts) Rules 1994
SAFraB Rules	The SATR (Television Broadcasts by a Franchise Holder) Rules 2009
SAPFra Rules	The SATR (Procedures for Granting a Television CBF) Rules 1992
SAPRL Rules	The SATR (Procedure for Granting a Radio Broadcasting License) 2006.
SAPTVL Rules	The SATR (Procedure and Conditions for Granting a Television Broadcast License) Rules 2011
SARaAD Rules	The SATR (Integrating Advertisements and Commercial References in Radio Broadcasts) Rules 1999

SARaF Rules	The SATR (Radio Broadcasts by a Franchise Holder) Rules 1999
SATak Rules	The SATR (Taking of Broadcast Time) Rules 2007
SaRaL Rules	The SATR (Radio Broadcasts by a License Holder) Rules 2006
SASpon Rules	The SATR (Sponsorships) Rules 2009
SATR	Second Authority for Television and Radio
SATRL	Second Authority for Television and Radio Law, 1990
SBL	Satellite Broadcast License
SC	Supreme Court

List of Abbreviations

General Introduction

§1. General Background of the Country

I. Political and Legal System of the Country

1. Israel was founded in 1948 as a parliamentary democracy. Its democratic foundations lie on the principle of separation of powers. The head of state is the President elected by the Knesset (the Israeli parliament) for a seven year term. The president's functions are mostly ceremonial and symbolic.[1]

2. The legislative branch, the Knesset, consists of 120 members. The Knesset is elected for a term of four years by secret ballot in national, direct, equal and proportional elections. Each citizen may cast a vote in favour of a party representing an electoral list of candidates. Each electoral list receives the number of Knesset members in proportion to the votes cast for it, subject to the condition that the list receives at least 2% of the total votes cast. Every citizen of 18 years of age or older has the right to vote; every citizen aged 21 years or older may be elected as a member of the Knesset. The minimum age for election as Prime Minister is 30.[2]

3. Following elections to the Knesset, the President consults with the various political parties represented in the elected Knesset and determines the leader of which party is most likely to raise the support of a majority of the 120 members of the Knesset in his government. The President then asks the leader of that party to form a government. The government must win a vote of confidence in the Knesset. It then serves until the next Knesset elections that are held after approximately four years unless it falls before that time by a vote of no-confidence. Early elections for a new Knesset without the fall of the government may be effected by passing a law disbanding the Knesset, which requires a vote of a majority of all Knesset members.

4. In addition, if the Prime Minister is in the opinion that the government is unable to govern he or she can appeal to the President to order the disbanding of the Knesset and the holding of new elections.

1. This chapter draws on Suzie Navot, *The Constitutional Law of Israel* (Kluwer-Wolters 2007) (hereinafter – Navot).
2. See generally *ibid.*, 99–108.

5. The executive branch is headed by the government. As no Israeli party has ever achieved a majority in the Knesset, the government has always been a coalition government. The government draws its powers from the Basic Law: The Government. The number of ministers and governmental ministries varies as a result of political coalition needs.

6. The Judiciary consists of a central system of courts dealing with civil, criminal and administrative matters. In addition there are specialized family courts, labour courts and a separate system of religious courts for the various religious communities. The regular court system is three-tiered and consists of Magistrate courts, District courts, and the Supreme Court. The Supreme Court also sits as the High Court of Justice. The Supreme Courts consists of fifteen Justices and in most cases sits in panels of three. In cases of unique importance the panel is expanded to larger odd numbers.

7. The Israeli legal system is considered to be a 'mixed' system combining sources derived from the English common law and the civil law system of continental Europe, along with influences of Jewish, Moslem and other systems of law. This multiplicity has historic roots. Before the First World War, the geographical territory that is now the State of Israel was part of the Ottoman Empire. Remnants of the continental legal order which characterized the Ottoman Empire remain in Israeli law.[3] The territory was later overtaken by the British Mandate which infused colonial common law into the region. Following the end of the British Mandate over Palestine on 14 May 1948 and the establishment of the State of Israel, the pre-existing legal structure was adopted into Israeli law and gradually revised, amended, replaced or repealed. While Ottoman law has been almost entirely replaced, British mandatory law is still a significant part of the Israeli legal system, especially with regards to ordinances designed to regulate security affairs and public order. The Knesset in its legislation and the courts in their interpretation of the law have referred to multiple sources of law including Jewish law, continental law, the common law of England, Canada and the United States, etc.

8. Israel lacks a formal constitution in the sense of having drafted and enshrined one written, unified document. The Declaration of Independence of 14 May 1948 expressly stated that the permanent and elected governmental organs of the State would be established under a constitution. However, due to an ongoing debate during the formative years on whether Israel is ripe for framing a constitutional document, a parliamentary compromise known as the 'Harari Resolution' has been reached. The resolution states that a constitution would be adopted piecemeal in a series of Basic Laws which will eventually be unified into one document.[4]

---

3. Another continental legal influence was introduced into the Israeli legal system by German-Jewish jurists that fled Nazi Germany and were involved in the formation of Israeli law during the formative years of the legal system.
4. Navot, *supra* n. 1, at 35.

9. To date, eleven Basic Laws have been adopted: The Knesset, The President, The Government, The Army, The State Economy, State Lands, Jerusalem the Capital of Israel, The Judiciary, The State Comptroller, Freedom of Occupation, and Human Dignity and Liberty.

10. The difficulty in drafting the constitutional documents is exemplified by the last two Basic Laws - Basic Law: Freedom of Occupation and Basic Law: Human Dignity and Liberty - that were adopted in 1992. The first was replaced in 1994 and the latter was amended on that year. These laws were the first constitutional laws directly concerned with the protection of human rights.

11. In what is often referred to as 'The Constitutional Revolution', the Supreme Court has held that under these Basic Laws courts have the authority to strike down or declare invalid ordinary laws or parts thereof which are in violation of those constitutional principles that are protected by the Basic Laws.[5]

II. Geography and Population

12. Israel is a small country on the western edge of the Asian continent. It is part of the region known as the Middle East. The state measures 424 km from north to south and at its widest point 114 km from east to west but only 15 km at the narrowest point.

13. Israel is surrounded by Arab states. Israel's southern border stretches along the Sinai Peninsula which is under Egyptian sovereignty and continues north to encompass the Gaza Strip which is governed by the Palestinian Authority (although it is controlled de facto by the Hamas movement) following Israel's withdrawal from this territory in 2005. The most southern point of Israel is the resort and port city of Eilat which lies on the northern edge of the Red Sea and borders with Egypt in the west and with Jordan in the east. The Jordan River runs from the north of Israel to the Dead Sea and acts as a natural barrier along most of Israel's eastern border with Jordan. The Dead Sea is divided between the two countries. The so-called West Bank (also known in Israel as Judea and Samaria) is an area lying at the middle of the country and bordering with Jordan. The West Bank was occupied by Israel in the 'Six Day War' in 1967. The western border of this area is delineated by the so-called 'Green Line' and parts thereof are lined by the 'The Fence' which is a wall-like security barrier designed to prevent unsupervised movement of Palestinians from the West Bank to Israel. Parts of the West Bank are currently governed by the Palestinian Authority (the Fatah movement) while other parts are controlled by the Israeli army and include Jewish Settlements in various sizes including cities such as Ariel. Israel's north borders with Lebanon and the Golan Heights plateau which was occupied from Syria in 1967 and annexed by Israel lies

5. CA 6821/93 *Bank Mizrachi v. Migdal* 49(4) PD 221 [1995]. Since 1995 approximately ten laws have been declared to be unconstitutional.

at the north-eastern part of the country and borders with Syria. The Mediterranean Sea is Israel natural border to the west with a coastline of more than 200 km.

14. Israel's capital is the city of Jerusalem, which lies at the centre of the country, as declared by Article 1 Basic Law: Jerusalem the Capital of Israel. The eastern part of Jerusalem is part of the West Bank but was annexed after its occupation in 1967. Basic Law: Jerusalem the Capital of Israel states that the capital is the 'unified' city. Jerusalem, along with the coastal metropolitan area of Tel Aviv and the coastal port city Haifa, are Israel's largest cities.

15. The north of Israel provides fruitful ground for agriculture. The south of the country is dominated by the Negev desert. Israel enjoys a warm climate year round but has low precipitation and therefore it is increasingly reliant on desalination plants for its drinking, industrial and agricultural water supply.

16. The statistical data by the Israel Central Bureau of Statistics (www.cbs.gov.il) regarding the population of Israel includes annexed East Jerusalem, the Golan Heights, and the settlements in the West Bank but excludes the rest of the population in the West Bank and Gaza Strip. In 2012 the population of Israel numbered 7.881 million according to estimates based on a 2008 census. The Jewish population numbered approximately 5.931 million residents (75.3% of the total population); the Arab population numbered approximately 1.623 million residents (20.6%); immigrants and their offspring who are not registered as Jews in the Ministry of the Interior account for 327,000 (4.1%).

17. Most of the population is located in the metropolitan areas and a minority lives in rural areas, including in 'Kibbutzim', a unique semi-socialist form of agricultural settlements.

18. Before 1948, most of the Jewish immigration to Palestine stemmed from European countries. During its early years, Israel's demographic growth relied heavily on Jewish immigration from a variety of countries, most notably from North Africa, Yemen, Iraq and Iran. However, the majority of the current population is native born. Israel does have a dominant minority of Russian speaking Jews and some non-Jews as a result of several immigration waves from the former-Soviet countries during 1989–2006. The Russian speaking population is estimated at 1.14 Million residents.[6] In addition, a significant portion of the Jewish population in Ethiopia has immigrated to Israel and forms another small ethnic Jewish minority. The Ethiopian Jews were estimated at approximately 120,000 in 2009.[7]

---

6. Oz Almog & Igor Yevdossin, *An Estimate of the Russian Speaking Population* (2008) at: http://www.peopleil.org/details.aspx?itemID=7577&index=26&searchMode=1. Most of this population now speaks Hebrew very well, especially the younger generation of Jews originating from former Soviet countries.
7. According to the Israeli Association for Ethiopian Jews, in 2009 about two third of Ethiopian Jews were immigrants and only 40,000 were native-Israeli descendants. Data available at: http://www.iaej.co.il/newsite/.

19. The Arab minority is comprised mostly of Moslem Arabs, descendants of the Arab-Palestinian population that resided in the geographical area of Palestine before the establishment of Israel. Approximately 10% of the Arab population is Christian Arabs and another 10% is Druze. A small group of Moslem Arabs (about 110,000) are Bedouin tribes located in the north and in the south of Israel and undergoing a government imposed transition from a nomadic way of life to permanent residence in designated towns.

III. Social and Cultural Values

20. Israel is a multicultural and multi-ethnic society. Since the 1980s Israel is undergoing a transition from a state sanctioned social melting pot policy that characterized its formative years to a policy recognizing social, ethnic and cultural pluralism. In spite of its now diminishing melting pot policy (or perhaps as a backlash against this policy) Israeli society remains deeply divided. There are six social and cultural divides that characterize the Israeli social landscape:

- *The national divide between Jews and Arabs.* This conflict stems from the fact that Israel defines itself as the 'State of the Jewish People', according to the Declaration of Independence, which also guarantees equal rights without discrimination due to 'religion, race or sex'. The Declaration of Independence is not a legally binding document. However, in Basic Law: Human Dignity and Freedom Israel is subsequently defined as a 'Jewish Democratic' state. The Arab minority enjoys de jure equal rights. De facto, the Arab minority population lags significantly behind the Jewish population in average income, education, representation in the civil service, investment in infrastructure, access to metropolitan areas, etc.
- *The religious divide.* Approximately one fifth of the Jewish population in Israel is religious or Orthodox. Within the secular population almost half of the Jews define themselves as 'traditional' which means they selectively observe religious precepts. Most orthodox Jews tend to reside in secluded Orthodox neighbourhoods or cities and they are absolved from the mandatory army service and receive state financed stipends for religious studies. The increasing numbers of Orthodox Jews enjoying this status generates criticism among secular Jewish population. In addition, personal status matters of Jews in Israel are governed my Jewish laws and by Orthodox Rabbinical institutions. The state refuses to recognize civil marriages conducted in Israel (although civil marriages conducted abroad are recognized. Another manifestation of the religious divide is the Labour and Rest Hours Law 1951 which forbids opening most businesses from the beginning of 'Shabbat' (which starts on Friday evening) until it ends (on Saturday evening). Thus municipal public transportation in Israel such as busses and trains ceases on *Shabbat*. With respect to broadcasts, in 1969 the HCJ overturned a government decision and allowed the IBA to broadcast on *Shabbat* in a

ruling that is considered to this day a secular victory over religious coercion.[8] Tension exists not only between secular and religious but also within the religious Jewish groups where Orthodox Jews dominate state institutions and Conservative and Reform Jews attempt to challenge the Orthodox hegemony.

- *The ethnic divide.* Israeli-Jewish society is characterized by persisting tension between Jews originating from European and western countries ('Ashkenazi') and Jews originating from Arab countries ('Mizrachi' or 'Sephardic'), most of whom immigrated to Israel after its foundation. The Ashkenazi Jews were the hegemonic group in the formative years of the state imposing a melting pot policy in which an 'Israeli' set of ideological and cultural components most of which stemming from Western culture and values were imposed on the Mizrachi Jews.
- *The political-ideological divide.* Israeli population is deeply divided between right-wing hawkish political views and left wing dovish views. The divide manifests itself in the position taken with respect to the occupied territories, with the right wing viewing the West Bank as an integral part of Israel and the left wing advocating withdrawal as a first step towards reconciliation between Israel and the Palestinians.
- *The socio-economic divide.* According to data collected by the OECD and published in 2011, Israel has a higher than average level of inequality in income with an increasing trend which is unique in that the real incomes of those at the bottom of the income ladder actually fell compared with the mid-1980s.[9] Economic inequality persists and increases as lower income households tend to reside in the peripheral areas of Israel with lesser access to quality education and health facilities; limited job market opportunities; distanced welfare services; inefficient public transport connectivity with the metropolitan business centres of the country, etc.
- *The native-immigrant divide.* Following the large immigration waves to Israel from former Soviet countries and from Ethiopia, more than a million immigrants

---

8. HCJ 281/69 *Adi Kaplan v. The Prime Minister* 23(2) PD 394 [1969]; HCJ 1514/01 *Gur-Arye v. The SATR* 55(4) PD 267 [2001] reiterates that freedom of speech outweighs the offence to religious feelings unless there is near certainty of severe harm. In this case the court acknowledged that broadcasts on religious days such as *Shabbat* (Saturday) offend religious feelings but the court maintained that this offence does not shatter the foundations of religious tolerance in Israel and that in a democratic society a certain measure of offence to religious feelings must be tolerated. The HCJ denied the petition of religious Jews recorded for a television programme on a weekday to ban the broadcast of the programme on *Shabbat*. In another recent example, following the same moderate approach, the Jerusalem District Court rejected a class action lawsuit against 'The Big Brother' cable channel (a channel following a group of people living together in a 24-hour camera monitored house), in which the representative plaintiff asserted that religious feelings were injured when the tenants of the house discussed the possibility of taking a bible to the restroom. Class Action (Jerusalem Dist. Ct.) 50876-02-11 *Erez v. Reshet Broadcasting Ltd.* (16.10.2012). Note that the protection of religious feelings and freedom of religion are constitutional rights according to the SC but they have no grounding in any Basic Law. See Navot, *supra* n. 1, at 211.
9. Israel and Japan were the only countries with a drop in the real income of the lower echelon. In the average OECD country, an individual on the highest income level earned nine times more than one on the lowest in 2011, whereas the Israeli top echelon earners earned 14 times more than the lowest echelon earners. See: *An Overview of Growing Income Inequalities in OECD Countries: Main Findings* 22 (2011) available at http://www.oecd.org/dataoecd/40/12/49170449.pdf.

either do not speak the native Hebrew language or belong to communities that share a culture, heritage and values which differ from that of the surrounding native-Israeli society. Due to the disintegration of the melting pot policy, more pluralistic approach by the state and protectionism by political parties representing some of the immigrants, they were able to develop sub-cultures within Israeli society.

21. National security issues have always captured a prominent role in the Israeli socio-political agenda as well as in the regulation of the media. Since its inception Israel survived nine armed conflicts (1948 War of Independence, 1956 Suez War, 1967 Six Day War, 1969 War of Attrition, 1973 Yom Kippur War, 1982 The Lebanon War, 2000 Gulf War, 2006 The Second Lebanon War, and the 2008 Gaza War) and two Palestinian uprisings. Israel maintains a peace agreements with Egypt (1979) and Jordan (1994) although the relationship with the former is tense due to the rising power of the Islamic movement following the overthrow of the President Hosni Mubarak in 2011.

§2. THE MEDIA LANDSCAPE

I. Overview of Media Markets and Main Actors

A. Introduction

22. The Israeli media market evolved from a relatively monolithic structure in the early years of the state to a vibrant and competitive market.[10]

23. The media market in Israel encompasses a large Jewish Hebrew speaking population which is served by the major media corporations. In addition, Arab-Israeli population which accounts for approximately one fifth of Israeli population is served by the mainstream media but an independent Arab language media market exists as well, in parallel to the Hebrew mainstream media market and with relatively few ties to the mainstream Hebrew media organizations. The Russian language speaking population which numbers more than one million people (although most of which speak Hebrew fluently) is another media market, which is catered for by Russian language Israeli media, some of which are tied to Israeli media conglomerates, but is also served by Russian language satellite channels.

24. Israeli media consumers are characterized by a heightened demand for news, which is reflected by relatively high ratings for television news programmes, high readership for newspapers and high attendance to internet news portals. Accordingly, significant regulatory efforts are directed particularly at the regulation of news and current affairs content.

10. Dan Caspi, *Israel: Media System*, in *International Encyclopedia of Communications* (Blackwell, update 21 Jun. 2010).

B. Broadcasting

25. The main public television broadcaster is the IBA. The IBA's main television channel is 'Channel 1' which broadcasts news, current affairs, films, drama, culture, arts and heritage programmes. The IBA also broadcasts 'Channel 33' which is carried only by satellite and cable multichannel television providers. The IBA television channels are financed by a levy and revenues from sponsorships and Public Service Announcements ('PSA') but only IBA radio channels may broadcast advertisements.

26. Another public broadcaster is the Educational Television ('ETV') which broadcasts its own channel ('Channel 23') on multichannel television platforms. Additionally, it has time slots allocated for its broadcasts on the commercial television channel, Channel 2 (but not on the second commercial channel, Channel 10) and on Channel 1. The ETV is a department of the Ministry of Education and relies on the ministry for its budget but it also sells advertisements on its allotted time in the commercial channels and sells sponsorships on its allotted time in Channel 1.

27. The Knesset Channel ('KTV') is carried by multichannel television platforms on Channel 99. It broadcasts the hearings of the Knesset and current affairs programmes. The KTV is entirely funded by the budget of the Knesset.

28. All public channels are part of a free bundle of channels transmitted by a DTT distribution system known as 'Idan Plus' that may be viewed by purchasing a DTT receiver. Channel 1 is also broadcasted terrestrially and some of its programmes are also broadcasted over the internet.

29. There are two commercial broadcast channels financed by advertisements. The first commercial channel, known as 'Channel 2' started its broadcasts in 1993. Channel 2 is currently operated by two private franchisees ('Reshet' and 'Keshet') dividing and rotating the broadcasting weekdays, with Saturdays alternating in each rotation. Channel 2 broadcasts a variety of programmes, some of which are obligated by quotas (see *infra* in part III, Chapter 2 and in Chapter 3 at §2).

30. The broadcasting of news by the commercial channels is uniquely regulated. Channel 2's two franchisees hold jointly a statutory subsidiary news corporation. The franchisees are obliged to finance the news corporation but its broadcasts are heavily regulated by the SATR, which has representatives in the news corporation's board of directors and appoints the chairperson of the board, in order to guarantee the news corporation's independence from the interests of the channel's owners (see *infra* part III, Chapter 3 at §1 and part IV).

31. The second commercial channel, 'Channel 10', started its broadcasts in 2002 and was conceived in order to promote competition in the market for commercial television advertisements and to promote pluralism in broadcasts. Channel 10 is operated by a single franchisee and also operates a news company according to a statutory framework similar to Channel 2.

32. Both commercial channels are part of the free DTT bundle and are also carried by the multichannel television providers. Channel 2 was broadcasted terrestrially while channel 10 was not but the terrestrial broadcasts of Channel 2 has been phased out and replaced by the DTT system. Some broadcast of the commercial channels is available in the internet and the news corporation of Channel 2 operates an independent CNN-style internet news channel.

33. There are two private competitors in the market for multichannel television infrastructure services for subscribers, but each has a monopoly on a type of platform.

34. Cable television is monopolized by the cable television company known as 'HOT' (HOT Cable Communications Systems Ltd.).[11] HOT is controlled by Kol Holdings Ltd, which is dominated by French businessman Patrick Derhy. HOT was a public company until 2012 and approximately a quarter of its shares were traded in the Tel Aviv Stock Exchange. In 2012 its public shares were re-acquired by Derhy and it became a private company.

35. Direct Satellite Broadcasting (DBS) is monopolized by the corporation known as 'YES' (DBS Satellite Services (1998) Ltd), which is a subsidiary corporation of 'Bezeq' (49.78%) and Eurocom DBS (50.22%). Bezeq is the former state owned monopoly and now privatized telecommunications company.

36. Both multichannel platforms offer their subscribers bundles of local and foreign channels including news, sports, dramas, arts and culture, music, heritage and history, foreign channels, etc. Both operators also offer interactive services including pay-per-view and the possibility to record programmes.

37. The competition between the two platforms is highly regulated. For example, HOT is allowed to offer subscribers a 'triple play' deal that includes cable television, landline telephony and internet connection infrastructure, whereas YES was prohibited from offering an identical triple play deal due to the fact that it is held by a telephony company with a strong market position.

38. According to the CSBC Annual Report 2010 HOT had slightly more than 900,000 subscribers while YES had slightly less than 600,000.

---

11. Following the abolishment of the original regional distribution of cable television broadcasters the firms were allowed to merge into a single entity. This led to the establishment of HOT in 2003. The reason for allowing the merger was to enable the merged cable company to offer telephony and internet services on its cable infrastructure, which is the only competing infrastructure vis-à-vis the telecommunications conglomerate Bezeq-YES which owns the only landline telephony network. See Eytan Gilboa, *The Evolution of Israeli Media*, 12 Middle East Rev. Intl. Affairs 88, 93 (2008) (hereinafter – Gilboa).

C. Radio

39. There are two public radio broadcasters in Israel. The largest one, 'Kol Israel'[12] (Voice of Israel) is operated by the IBA and the other, 'Galei Zahal' (IDF Radio) ('GLZ') is an army unit supervised by both the Minister of Defence and the IBA. Both broadcasters operate their own websites and broadcast over the internet as well as over the airwaves.

40. Kol Israel broadcasts nine channels including a general education, art and cultural programmes channel (Alef), a news channel (Bet), Israeli music channel (Gimel), programmes in Arabic (Dalet), a classical music channel (Kol Hamusicah), a popular music and traffic reports channel (88FM), a Jewish heritage channel (Moreshet) and an immigrants absorption channel (REKA) which broadcasts programmes in Yiddish, Ladino, Spanish, French, English, Amharic, Farsi, etc. Kol Israel is financed by a levy and by advertisements.

41. GLZ broadcasts two channels – a news and general programmes channel and a popular music channel with traffic reports. GLZ is operated by a combination of young soldiers and army-employed civilian media personnel. The soldiers recruited to GLZ are given on-the-job practical media and journalism training by experienced media personnel during their three year mandatory army service. Therefore GLZ has produced and supplied large and influential cadres of experienced media and journalism personnel to other media organizations over the past decades. GLZ's programme schedule includes some daily programmes on military and defence issues. As an army unit, GLZ is obliged to submit content concerning military affairs to prior approval by the IDF spokesperson before broadcasting it. GLZ is financed by the defence budget and sponsorships.

42. Commercial radio broadcasts in Israel are regulated by the SATR. There are 16 commercial radio stations, all regional and all of which are operated by franchisees. The highest number of radio franchises is concentrated in the central coastal region surrounding the metropolitan area of Tel Aviv. Although each regional CRF holder has a distinct geographical broadcast franchise the radio stations are de facto competitors due to the relative small size of the country and the wide range of the radio signal reception.[13] In addition to the regional radio stations there are three radio franchises directed at minority groupings although they are also regional stations in legal terms. Those are the Arabic radio franchise (Radio A-Shams) which broadcasts in the north of Israel and two commercial stations dedicated to religious and ultra-Orthodox Jews (Kol Chai and Kol Barama), which broadcast in the centre of Israel.

12. 'Kol Israel' is the Israeli re-incarnation of the 'Palestine Broadcasting Service' which was inaugurated by the British Mandate in 1936. For a brief history of radio broadcasting in Israel see: http://www.israelradio.org/history/history.html.

13. De facto competition between regional radio stations is also affected by their online transmission and the fact that they are transmitted nationally by multichannel television providers as well as by the DTT service.

43. Alongside with the development of commercial radio broadcasts the government moved to shut down 'pirate' radio stations that were increasingly active during the early 2000s. Operators of illegal radio stations were criminally indicted for violating the Communications Law. A unique case concerned the illegal radio station 'Arutz Sheva' (channel seven), a right-wing station slanted to represent the positions of the Jewish settlements in the West Bank and Gaza and run by settlers and religious activists. After the Knesset passed a law legalizing the station in 1999, the SC disqualified the law in 2002.[14] Arutz Sheva's terrestrial broadcasts were shut down but it now broadcasts as an internet-based radio and offers a website with news and commentary in Hebrew, English and Russian as well as video content.

D. Print Media

44. There are four major Hebrew newspapers, all of which are controlled by dominant owners. Most of the daily newspapers in Hebrew to date are general newspapers without a distinct political affiliation, although some have a political line. This is a significant change as compared to the mainstream print landscape before 2000 which was dominated by partisan newspapers. The last mainstream partisan newspapers collapsed during the 1990s.[15]

45. Competition in the print market has increased in the recent decades due to several changes including *inter alia* the shift of media consumption from print to internet; the shifting of advertisements from print media to television and internet; the rising cost of paper; global financial slowdown effects on local media consumption.

46. A dramatic change in the Israeli print landscape has been the introduction of the daily tabloid 'Israel Hayom' (Israel Today) owned by the American-Jewish billionaire Sheldon Adelson and distributed free of charge as of July 2007. As of 2011 it is the newspaper with the highest exposure, slightly above its closest rival.[16] Indeed, Israel Hayom has rocked the monopolistic market domination of the daily 'Yediot Ahronot' (Latest News), also printed in tabloid format. Yediot Ahronot is controlled by Arnon Mozes, the son of the newspaper's founder, and other members of the Mozes family. A minority stake is held by businessman Eliezer Fishman (who owns a financial newspaper as well). The Mozes family also owns a publishing house, local newspapers, a financial newspaper, newspapers in Russian and Arabic, popular websites and stakes in other media. The third largest newspaper in terms of exposure, 'Maariv' (Evening), lags significantly behind its two competitors. Maariv is also distributed in tabloid format. Maariv is the only newspaper

14. HCJ 1030/99 *Oron v. The Chairperson of the Knesset*, 56(3) PD 640 [2002]. Some of the owners, directors and operators of Channel 7 Radio were also convicted in 2003 in criminal felonies with regards to the illegal broadcasting.
15. The last bastion of partisan newspapers, 'Davar', the Labor Union's newspaper, shut down in 1996.
16. Media exposure in Israel is measured semi-annually since 1998 by 'TNS TeleGal' which conducts a representative survey primarily for marketing purposes. The results of the survey known as 'TGI survey' reflect the answers of respondents and therefore rely on the respondents' candour.

which shares have been floated in the Tel Aviv stock exchange. Its ownership has changed several hands in the recent years as its financial situation deteriorated. In 2011 it was acquired by one of Israel's major financial conglomerates, IDB, which is controlled by businessman Nochi Dankner. Although IDB Group initially promised to invest substantial funds in Maariv and turn it into a profitable newspaper, in 2012 the group itself faced substantial financial difficulties and moved to declare that Maariv was insolvent. Maariv employees protested attempts to sell or shut the newspaper down and even declared an unprecedented one day strike in which the newspaper was not distributed. Maariv was eventually sold under a court supervised proceeding to Shlomo Ben-Zvi, owner of the daily newspaper 'Makor Rishon' (first Source), which is known for its hawkish inclination. Ben-Zvi significantly downsized Maariv's staff and is moving to consolidate some of Maariv's editorial systems with Makor Rishon. The IDB Group subsidiary through which Maariv was acquired in 2012, Discount Investment Ltd, and the directors and officers of this corporation, are now the target of a derivative lawsuit. The plaintiff alleges that investing in Maariv, a newspaper that displayed an ongoing loss, was not a justifiable business decision. In spite of its name, Maariv and all the other major newspaper are distributed in the morning. Finally, 'Haaretz' (The Nation) is a high-brow broadsheet daily newspaper characterized by a liberal political slant and positioned fourth with respect to daily exposure. Haaretz has diversified its media portfolio under Haaretz Group with a financial newspaper ('The Marker'), websites, magazines and a publishing house. Haaretz Group is controlled by publisher Amos Schocken and members of the Schocken family, with minority stakes held by German publishing group Dumont-Schauberg and by the Israeli-Russian businessman Leonid Nevzlin. 'Israel Post' (formerly 'Metro') is a Hebrew tabloid distributed free of charge in gas stations and supermarkets, owned by businessman Eli Azour, who also owns the weekly magazine 'Sof Hashavua' (The Weekend), established in 2012 with many journalists from Maariv on its staff.

47. The financial print media has been one of the fastest growing media industries in Israel in the first decade of the millennium and displays strong competition. There are three main competitors in this arena. The financial newspaper 'Globes' is currently the only daily newspaper in Israel published and distributed in the evening. It is controlled by Eliezer Fishman (who holds a stake in Yediot Ahronot). As of 2012, Globes supplies financial news content to Maariv after Maariv's new owner Shlomo Ben-Zvi closed down its financial section in an attempt to cut costs. 'The Marker' is the financial newspaper of Haaretz Group and it is distributed to Haaretz subscribers and also sold separately. 'Calcalist' (a Hebrew variation on the word 'economist') is the financial newspaper of Yediot Ahronot group.

48. There are two daily newspapers in English. 'Haaretz in English' is an English daily version adapted from the original Hebrew version of Haaretz and owned by the Haaretz Group and the International Herald Tribune. Its main competitor is 'Jerusalem Post' which is controlled by Eli Azour.[17] The Russian speaking population is catered for by several daily newspapers with 'Vesti' (News), controlled by Yediot Aharonot, being the most dominant.

49. The Arab population is catered for by numerous daily and weekly national and local newspapers. Arabic print media have been dominated by political newspapers but those have been pushed aside in the recent decade by private media groups. There are three competing private weekly magazines – 'Panorama', 'A-Sinara' (The Lighthouse) and 'Kul El-Arab' (All the Arabs) – each also owns a popular website in Arabic. Among the Arabic daily newspapers, the prominent 'Al-Ittihad' (The Union) is affiliated with the Communist Arab-Israeli party.

50. There is a prosperous religious and orthodox print media in Israel, partly due to the fact that orthodox Jews refrain from watching television and some also avoid using the internet as part of their faith's precepts. Religious and orthodox newspapers are usually owned or strongly affiliated with political parties. 'Makor Rishon' is a daily affiliated with right-wing national religious political views, 'Yated Neeman' (Faithful Stake) and 'Hamodi'a' (The Informer) are affiliated with the Ashkenazi orthodox right-wing parties 'Degel Hatora' and 'Agudat Israel', and several daily and weekly newspapers are affiliated with the Sephardi-orthodox 'Shas' party.

51. In addition, there are hundreds of local newspapers, some of which are owned by the major print media groups but most of which are independent.

E. Concluding Remarks

52. The Israeli media market displays a tendency towards concentration of ownership and cross media expansion of major media groups due to its small size and its geographical and linguistic seclusion. The latter implies that international expansion possibilities for Israeli media outlets are extremely restricted given that Israeli media content is almost entirely in the Hebrew language. Affiliation of Israeli media organizations with international media groups is insignificant and practically non-existent. However, the relatively cheap and available foreign audio-visual and online content poses a threat to local television industry and serves to justify the regulatory intervention in favour of local production quotas for Hebrew language television programmes.[18]

---

17. The Jerusalem Post is the current incarnation of the 'Palestine Post', a Jewish-Zionist newspaper established in 1932 in Jerusalem. The newspaper changed its name to Jerusalem Post in 1950. Historical survey of the Jewish newspapers in Palestine and in Israel as well as archives of the newspapers can be found at: http://jpress.org.il/view-english.asp.
18. Yoav Hammer, *Local Culture, Minority Cultures and the Law: Regulation of Television and Radio Content in Israel*, 14 Mishpat Umimshal 149 (2012).

53. Media outlets remain an efficient means of influencing public opinion due to their popularity. However, the professional independence of media organizations is threatened by several trends that have weakened the financial basis of Israeli media. Print media has lost much of its financial stability due to the shift of readership from print newspapers to online content and loss of advertising revenue. While most newspapers have developed popular online versions they have so far been unable to recoup online the sliding revenues from the decline in demand for advertisements in print editions. As of 2013, Haaretz Online was the only online newspaper to introduce a 'pay wall' requiring online readers who wish to read the full content of the newspaper to pay a fairly modest monthly subscription fee.

54. In spite of the popularity of commercial and multichannel television, the competitive nature and the relatively small size of the advertising market alongside with the required expenditures on local and original productions has contributed to the erosion of the profitability of television corporations.

55. Consequently, Israeli media outlets have become the potential target of local and foreign businessmen who are interested in gaining influence over national public opinion, for political or other reasons. While partisan mainstream newspapers disappeared it is not uncommon to find general newspapers take sides in political, economic, social and legal affairs in accordance with the interests of their owners. Additionally, the government is able to exert political pressure on financially distressed media outlets dependent on its licensing authority such as commercial television broadcasters.

56. As a response to the erosion of labour conditions, wages and job security in the media market, and under the influence of popular demonstrations for national social reforms in 2011, collective action of journalists to protect their livelihood surged. A legally representative Journalists Organization (itonaim.org.il) was established in April 2012 with memberships from newly formed labour unions representing employees from more than 10 media organizations. In one case, the labour court intervened to nullify the dismissal of a reporter in Ynet website, a subsidiary of Yediot Ahronot, who was one of the founders of the labour union in the organization. The court held that the reporter and three other members of the newly formed labour union were dismissed in the initial stage of their attempt to form a labour union, which constituted an infringement of the employees' freedom of association and could deter other employees from joining the union.[19]

57. A highly influential trend on Israeli media has been the tremendous online content consumption and creation as well as the increased tendency to access internet content via cellular phones and other handheld devices such as tablets. One of every five Israelis tracks news events on the internet and many Israelis follow more

19. Regional Labor Ct. (Tel Aviv-Yafo) Case 32893-02-12 *Histadrut Haovdim v. Yediot Internet* (2012).

than one media outlet for their news.[20] Social media has also become a significant source of information and news to Israelis in particular. In 2011 Israel was ranked first in the world in a global survey of social media engagement with an average 11.4 hours per month spent by individuals using social networking websites (facebook.com being the most popular).[21]

58. A unique trait of Israeli online media is the high engagement of viewers from outside Israel, due among other reasons to the large Jewish diaspora and its intensive interest in the developments in Israel. Some mainstream media outlets provide English online editions that cater this share of viewers (Most notably www.haaretz.com).

59. Finally, freedom of the press is a matter of heated debate and ongoing concern. In an effort to exert political pressure on the media, a host of bills were proposed in 2012, mostly by right-wing Knesset Members, including most notably a proposal to increase the amount of exemplary damages in the Law of Defamation. This legislative offensive on the press was generally unsuccessful, although it contributed to the overall public distrust of the media in Israel. The Israeli Democracy Index 2012 (Tamar Herman, Ed.) ranked the media as the second least trusted institution in Israel with only political parties passing the media as the least trusted institution on the list. In a response to the legislative offensive, left wing opposition Knesset Members proposed a mass of bills aimed at strengthening the media, including exempting newspapers from Value Added Tax, fortifying the protection of confidential sources, etc. These proposed bills were also unsuccessful as of yet.

II. Infrastructure

A. *Cable Penetration*

60. Television broadcasts are disseminated in Israel in a variety of transmission methods including terrestrial broadcasting, cable and satellite, both analogue and digital. However, due to the fact that a very high share of households is connected to the cable infrastructure, terrestrial analogue broadcasting is being phased out.

61. In 2011 cable penetration in Israel has been estimated at 92%. The cable corporation, HOT, enjoys an advantage over the satellite corporation, YES, due to its ability to offer consumers an attractive 'triple play' bundle of services including

20. Data available on the Israeli Internet Association (ISOC IL) website at: http //data.isoc.org.il. In a survey of 992 Israelis conducted by Google and Shiluv Millward Brown in 2011, responses regarding media consumption indicated that 36% of the respondents use internet via computers as their main consumption medium, another 8% surf via cellular smartphones and similar devices, 29% watch television, 13% indicated the radio as the main medium and 9% opt for the newspaper. See: http://www.google.com/think/research-studies/media-consumption-in-israel.html.
21. Data collected by ComScore available at: http://www.comscore.com/Press_Events/Presentations_Whitepapers/2011/it_is_a_social_world_top_10_need-to-knows_about_social_networking.

multichannel television, broadband internet access and landline telephony. HOT is a declared monopoly in the market for multichannel television providers with approximately 55% to 65% of the market share.[22]

62. YES is held by the giant telephony corporation 'Bezeq' which has an existing nationwide landline infrastructure network, and also provides internet infrastructure, internet access, international telephony and cellular telephony services through a conglomerate of affiliated corporations. [23] In order to encourage HOT to become a significant competitor in the landline telephony market (and to encourage Bezeq to enter the multichannel platform market) YES has been prohibited from offering its client a 'triple play' bundle in conjunction with Bezeq although the two corporations are not enjoined from offering their services to the same consumer in a 'basket of services', which means a client may purchase a dual play bundle of television and internet access from YES and add a landline telephony service from Bezeq.[24]

63. Multichannel media and telecommunications providers are enjoined from conditioning one service upon a subscription to another service (e.g., requiring a subscription to landline telephony as a prerequisite for an internet infrastructure subscription) (Article 4g Communications Law).

B. Mobile Market

64. The Israeli mobile market has undergone a dramatic change in 2012. Prior to this change, the market was dominated by three cellular companies: Pelephone (a subsidiary of the telephony giant Bezeq), Cellcom (a subsidiary of IDB Group), and Partner/Orange (controlled by businessman Ilan Ben-Dov through the holding company Skylax). During the last four years, the Ministry of Communications has taken aggressive steps to increase the competition in the cellular market. This included intervention in pricing of cellular services and regulation of competition.

65. Most recently, the Ministry of Communications granted two licenses to new cellular service providers committed to construct a national cellular infrastructure and compete with four existing cellular service providers. In addition, several

22. CA 2082/09 *Eurocom DBS v. The Commissioner of Competition* (2009), sec. 19 of Justice Hayut's decision for the court.
23. In order to increase competition and facilitate an easier shift of consumers between cable and satellite television providers, Art. 4h Communications Law was added in 2001 stipulating that the physical wiring installed by the service provider in the consumer's home may be purchased from the installing service provider and used in order to connect the consumer to another service provider, thereby reducing the shifting cost. The purchase price of the wiring is regulated by law (Art. 4h(e) Communications Law).
24. A similar approach has been adopted in the cellular telephony market in order to encourage competition. Hence HOT which owns a subsidiary cellular company, 'Mirs', has been enjoined from bundling its cellular telephony services with its other products thereby preventing it from offering a 'quadra play' bundle (television, internet access, landline and cellular telephony) which would have presumably had a chilling impact on other competitors in the cellular telephony market.

licenses were granted to 'virtual' cellular service providers which offer attractive cellular subscription at low fees by renting bandwidth from the incumbent cellular network operators. The increased competition had dramatic effects on the prices of cellular services. At the same time, the market value of the incumbent cellular operators, all of which are publicly held corporations, has deteriorated significantly, indicating that some of them were heading towards financial dire straits.

66. The Ministry of Communications foresees that cellular network operators will shift their efforts into the broadcast market, by offering cellular internet television services. Although some of the incumbent cellular operators entered into cooperation agreements with regards to broadcast content production and dissemination on cellular platforms, this development is still in its infancy.

III. Technological and Economic Developments on the Media Markets

A. Digital Television

67. All major daily newspapers and all the financial newspapers have digital presence on the web with real time updates. Almost all newspapers use the print editorial staff to produce the internet editions. The exception is Yediot Ahronot which operates separate websites (www.Ynet.co.il for news and www.Xnet.co.il for entertainment and leisure) with their own editorial system.

68. Additional independent news portals include Mako (which is owned by Channel 2 television franchisee Keshet), Walla!, Arutz Sheva and NFC. Mako, Walla! and Nana10 are popular websites. The latter enjoys a cooperation agreement with commercial television Channel 10 whereas Mako offers content from Keshet's Channel 2 programmes. Other popular websites include One (a sports website) and the lifestyle websites Saloona and Onlife.

69. Although technology allowing multichannel television broadcasts via the internet such as IPTV is still in its infancy, the Communications Law foresees (in Article 5(9)) the need to empower the Minister of Communications with the authority to compel broadband internet infrastructure providers to allocate sufficient bandwidth in order to enable the imposition of 'must carry' obligations.

70. As discussed *supra* in the previous section, the Israeli Competition Authority and the Ministry of Communications are striving to encourage the entrance of an additional competitor to the duopolistic market for multichannel television providers. This has been the reason for the objection of the Competition Authority to the attempt of Bezeq to increase its current stake of 49.78% in YES to a controlling stake of 58%. The move constitutes a 'merger' under the definition of the Israeli competition legislation and therefore required the prior approval of the Competition Authority, which was denied. Bezeq appealed the decision to the SC, which eventually upheld the Competition Authority's refusal.[25] The Competition Authority asserted that Bezeq is the only likely potential competitor in the multichannel platform market in the foreseeable future due to its ability to upgrade its nationwide ADSL network infrastructure to provide IPTV services.[26] The Competition Authority asserted that Bezeq would have no incentive to develop the competing IPTV infrastructure once it is permitted to merge with and control YES which already competes in the multichannel platform market. Alternatively, the Competition Authority claimed Bezeq might transfer its potential IPTV infrastructure to YES after the merger in order to block potential entrants in the market.[27] In contrast, Bezeq claimed that it does not have an incentive to develop the IPTV platform as long as it is prohibited from applying for a general broadcast license. Indeed Article 6(8)4(a)(2) Communications Law prevents granting a multichannel broadcaster license to a corporation that holds a significant interest in an existing broadcaster (as Bezeq holds in YES). The SC upheld two responses provided by the Competition Authority to Bezeq's claim. The court noted that if the merger was denied Bezeq could transfer its IPTV activity to a new subsidiary in which case the Minister of Communications would have the power to grant the subsidiary a multichannel broadcaster license as stipulated in an exception in the Communications Law (Article 6(8)4(a)(5)) which is justified by furtherance of competition in the market.[28] Second, Bezeq itself made several earlier documented and binding statements about its intention to develop the IPTV infrastructure regardless of the merger or of the ability to receive a multichannel broadcast license.[29] Since the ruling in August 2009, the multichannel platform market remains duopolistic.[30] Although Bezeq improved its Internet infrastructure it did not as yet upgrade its network with micro-optic fibres that enable the type of IPTV service discussed in the court's ruling.

B. Convergence of Media Products

71. Global media convergence trends did not skip the Israeli media market. Two principal trends can be delineated. On the consumer side, the most influential trend is the ability to receive various types of content (print, audio and audio-visual) via the internet on portable and non-portable devices. In the Israeli market this trend is characterized by constant increase in the quality of the offered content, the breadth of offered content and a reduction in the consumption costs due to regulatory induced competition. On the supply side, the trend is manifested by traditional media content providers such as newspapers, radio and television offering internet versions of their content or controlling internet media outlets. For example, aside

---

25. CA 2082/09 *Eurocom DBS v. The Commissioner of Competition* (2009).
26. *Ibid.*, sec. 29 per Justice Hayut.
27. *Ibid.*, sec. 2 per Justice Hayut.
28. *Ibid.*, sec. 31 per Justice Hayut.
29. *Ibid.*, sec. 33 per Justice Hayut.
30. According to experts quoted in the court's decision, Bezeq was capable of entering the multichannel platform market within three years. *Ibid.*, sec. 29 per Justice Hayut.

from broadcasting its terrestrial radio broadcasts on the internet the IBA also transmits some popular radio talk shows as audio-visual broadcasts on the internet; news websites such as Ynet, Walla! and The Marker provide video reports on the internet; in 2012 Channel 2 News Company launched a round the clock online television news channel which complements its news broadcasts on Channel 2; as of the national elections held on January 2013, Ynet, Walla! And Mako also broadcast live newscasts.

72. The existing regulation of audio-visual content does not apply to online broadcasting. The major regulatory entities in Israel have already noted the need to re-examine the existing regulation in light of the expansion of internet-based audio-visual content. In 2009, a team headed by the Chairperson of the CSBC was charged with this re-examination (the 'Chen Report').[31] The Chen Report pointed out that global convergence trends apply to Israel media market; that particularly technological development increasingly enables broadcasting video content with high download speed or streaming possibilities; that there is an ever growing increase in the bandwidth offered by the land and cellular networks. However, according to the Chen Report the internet-based video content is still not sufficiently substitutive to television broadcast content and therefore the report offers guidelines and a 'road-map' for the future regulation of broadcast content without prescribing immediate implementation.[32]

73. The Chen Report proposes to substitute the existing regulatory regime which is based on the medium by which the broadcasts are disseminated (terrestrial, satellite, cable, digital, etc.) with a regime based on the nature of the broadcasted product (television or quasi-television products). However the Chen Report conditions such a change in a re-evaluation of the entire media market regulation in order to guarantee a harmonized fair and equal treatment to all broadcasters.[33] The Chen Report proposed that a new team encompassing all broadcast regulators will be established in order to conclude the task.[34] Such a team has not been established to date.

31. Report of the Joint Team of the CSBC and the MOC on the Dissemination of Visual Content to the Public via Electronic Communications Networks (October 2011) (hereinafter – the Chen Report).
32. Chen Report, *supra* n. 31, at 7. One exception is the VOD service provided by the satellite corporation YES to subscribers which relies on special reception equipment, MPEG-4 formats, and progressive download systems with protocols that overcome packet loss problems It could be asserted that since YES operates its VOD services on internet infrastructure it is not subject to any particular telecommunications regulation since this regulation applies only to terrestrial, cable or satellite transmission. To date, YES has not taken advantage of this regulatory lacuna.
33. In a significant dissent from the team's proposals the legal adviser of the MOC, Noga Rubinstein, proposed a different regulatory regime according to which internet broadcasters will be subject to lax regulation in order to encourage a wider offering but stressed that some market failures should be addressed also with respect to internet television content such as the need to promote local productions and the need to protect minors against unsuitable content.
34. Chen Report, *supra* n. 31, at 8.

74. One of the by-products of media convergence has been the increased participation of media consumers in interacting with content and in user generated content. As internet websites remain relatively unregulated, the regulation of consumer participation is mostly limited to the general rules of private law (defamation, privacy, copyright, etc.) and to some unique rules regarding participation of viewers in audio-visual media. For example, an amendment of the BCL Rules from 2004, applicable only to multichannel television providers, guarantees that viewer messages (broadly defined as phone calls, text messages and any other messages transmitted via data transmission systems) will be aired without content discrimination such that the freedom of speech is guaranteed; without discriminating one type of messaging technology over another; and in compliance with all legal restrictions and prohibitions in the general legislation (Rules 33h-33j BCL).[35]

75. Another phenomenon that can be discerned as a result of media convergence is the referral of consumers from one medium to another. One of the concerns that such activity raises is regulatory arbitrage. For example, the possibility of broadcasting on the internet fuller versions of programmes which were censored or edited due to various regulatory requirements on other audio-visual media platforms. This issue has also been regulated exclusively with respect to multichannel television providers and minor-related content, by prohibiting the referral from television broadcasts directed at minors to internet websites that may include content which is unsuitable to minors.[36]

76. Interestingly, the IBA is prohibited from airing full programmes on its internet website prior to their initial broadcasts on its radio or television channels (although broadcasting promos or short excerpts is allowed). Article 44f IBA Law stipulates that the IBA may only broadcast programmes on the internet simultaneously with or after their initial broadcast.

35. The BCL Rules also require multichannel television providers to screen messages inappropriate for minors in *programmes* oriented at such viewers (Rule 33l BCL); to remove offensive content at their discretion in the event that an individual claims to be offended by a message (Rule 33m BCL); to clarify to the audience the costs of sending the messages, how the messages are broadcasted and whether the broadcaster reserves the right to edit or intervene in the content of the message, etc. (Rules 33p-33r BCL).

36. For example, the CommAD Rules which apply to designated channels on cable and satellite television devote a chapter to references of websites in programmes. Unless the website belongs to the channel licensee or to the programme producer, the referenced website must be shown visually; be directly related to the programme; shown no more than four times during the programme and no longer than 10 seconds each time (Rule 74 CommAD). In a programme directed at minors the referenced website will not contain content inappropriate for minors (Rule 76 CommAD); the website will not advertise products or services shown in the programme (Rule 77 CommAD) nor contain information or an advertisement by a sponsor of the programme (Rule 78 CommAD).

§3. Sources of Media Law

I. Legislation

77. The legislation of Israel is published in print by the formal government gazette 'Reshumot' (loosely translated as notifications) and on the Knesset website (www.Knesset.gov.il) which also includes minutes of Knesset committees discussing the legislation and the text of the initial legislation proposals. Legislation is most commonly accessible on private online legal databases in Hebrew, some of which offer content free of charge. There is no official publication of Israeli legislation in languages other than Hebrew.

78. Israel does not have a single unified constitutional document. However, the Knesset has enacted several constitutional Basic Laws. Two of these laws are relevant to matters of freedom of expression and the protection of privacy:

- Basic Law: Human Dignity and Freedom
- Basic Law: Freedom of Occupation.

79. The most prominent law regulating print media is the Press Ordinance 1933. The direct regulation of radio and television is divided between three laws:

- The Broadcasting Authority Law 1965 ('IBA Law'), which regulates the government's radio and television broadcasts;
- The Communications (Telecommunications and Broadcasts) Law 1982 ('Communications Law'), which regulates cable and satellite broadcasts to subscribers;
- The Second Authority for Radio and Television Act 1990 ('SATR Law' or 'SATRL'), which regulates commercial radio and television broadcasts.

These laws and the intricate web of regulations and rules promulgated according to the authority granted by these laws are available in Hebrew on the websites of the pertinent government ministries or regulatory authorities (www.moc.gov.il; www.iba.org.il; www.rashut2.org.il). The main rules and regulations discussed in this monograph are listed here:

- The Communications (Telecommunications and Broadcasts) (Broadcast Licensee) Rules 1987 ('BCL Rules').
- The Communications (Telecommunications and Broadcasting) (Advertisements, Public Service Announcements and Sponsorship Announcements in Designated Channels) Rules, 2004 ('CommAD').
- The IBA (Radio Advertisements and Announcements) Rules 1993 ('IBARadA Rules').
- The SATR (Integrating Advertisements in Television Broadcasts) Rules 1992 ('SAAD Rules').
- The SATR (Ethics in Radio Advertisements) Rules 1999 ('SAERAD Rules').
- The SATR (Ethics in Television Advertisements) Rules 1994 ('SAEthAD Rules').

- The SATR (Ethics in Television and Radio Broadcasts) Rules 1994 ('SAEthic Rules').
- The SATR (Television Broadcasts by a Franchise Holder) Rules 2009 ('SAFraB Rules').
- The SATR (Procedures for Granting a Television CBF) Rules 1992 ('SAPFra Rules').
- The SATR (Procedure for Granting a Radio Broadcasting License) 2006 ('SAPRL Rules').
- The SATR (Procedure and Conditions for Granting a Television Broadcast License) Rules 2011 ('SAPTVL Rules').
- The SATR (Integrating Advertisements and Commercial References in Radio Broadcasts) Rules 1999 ('SARaAD Rules').
- The SATR (Radio Broadcasts by a Franchise Holder) Rules 1999 ('SARaF Rules').
- The SATR (Taking of Broadcast Time) Rules 2007 ('SATak Rules').
- The SATR (Radio Broadcasts by a License Holder) Rules 2006 ('SaRaL Rules').
- The SATR (Sponsorships) Rules 2009 ('SASpon Rules').

80. In addition there is a host of legislation dealing directly or indirectly with matters of freedom of speech, media and communications. These include, in chronological order:

- The Cinematographic Films Ordinance 1927.
- The Defence (Emergency) Regulations 1945.
- The Elections (Methods of Electioneering) Law 1959 ('Elections Law').
- The Prohibition of Defamation Law 1965 ('Law of Defamation').
- The Wireless Telegraph Ordinance (New Version) 1972.
- The Penal Law, 1977.
- The Protection of Privacy Law 1981.
- The Restrictions on the Advertisement of Tobacco and Smoking Products Law 1983.
- The Courts (Integrated Version) Law 1984 ('Law of the Courts').
- The Prohibition of Holocaust Denial Law 1986.
- The Freedom of Information Law 1998 ('FOIL').
- The Classification, Marking and Prohibition of Harmful Broadcasts Law 2001.
- The Copyright Law 2007.

II. Case Law

81. All the decisions of the Supreme Court of Israel are available online in Hebrew on the website of the judicial branch (www.court.gov.il) and on online legal databases. Some notable decisions have been translated informally into English but otherwise there is no official publication in languages other than Hebrew. Selected decisions of the Supreme Court and of the lower courts were printed in official bands known as 'Piskey Din' (Rulings) but the publication ceased more than ten years ago.

Part I. Freedom of Speech

§1. Constitutional Framework

82. Freedom of speech is not enumerated in Israel's constitutional legislation nor is it mentioned in a regular law of the Knesset. On the other hand there are countless laws limiting or curtailing the freedom of speech. The bulk of these laws were legislated near the establishment of the State of Israel in 1948 and some of them are remnants of the British Mandate over Palestine (1917–1948).[37]

83. In 1992, the Knesset enacted two Basic Laws, namely, Basic Law: Human Dignity and Liberty and Basic Law: Freedom of Occupation. Both Basic Laws are considered to be part of the unfinished constitution of Israel. Neither freedom of expression nor freedom of the press is mentioned in either Basic Law, which lends force to the claim that these rights have not been afforded constitutional protection.[38] Although the opinion that freedom of speech is part and parcel of human dignity and therefore is protected by Basic Law: Human Dignity and Liberty has been voiced quite often,[39] it has also met occasional resistance in the Israeli SC.[40]

84. Nevertheless, freedom of speech has been recognized as a fundamental tenet of the Israeli legal order by the SC in numerous cases and in that sense it is

---

37. Moshe Negbi, *Freedom of the Journalist and Freedom of the Press – Media Law and Ethics* 44 (Open University Press 2011) (hereinafter – Negbi).
38. This claim is most eloquently asserted in Hillel Sommer, *The Un-enumerated Rights – On the Scope of the Constitutional Revolution*, 28 Mishpatim 257, 318 (1997).
39. Negbi, *supra* n. 37, at 44; Aharon Barak, *Human Dignity as a Constitutional Right,* 41 Hapraklit 271 (1994).
40. The fortification of freedom of speech as a constitutional right has been attributed to the era of Justice Aharon Barak in the SC and the influence of American jurisprudence on the Israeli SC. See: Eli Salzberger & Fania Oz Salzberger, *The Tradition of Freedom of Speech in Israel*, in Be Quiet, Someone Is Speaking! 27 (Michael Birnhack ed., Remot 2012) (hereinafter – Be Quiet). The opposition to the granting of a unique status to freedom of speech can be found in the dissenting opinion of Justice Mishael Cheshin in CFH (Civil Further Hearing) 7325/95 *Yedioth Ahronot Ltd. v. Kraus* 52(3) PD 1 [1998] in which the influential justice asserted that excessive weight has been given to freedom of speech at the expense of other rights, also protected by the principle of human dignity, such as the right to reputation. For a discussion of the balance between freedom of speech and the right to reputation see also Elad Peled, *The Israeli Law of Defamation: A Comparative Perspective and a Sociological Analysis*, 20 Transnational Law & Contemporary Problems 735 (2012) (asserting that the legislature gives more weight to the right to reputation whereas the courts under the influence of U.S. jurisprudence give greater weight to freedom of speech).

presumed to be entrenched as a constitutional right.[41] The court's grounding of freedom of speech as a 'supreme right' can be traced to the 1953 landmark *Kol Ha'am* decision which founded the right to freedom of speech on the democratic rationale, according to which a democratic decision making process is the result of open public discourse from which the truth can only emerge when the right to free exchange of views and opinions is guaranteed.[42] In his opinion for the HCJ, President Shimon Agranat held that freedom of speech stems from the democratic nature of the State of Israel as declared by the state's Declaration of Independence. It should be noted that the Declaration of Independence does not mention freedom of speech expressly nor is it a binding source of law although it is enumerated as a fundamental interpretative instrument in Article 1 of both Basic Law: Human Dignity and Liberty and Basic Law: Freedom of Occupation.

85. Freedom of speech is not an absolute right and it should be balanced and weighed against conflicting rights. This balancing act tends to be especially challenging when freedom of speech conflicts with a constitutionally protected interest such as privacy or property rights. In practice, however, the most challenging balance for Israeli courts has been that of freedom of speech vis-à-vis interests of national security.

86. The HCJ in *Kol Ha'am* held that laws curtailing freedom of speech should be narrowly construed. Consequently, the court held that the Minister of Interior's authority according to Article 19(2) of the Press Ordinance to shut down a newspaper if a publication is 'likely' to upset public peace or public order should be construed to apply only when the likelihood of the upsetting result exists with 'near certainty'. The 'near certainty' test governs the court's balancing of freedom of expression versus other interests such as national security, public order, protection of public feelings, etc., to this day. The test is often equated to the American 'clear and present danger' test.[43]

§2. Scope

87. Due to the lack of legislative grounding, the scope of freedom of speech is not statutorily defined. The scope of freedom of speech is therefore developed casuistically.

---

41. Navot, *supra* n. 1, at 210–211, noting that to date no law has been invalidate for infringing on the constitutional freedom of expression but that this may be due to the fact that laws enacted before 1992 are protected from such invalidation and most laws curtailing freedom of speech have been enacted before 1992. See also CA 4463/94 *Golan v. The Prison Service* 50(4) PD 136, 152 [1996] in which the SC noted specifically that 'even without a particular reference, freedom of expression is included in human dignity according to its meaning in Arts 2 and 4 of the Basic Law' (author's translation).
42. HCJ 73/53 *Kol Ha'am v. Minister of the Interior*, 7(2) PD 871 [1953]. English version available at: http://elyon1.court.gov.il/files_eng/53/730/000/Z01/53000730.z01.pdf.
43. Amnon Reichman, *The Voice of America in Hebrew? On the Israeli Court's Reference to the United States Law in Matters of Freedom of Speech*, in *Be Quiet* 185 (Remot 2012).

88. The Israeli SC seems to make no distinction between print and electronic media in its application of freedom of speech. In light of its emphasis on open discourse as the foundation of freedom of speech, the HCJ has determined that the scope of the right should be broad. Hence, racist expression falls within the scope of the right to freedom of speech, and is protected as long as there is no near certainty that this speech will upset public peace and public order. The strength of protection given to hate speech thus differs in comparison with other types of expression. The HCJ protected racist expression when it nullified the decision of the Managing Committee of the IBA to forbid the broadcasting of comments by the racist Member of Knesset Meir Kahane or inviting him to news and talk shows. The court held that 'Indeed racism is founded on a lie, but this truth shall only emerge through the free battle of ideas and opinions'.[44] The court nevertheless recommended that Kahane would not be interviewed or broadcasted on live broadcasts in order to allow the editors sufficient time to filter out racist comments that do not pass the 'near certainty' test.

89. The HCJ protected pornographic content, by approving the decision of the CSBC to allow the broadcasting of a pornographic cable television channel, subject to controlling the access to such channels by an access code.[45]

90. The SC also noted that anonymous speech furthers public discourse and should therefore be considered part of the protected freedom of speech.[46]

§3. *A Priori* Censorship

91. Considering the strong influence of British Mandate legislation, it is not surprising that Israeli law contains a plethora of provisions retraining free speech *a priori*. The most salient *a priori* censorship is the Military Censorship. The legal foundation for the operation of the Military Censorship is laid in the Defence (Emergency) Regulations, 1945, which is a far-reaching emergency legislation instated by the British Mandate government to empower the executive branch with extensive authorities. Although they are entitled 'regulations', the Defence (Emergency) Regulations, 1945, have the force of primary legislation and as such they are subject to judicial interpretation according to the basic principles of Israeli law.[47] The Military Censorship is a unit within the Israeli Defence Force ('IDF'), headed by an army officer with the rank of colonel or lieutenant-General, known as the Chief Military Censor.

---

44. Author's translation. HCJ 399/85 *Kahane v. The Managing Committee of the Israeli Broadcasting Authority*, 41(3) PD 255 [1987].
45. HCJ 5432/03 *Shin v. The Council for Cable and Satellite Broadcasting* 58(3) PD 65 [2004].
46. LCA 4447/07 *Rami Mor v. Barak E.T.C (2009) per Justice Eliezer Rivlin's opinion*, sec. 11. The opinion of the court was delivered by Justice Rivlin against the dissenting opinion of Justice Elyakim Rubinstein.
47. Navot, *supra* n. 1, at 300.

92. Regulation 97 of the Defence (Emergency) Regulations, 1945 empowers the Chief Military Censor with a broad authority to require any person about to publish or print any material to submit the said material to the Military Censor. The language of the regulation is not uniquely aimed at publications concerning military or defence issues. Violation of the Military Censor's submission request is a criminal offence. In an order published by the Chief Military Censor and implementing the authority granted by Regulation 97, every person must submit for prior review any publication concerning state security, public peace and public order in Israel, West Bank and the Gaza strip, as well as any publication concerning Arab-Israeli relations. The publication must be submitted regardless of whether the information has been published in the past and applies to Israeli as well as non-Israeli media and on publication within the state of Israeli and in foreign countries.[48]

93. Regulation 87 of the Defence (Emergency) Regulations, 1945 empowers the Chief Military Censor to ban either particularly or by general decree the publication of material which may be in his opinion detrimental to the defence of Israel, the public peace or the public order.[49] Violation of such a decree is a criminal offence by the author of the material as well as the editor and the owner of the publication.

94. It should be noted that the Military Censor's authority to suppress a publication is slightly more limited than his or her authority to require submission for prior review, yet it is still highly expansive and overbearing.

95. The HCJ narrowed the scope of the Chief Military Censor's discretion to strike down publications in the 1989 landmark *Schnitzer* case, holding that the Military Censor may only suppress a publication when the probability of harm exists with 'near certainty' and the expected harm is 'harsh, serious and severe'.[50]

96. The free dissemination of information on the internet has also significantly undermined the effective power of the Military Censorship and in practice the Chief Military Censor often concedes and allows the publication of information that has been disseminated in the internet. However, as I elaborate in this chapter henceforth, in some cases the State Prosecution has moved to override the Military Censorship in matters of national security and was granted prior restraint orders by

48. Emergency Decree (Submission of Printed Material and Publications to Prior Review and Banning of Print and Publication), 1988.

49. Regulation 87 is the heart of the Military Censorship's power while Regulation 97 is the technical instrument by which the prior restraint is implemented. See generally David Ronen, *Censorship Law – the Media, Freedom of Expression and National Security* (Perlstein-Ginosar 2011) (hereinafter – Ronen).

50. HCJ 680/88 *Schnitzer v. The Chief Military Censor*, 52(4) PD 617 [1989]. The case concerned the publication of a critical reportage about the head of the Israeli intelligence agency, the 'Mossad'. At the time, even publishing the name of the head of the Mossad was not permitted by the Chief Military Censor. Among other things, the SC held that the Military Censor cannot suppress the publication of the expected date of the head of the Mossad's retirement.

courts suppressing information that was previously approved by the Military Censorship.[51]

97. Due to the draconian power of the Military Censorship which stands in stark contradiction to Israel's self-perception as a democratic state, a parallel contractual substituting agreement between the press and the Military Censorship emerged in 1949. The agreement has been revised several times until its last version from 1996,[52] and it watered down the Military Censor's powers, yet the agreement covers only parts of the Israeli media landscape. The agreement states that:[53]

(a) The purpose of the censorship is to prevent the publication of defence-related information that may cause with near certainty real harm to the security of the State of Israel.
(b) Censorship shall not apply to political matters, opinions, commentary, assessments or any other matter unless defence-related information can be deduced from such publications.
(c) The censorship is based on a mutual understanding between the defence system and the media with regards to the purpose of the censorship.
(d) The censor will update from time to time the list of topics that must be submitted for prior review and notify the media.
(e) A committee will be established which will be comprised of three members as follows:
   (i) A public representative, jurist, will be appointed by the Minister of Defence and the chairman of the editors' committee and will serve as then chairman;
   (ii) An army representative appointed by the Chief of Staff;
   (iii) A media representative appointed by the chairman of the editors' committee.
(f) Appeals by the media with regards to material suppressed by the Military Censor as well as complaints of the Military Censor against a media organization that is a party to the agreement will be brought before the three member committee.
(g) The committee shall have the power to:
   (i) Adjudicate the Military Censor's complaint against a media organization and, should it find that the complaint is justified, impose a penalty (warning, fine, reprimand, citation, etc.) including probation;
   (ii) Adjudicate a media organization's editor's appeal on the Military Censor's decision and approve the Military Censor's suppression or dismiss the suppression in whole or in part.
(h) The committee will convene no later than twenty-four hours from the time of the request and render its decision the same day.

51. For a discussion of this phenomena see Karin Barzilai-Nahon and Gad Barzilai, *The Practical and Imaginary Freedom of Speech in the Internet, in Be Quiet* 483 (Remot 2006).
52. Negbi, *supra* n. 37, at 105.
53. Author's translation.

(i) The committee will elaborate the reasoning of its decisions.[54] The committee's discussion will be secret and it is not obligated to publish its decisions. A party can request permission for the publication of a decision in part or in whole. The permission shall include the text permitted for publication and will be subject to censorship. The committee's chairman is in charge of executing the committee's decisions.

(j) The agreement does not prevent a media organization from filing a petition to the HCJ if the committee rejected the media organization's appeal against the Military Censor. In such cases, the Military Censor's decision shall be in force so long as the court does not hold otherwise.

98. As a result of the so-called Censorship Agreement, the Military Censor waived his power to shut down or sanction in any other way a media organization without due process. However, the agreement applies only to the major media organizations in Israel whereas foreign media, internet-based media, and media organizations that are not part of the agreement remain subject to the Defence (Emergency) Regulations regime.[55]

99. The Chief Military Censor's current list of issues that must be submitted to prior review includes information about:

- The Israeli Defence Force including *inter alia* the size of military and reserve forces; alert levels; military operations; appointments and retirements of high ranking officers; casualties; rumours and complaints that may harm the army or its commanders; letters and commentaries by army soldiers on issues relating to their army service; development, experimentation, manufacture, acquisition and sale of arms; training and courses in Israel or abroad;
- Israeli defence industries; development, experimentation, manufacture, acquisition and sale of defence products including contacts with foreign countries; location of factories; identification of employees whose identity is confidential; the use of civil aircrafts belonging to the national airline for military purposes; research facilities and any research with defence significance;
- The intelligence community (including the military intelligence, the Mossad, Israeli Security Service, etc.), its structure, objectives, locations, employee names, intelligence information and its evaluation by these organizations;
- 'The enemy' – Arab state armies and terror organizations, their size, plans and activities including information about their defence systems and industries with defence significance; prisoners of war, captives and infiltrators, where they were captured, detained, arrested, interrogated, where they are held, how and where

54. The reasoning is essential to enable judicial review of the decision by the HCJ should one of the parties decide to challenge the decision.

55. Various proposals, including legislative proposals, to supplant both the relevant regulations of the Defence (Emergency) Regulations and the agreement failed to materialize. See Negbi, *supra* n. 37, at 107-109; Ronen, *supra* n. 49, at 66–70. See also Hillel Nossek and Yehiel Limor, *Fifty Years in a "Marriage of Convenience": News Media and Military Censorship in Israel*, 6 Comm. L. & Policy 1 (2001) asserting that the current relatively flexible and loosely defined boundaries of the Military Censorship are preferred by both the media and the government over any other solution.

they are deported. Similar requirements apply to members of terror organizations including prisoners and detainees of such organizations;

- General security matters, including security arrangements, bombing attempts, weakly protected locations, fuel pipelines and storage locations, power stations, communications facilities, ports, airports, bridges; accidents in the army; prior information about movements of important officials and army officers near border zones and abroad; the defence budget; government and parliament discussions on defence issues; aerial photographs and maps; military court hearings that were held in closed doors; detention of soldiers for defence related reasons; information about persons about to cross state borders or caught doing so and persons caught by the enemy and negotiations for their return; information about the Military Censorship;
- The ministerial defence committee's discussions; the Eilat-Ashkelon oil pipeline; immigration stemming from countries from which exit is limited including plans to arrange the exit of Jews from such countries; foreign loans to the state or to Israeli financial institutions including negotiations for such loans.

100. Military Censorship aside, there are nevertheless additional prior restraint measures in the Israeli legislation.[56] These measures all require approaching the court and are thus subject to judicial discretion and review. In addition, there are *a priori* authorization procedures for the publications of newspapers, discussed *infra* in sub-Chapter §5.

101. The Prohibition of Defamation Law 1965 in conjunction with the Rules of Civil Procedure 1984, allow a plaintiff to move for a civil injunction against the publication of an allegedly defamatory publication. Nevertheless, the SC has made it difficult for a plaintiff to succeed in such a motion. The SC held that the plaintiff must overcome the burden of proving that there is no public interest in the disputed publication or that the publication is evidently false. However, the defendant is not obligated to produce the publication to the plaintiff or even to the court for prior review, thereby making the plaintiff's burden practically insurmountable.[57]

102. The court's willingness to apply prior restraints on publications breaching the right to privacy is slightly less lenient towards the media compared to its treatment of defamatory information.[58] This discrepancy can be attributed to the fact that the right to privacy is protected not only by the Protection of Privacy Act 1981, but also granted constitutional protection according to Article 7 of Basic Law: Human Dignity and Liberty. It therefore follows that when information of public interest has been obtained by the media through an invasion of privacy, this in itself would not

---

56. Ronen, *supra* n. 49, at 55–57, surveys some of this legislation and notes that most of it is dead letter law.
57. CA 214/89 *Avneri v. Shapira* 43(3) PD 840 [1989].
58. For a recent example see: Civ. Case (Mag. Ct. Tel Aviv) 171305-09 *Dr. R. v. Israeli Medical Association* (2012) in which the court ordered that a story about to be published in a daily newspaper concerning an alleged inappropriate relationship between a psychiatrist and her patient will be submitted to the court's prior approval due to a potential infringement of privacy.

be sufficient cause for prior restraint whereas a court would consider suppressing information when its content presents a severe intrusion of privacy.[59]

103. Article 3 Basic Law: The Judiciary stipulates that hearings before the courts shall be open to the public unless stated otherwise.[60] Nevertheless, in matters brought before the judiciary, a wide array of publications requires the prior authorization of the court. Article 70(a) of the Law of the Courts [Combined Version] 1984 states that matters heard 'in closed doors' may not be published without the prior consent of the court. Article 68 of the said statute specifies a list of concerns that may induce the court to hold a hearing 'in closed doors' in part or in whole. These include *inter alia* state security; state foreign relations; protection of moral ethic; protection of a minor or a mentally or physically disabled person; protection of a complainant or accused in a sex offence;[61] a situation in which a hearing in open court might deter a witness from testifying freely or from testifying at all; protection of a trade secret; protection of a complainant or a victim in a human trafficking offence; protection of a witness in a witness protection plan.[62] In addition, tax appeals are held in closed doors although the court's final ruling is made public and includes the identity of the parties. In family courts hearings are held in closed doors, decisions are available to the public but parties' names are deleted.

104. Article 70 of the Law of the Courts further empowers the courts to ban publications of information from public hearings held in open court. Hence, the court can forbid a publication in order to ensure the security of a party, a witness or a person mentioned in the hearing or to prevent a serious harm to the privacy of the said person or a person with mental or physical disability. The court may prevent the publication of a suspect's identity, prior to the filing of an indictment, if the publication may interfere with an ongoing investigation or if the publication might cause a severe harm to the suspect and the court concludes that this harm overweighs the public interest in the information.[63]

105. As of January 2012, an amendment to the Law of the Courts prohibits to publish the name of a suspect that has not been indicted before forty-eight hours from his initial investigation had elapsed or before he is brought for arraignment before a judge, whichever happens earlier.[64] The purpose of this stipulation is to

---

59. Negbi, *supra* n. 37, at 191–192.
60. It is however forbidden to take photographs inside a courtroom without the prior consent of the judge according to Art. 70 of the Law of the Courts [Combined Version], 1984.
61. Note that according to Art. 352 of the Penal Law, 1977, and Art. 5(e) of the Law on the Prevention of Sexual Harassment, 1998, it is strictly forbidden to publish the name of a complainant or a victim in a sex offence and even the court cannot authorize such a publication unless the complainant declares in court that he or she allows the publication.
62. In addition, hearings before family courts are held in closed doors as a general rule, with very minor exceptions, and therefore may not be published without the family court's prior consent.
63. The Ministry of Justice is currently considering legislation that will forbid the publication of any information which emanated from criminal investigations until the finalization of the criminal process. This proposal aims specifically to prevent the media from broadcasting audio and visual recordings of suspects in police interrogations.
64. Article 70(d1)(1) Law of the Courts [Combined Version], 1984.

allow a suspect sufficient time to petition the court for a ban on the publication, which will remain in force until an indictment is filed. The language of the amendment seems to prohibit identifying suspects in earlier stages of investigation, e.g., when the police already suspects an individual of committing an offence but has not decided to summon the individual to a formal investigation. To date, there is no case law on the matter.

106. It should be noted that in recent years there has been a significant surge in the number of closed doors hearings and orders by courts curtailing media reports on judicial proceedings in whole or in part, particularly at the request of internal security authorities and in matters concerning police investigations.[65] Courts tend to uphold such orders even if the suppressed information has been disseminated incidentally or systematically in the internet.[66]

For example, on February 2013 a broadcast by an Australian investigative television programme claimed that an Australian-Israeli person was held under a false name in a secluded cell in an Israeli prison and committed suicide in that cell in 2012. The person was identified as Ben Zigier and the Australian programme claimed that he was a Mossad agent. In the Israeli media reports about the affair were suppressed by a court order given by the President of the Central District Court from 2010, that was later affirmed by the SC, that banned any publication on the matter, including publications quoting foreign media sources or referral to foreign internet websites. The court also banned the publication of its own order, thereby preventing any mentioning of the affair that was later entitled 'Prisoner X' by the media. The gag order concerning the suicide of Ben Zigier was removed at the request of the state shortly after the airing of the Australian programme but the circumstances of his incarceration are still suppressed. In an unusual move, on 21 February 2012, the AG publicized a letter that was sent to the editor of Haaretz newspaper concerning the alleged violation of the initial gag order by Haaretz Online website. The AG asserted that Haaretz published the details of the Australian investigative report before the gag order was removed and therefore committed a criminal offence. The AG clarified that he considered indicting the newspaper but decided not to do so in light of the restrained prosecutorial approach in matters of freedom of speech and the fact that the website took the report down after three hours, after a request from state officials. The AG added that similar violations in the future shall meet a less tolerant approach.

Less than a week after this letter, SC Justice Uzi Vogelman noted in obiter dictum that when issuing gag orders in matters of high public profile the court should bear in mind the fact that such injunctions may be violated on the internet. Justice

65. Negbi, *supra* n. 37, at 200.

66. A case in point is the suppressed identity of the state's principle witness in a highly publicized corruption trial that started in 2012 against businessmen and government officials including *inter alia* former Prime Minister Ehud Olmert and former Mayor of Jerusalem Uri Lopolyansky. The courts persistently refused to allow the publication of the witness's identity in spite of the fact that information about his identity was available on the internet to such an extent that entering the Hebrew words 'state witness' in the Google search screen automatically suggests the witness's name as one of the top search results. The witness eventually passed away during the trial, which is ongoing as of this writing, and the court subsequently allowed the publication of his name.

Vogelman nevertheless observed that gag orders are generally being complied with even at this day and age.[67]

107. Article 70(c) of the Law of the Courts forbids the publication of the name of a minor less than 18 years of age who is accused or is a witness in a criminal case without the prior consent of the court.

108. Broadcasting a recorded audio or visual documentation of a suspect's investigation by the police is forbidden during the course of a criminal proceeding unless expressly authorized by the court.[68]

109. Prior to election days, limitations on propaganda apply. The prohibition on political propaganda in the Election Law (Means of Electioneering) 1959 has different applications in print, internet and audio-visual media (the limitations of audio-visual media are discussed *infra* in part III, Chapter 4). Limitations apply ninety days before the elections (Article 2 Elections Law) with respect to print media. There are no limitations on propaganda in print media, but Article 10b Elections Law limits the number of advertisements by political parties to one per day per newspaper, and a size limitation is also included. The law does not expressly prevent a newspaper from distributing an advertising 'insert' of any size (which is not part of the newspaper itself) thereby allowing a circumvention of the advertisement limitation. No limitation on advertisement applies to advertisements on internet websites.

§4. Spectrum of *A Posteriori* Restrictive Measures

110. Defence and security concerns lie at the heart of many *a posteriori* restrictive measures and consequently these measures include harsh criminal and administrative sanctions. Violating the decrees of the Chief Military Censor is a criminal offence punishable by up to five years of imprisonment and/or a fine. However, the Chief Military Censor has a much more powerful sanction at his or her disposal. According to Regulation 100 of the Defence (Emergency) Regulations 1945 the Chief Military Censor has the authority to shut down without due process any publication that did not comply with the Military Censor's submission decree or violated an order to suppress a publication of material. The SC noted that this oppressive authority must be reserved to 'very rare' and 'unusual' occasions, yet the court has affirmed the use of this authority more than once.[69]

67. Cri. A. 8225/12 *Plonit (minor) v. Ploni* (2013).
68. Article 13 of the Criminal Procedure (Investigation of Suspects) Law, 2002.
69. The most notable case was HCJ 234/84 *Hadashot v. Minister of Defence* 38(2) 477 [1984]. In this case in 1984 the newspaper 'Hadashot' did not submit to prior review by the Military Censor a report about the decision of the Minister of Defence to set up an inquiry commission to investigate the murder of two terrorists who hijacked a bus in March of that year and were captured alive by the Israeli Security Service and later declared dead. The court affirmed the Chief Military Censor's decision to shut the newspaper down for a period of four days. In later criminal proceedings against the newspaper, its editors and its reports the court noted that the violating publication had in fact contributed

111. There are several penal laws limiting freedom of speech. It should be noted, however that the criminal prosecution adopted a restrained enforcement policy regarding penal laws curtailing freedom of speech in light of the SC's high regard to this right and its fundamental democratic significance.[70] Here are some examples of such laws:

(a) Rebellious publications are a criminal offence punishable by up to five years of imprisonment.[71] This offence applies to any publication which intends to inflame hatred, disloyalty or contempt with regards to the government; attempts to bring about changes to legal order through illegal activities; spreads discontent among the population or inflames hatred among various parts of the population.[72]
(b) Publishing a report or even a rumour that may cause public fear, panic or a public disturbance is a criminal offence when the publisher is aware that the publication is false.[73]
(c) Inciting against serving in the army is punishable by up to five years in prison.[74] Inciting insubordination is punishable by up to one year imprisonment. When the latter is done with the purpose of harming national security the maximum penalty increases to five years and when it is done during a time of hostilities the maximum term is seven years.[75]
(d) Racial incitement was criminalized in 1986 through the legislation of Articles 144A to 144C of the Penal Law, 1977, and it is punishable by up to five years in prison, but an indictment for such an offence requires the prior authorization of the Attorney General personally.[76] The law states that a fair and true report about an act of incitement will not be considered an offence provided that it was not made for the purpose of inciting to racism. The language of the law requires that the offender had acted with the intent of inciting to racism but the SC held

to revealing a cover up scheme in connection with the inquiry commission and revoked a fine against the accused. See Negbi, *supra* n. 37, at 103–104.

70. In HCJ 6271/96 *Beeri v. The Attorney General*, 50(4) PD 425 [1996] the court affirmed the Attorney General's refusal to indict the publishers of a political advertisement blaming Prime Minister Benjamin Netanyahu for inciting and bringing about the murder of Prime Minister Yizhak Rabin.
71. Article 134 of the Penal Law, 1977. The Attorney General applies a restrained policy to hate speech and incitement. See Elyakim Rubinstein, *On Freedom of Expression and the Policy of the Prosecution in Incitement to Violence Offences*, 44 Hapraklit 5 (1998); Raphael Cohen-Almagor, *Regulating Hate and Racial Speech in Israel*, 17 Cardozo J. of Int'l & Comp. Law 405, 413 (2009).
72. Article 136 of the Penal Law, 1977. However, propaganda and critical publications about the government supporting political changes in legal activities are expressly permitted according to Art. 138.
73. Article 159(a) of the Penal Law, 1977. This article has never been implemented.
74. Article 109 of the Penal Law, 1977.
75. Article 110 of the Penal Law, 1977. The Attorney General has refused time and time again to implement this offence. In 1993 following the Oslo Accords between Israel and the Palestinian Liberation Organization former Chief Rabbi (the highest rabbinical authority within the government) Shlomo Goren declared that a soldier must refuse an order to evict settlements in Judea, Samaria and Gaza. In 2005 similar calls were made by influential Rabbis prior to the Israeli eviction and retreat from the Gaza strip. In both occasions the prosecution refused to act. Negbi, *supra* n. 37, at 121–123.
76. Article 144E of the Penal Law, 1977.

that it is sufficient for the prosecution to show that the offender should have expected with near certainty that his publication will be interpreted as inciting to racism by the relevant audience.[77] There is a certain overlap between this offence and the offence of rebellious publications aimed at inflaming hatred.[78]

It is important to note that holding racial views is not criminal in and of itself according to the Israeli Penal Law. However, within the definition of 'Prohibited Association' in Article 145(2a) of the Penal Law, 1977, there is a list which includes an organized association of persons who advocate or promote racism or principles of Nazism. Membership, support or dissemination of the publications of such an association is a criminal offence.

Racial discrimination in the provision of products or services is also a civil tort and an offence punishable by a fine according to the Prohibition of Discrimination in Products, Services, Entrance to Entertainment Venues and Public Locations Law, 2000. According to Article 3 of the law, the same is true for discrimination on the basis of religion, religious affiliation, nationality, sex, sexual inclination, age, country of origin, opinion, partisan affiliation, marital status or parenthood. Article 4 prohibits discriminatory advertisements.

(e) Inciting violence or terror when there is a 'real possibility' that such a publication will lead to a violent or a terror act, is punishable by up to five years in prison according to Article 144D2 of the Penal Law, 1977. This article expressly protects the media by noting that a fair and true account of such incitement is not an offence.

(f) Publications injuring the faith or 'religious feelings' of others are a criminal offence according to Article 173 of the Penal Law, 1977. This offence is also rarely enforced. In one case, however, the SC affirmed the conviction of a woman that printed pamphlets depicting a pig with the name of Mohammed on them, with the intention of spreading them on Palestinian shops in the occupied city of Hebron.[79]

112. Offending a public official in words or actions with regards to his or her duty or in the course of performing their duty is punishable by up to six months in prison.[80]

---

77. Cr. A 2831/95 *Rabbi Iddo Alba v. The State of Israel*, 50(5) PD 221 [1996].
78. For example, Benjamin Kahane was convicted of rebellious incitement rather than racist incitement for publishing an election pamphlet calling for the bombing of Arab towns and communities in Israel in retaliation to terrorist attacks and describing these towns as 'nests of wasps' and 'nests of killers'. Cr. F.A. (Criminal Further Appeal) 1789/98 *State of Israel v. Benjamin Kahane* 54(5) PD 145 [1998]. In addition, Art. 4 of the Law of Defamation states that defaming a public group is a criminal offence punishable by up to one year in prison.
79. Cr. A 697/98 *Tatiana Sotzkin v. State of Israel* 52(3) PD 289 [1998].
80. Note that offending remarks constitute an offence regardless of whether they are true or false. It therefore follows that proving the truthfulness of an offending statement does not constitute a defence against a criminal indictment. It comes as no surprise that in reflection of the restrained application of the law, the Attorney General announced in 1998 that this offence will not be enforced when the offended person is an elected public official. This policy reflects both the ability of the offended public official to confront offending allegations in the public domain and the prosecution's acquiescence of the problematic nature of the offence.

113. In some cases the limitation on the freedom of speech is directed at particular groups. For instance, Articles 1(4) and 1(5) of the Public Service Law (Limitation on Partisan Activities and Fund Raising) 1959 forbid employees of the public service from partaking in public electioneering activities, criticizing the government's policy in public, especially in a journalistic interview or a similar publication. Offenders may be subject to disciplinary sanctions, up to dismissal. However, the courts have confined this limitation on civil servants' critical speech to cases where the expression will harm the public service or its interests with high probability.[81]

114. Several articles of the Penal Law serve as barriers preventing information from reaching the media. For example:

(a) Any person disseminating secret information without the authority to do so is exposed to a punishment of up to fifteen years in prison.[82] If the information concerns state security, the act is defined 'severe espionage' and is subject to life term imprisonment.[83] Obtaining such information and holding it, as journalists often do, is in itself a crime subject to a punishment of fifteen years in prison.[84] It should be noted that government officials drafting a document can generate a barrier to its dissemination by simply entitling the document 'top secret', whereby a media person accused of obtaining such a document will bear the burden of proving that there is no security reason for the document's classification. There is no specific legislation as to who has the authority to classify

81. Daphne Barak, *The Freedom of Speech of Civil Servants*, 16 Iyunei Mishpat 389 (1991) supports a restricted application of these limitations in a manner that allows civil servants to criticize the government but limits their political and partisan activities.
82. Article 113A of the Penal Law, 1977.
83. Article 113 of the Penal Law, 1977.
84. Indeed there have been several attempts to use Art. 113 against journalists. See Negbi, *supra* n. 37, at 156–157. The most recent and highly publicized case involved the dissemination of secret military documents by a former soldier named Anat Kam, who copied these secret documents when she served as a secretary in the office of the General in charge of the IDF Central Command. Kam delivered a portable memory device with approximately 1800 documents to Haaretz correspondent Uri Blau, who published articles on the basis of the information including photos of the documents. The reports concerned the IDF policy regarding the targeting and elimination of leaders of Hamas terrorism cells in the Occupied Territories. The reports were cleared for publication by the Military Censorship, which indicated that their publication did not pose with near certainty a clear and present danger to national security. However, the security services conducted an investigation and were able to trace the leak to Kam, who was indicted, convicted and sentenced to a prison term for severe espionage. Blau fled Israel to England enabling the newspaper to negotiate the handover of the secret documents and Blau's return to Israel in return for the prosecution's lenient treatment of the case. On July 2012 Blau was convicted according to Art. 113 (although the prosecution avoided entitling his actions as severe espionage and defined his violation as 'possession of a secret document') and sentenced to a term of four months of community service work. The court explained the lenient verdict by noting, *inter alia*, that punishing a journalist for actions that were part of his journalistic work has a chilling effect on the freedom of speech. Cr. Case 10677-07-12 *(Magistrate Ct. Tel Aviv) State of Israel v. Blau* (2012). In the beginning of 2013 Kam filed a lawsuit against Blau and Haaretz alleging that her identity was revealed as a result of the newspaper's negligence in protecting her confidentiality as a source.

documents as secret or as to the level of secrecy that should be attached to sensitive documents.

(b) Civil servants are forbidden from communicating any information they receive in the course of their duty to an 'unauthorized person', according to Article 117 of the Penal Law, 1977. It is therefore a criminal offence punishable by up to three years imprisonment to leak information to the press. This limitation applies for a period of five years after the civil servant's retirement and encompasses all types of information regardless of their potential harm or importance to the public. A journalist persuading a civil servant to leak information might be accused of committing a criminal offence himself. Several legislative proposals to water down Article 117 have not materialized.[85]

115. Defamation is not only a civil tort according to the Prohibition of Defamation Law 1965, but it can also be a criminal offence punishable by up to one year in prison.[86] Article 8 of the Prohibition of Defamation Law allows victims to initiate a private criminal proceeding when the public prosecution refrains from such an action. However, as the burden of proof on the injured party is significantly higher in a criminal proceeding compared to a civil claim it is a rarely used and less appealing alternative from the offended party's point of view. The private criminal proceeding is sometimes used as a strategic measure by plaintiffs to exert pressure on defendants in order to induce a higher compensation in settlement agreements.[87]

116. A breach of privacy could constitute a civil tort as well as a criminal offence under the Privacy Protection Law, 1981, much like defamation. Similarly, a criminal proceeding can be initiated by the victim, but there are no documented cases to this effect. Article 5 of the Privacy Protection Law, 1981, states that such an offence is punishable up to five years in prison.

117. Several legal *a posteriori* restrictions apply to the coverage of legal proceedings. These include:

(a) Article 71(a) of the Law of the Courts, also referred to as the '*Sub Judice* rule' criminalizes reporting about an ongoing criminal proceeding (but not on a civil proceeding) when such a report is done with the purpose of influencing the outcome of the case or when such an influence is foreseeable with near certainty, provided that the state can prove that the publication can, in fact, influence the

85. Negbi, *supra* n. 37, at 142–143. Since the legislation of Art. 117, only two civil servants have been accused and convicted of committing this offence.

86. Article 6 Law of Defamation.

87. There is no law dealing with strategic lawsuits against public participation ('SLAPP') in Israel. In a report published in 2012, the Association for Civil Rights in Israel found that SLAPP lawsuits were a common phenomenon and that they were directed not just at media organizations and journalists but also against employees who complained about their work conditions, social activists, consumers and members of the academic community. In most SLAPP cases, the plaintiffs were unsuccessful, but the mere imposition of legal costs on the defendants has a chilling effect on freedom of expression.

judicial process. The language of the prohibition echoes its original English origin,[88] but the enforcement of this prohibition is extremely rare.[89]

(b) Contemptuous publications against a judge or a court, as opposed to polite criticism, are criminalized in Article 255 of the Penal Law, 1977 and punishable by up to three years, but enforcement of this offence is rare.

118. Disseminating pornography is prohibited by Article 214 of the Penal Law, 1977. The punishment for this offence is up to three years imprisonment. In case of child pornography, including illustrations, the maximal punishment increases to five years. Additionally, showing violent, humiliating or abusive sexual relations is prohibited by the Communications Law. Nevertheless, this prohibition has been interpreted narrowly and the HCJ affirmed the broadcasting of erotic and pornographic television channels with code-restricted access.[90]

§5. PRIOR AUTHORIZATION FOR PUBLISHING

119. There is no law directly regulating the practice of journalism but publishing a newspaper is subject to prior registration and authorization. This is the result of British Mandate security-oriented legislation that has not been abolished in spite of its anti-democratic and obsolete nature. Article 4 of the Press Ordinance 1933 states that no newspaper may be printed without the prior permission of the District Commissioner. Article 2 defines the term 'newspaper' broadly to encompass any non-governmental printed publication containing news, information, opinion, commentary or matters of public importance, in any language, sold or distributed free of charge frequently or infrequently.

120. Article 5 of the Press Ordinance states that permission to publish a newspaper will only be given subject to the submission of a sworn declaration containing:

- The name, age, place of residence and postal address of the applicant.
- The applicant's declared ownership of the newspaper.
- The name of the newspaper.
- The location in which the newspaper is edited and printed.
- The topics with which the newspaper will be concerned.
- The language and the frequency of the publication.

---

88. Note that the English *Sub Judice* rule addresses the concern of influencing the jury in criminal trials whereas in Israel criminal defendants are tried before professional judges. See also: Reem Segev, *Freedom of Expression: Justifications and Restrictions* 639 (Israeli Democracy Institute 2008) (hereinafter – Segev).

89. In Civ. A. 409/13 *Keshet Broadcasting Ltd v. Shimon Cooper* (2013) the SC overruled a District Court's decision to issue an injunction against the broadcasting of a television programme that included interviews with witnesses and with the accused in a murder trial that was about to begin. The SC President Grunis overruled on procedural grounds but reiterated that even where the *Sub Judice* rule is concerned, *a posteriori* enforcement should be preferred over prior restraint in matters of freedom of speech.

90. HCJ 5432/03 *Shin v. The Council for Cable and Satellite Broadcasting* 58(3) PD 65 [2004].

- That the applicant is not the owner of a newspaper the publication of which has been stopped or banned.
- If the applicant is a local legal entity the declaration must be signed by its director and its secretary.
- If the applicant is a foreign legal entity the declaration must be signed by its local legally empowered representative.

121. Article 5 of the Press Ordinance further requires a sworn declaration by the chief editor of the newspaper confirming *inter alia* that he or she is at least 25 years of age; has passed the Israeli high school graduation exams ('Bagrut') or an equivalent exam; can speak, read and write the language of the newspaper; has never been convicted and sentenced for longer than three months imprisonment; has not been disbarred from practicing as a lawyer or a medical doctor; etc.

122. This strict legislation is bolstered by Regulation 94 of the Defence (Emergency) Regulations, 1945, also originating from the British Mandate and incorporated into the existing Israeli law due to the state's ongoing perceived existential security threats. The regulation allows the District Commissioner to refrain from permitting the publication, to add whatever conditions deemed fit to such a permit or to stop the publication of a newspaper altogether, without cause. The HCJ has voiced its strong discontent with Regulation 94, but it has never forced the authorities to provide cause for their decision to refuse newspaper permit requests.[91] Nor has the HCJ applied the 'near certainty' test to the application of this regulation.[92] Consequently, it has become routine for the state authorities to use this regulation in order to prevent the publication of newspapers or shut them down, instead of applying the Minister of Interior's parallel authority to desist a publication which has been significantly curtailed by the *Kol Ha'am* ruling. In spite of several political and government-driven proposals to supplant Regulation 94's permit regime with a registration-only regime, the existing legal situation persists.[93] The HCJ's willingness to accept, de facto, a prior authorization regime is incongruent with its liberal approach towards minimizing prior restraint, as discussed *supra* in sub-chapter §3. This can be explained by the HCJ's tendency to limit its scrutiny of matters concerning the nation's ongoing declared state of emergency. Additionally, considering the fact that the prior authorization regime is unusual among modern democracies, the HCJ has deferred the matter to the hands of the legislature. While some state law commissions and state officials suggested abolishing the prior authorization regime and substituting it with a registration regime, this has not happened.

---

91. Petitions against permit denials are often denied due to the inability of the petitioners to refute the state's unknown causes for denying the permit. See: HCJ 39/64 *El Ard Company v. Commissioner of the Northern District*, 18(2) PD 340 [1964] and HCJ 322/81 *Machul v. Commissioner of the District of Jerusalem*, 37(1) PD 789 [1981]. In an unusual case, HCJ 2/29 *El Asad v. Minister of Interior* 34(1) PD 505 [1979], the state voluntarily disclosed that the reason for denying the permit was its claim that the applicant was a senior member of a communist terrorist organization. The petitioner was able to refute the state's claims and the petition was granted. See also Negbi, *supra* n. 37, at 71-72.
92. HCJ 541/83 *Asli v. Commissioner of the District of Jerusalem*, 37(4) PD 837 [1983].
93. Negbi, *supra* n. 37, at 76–77.

123. A Special prior authorization regime applies to films, when they are shown in cinemas. Films and theatre plays were subject to prior authorization and prior censorship by the Council for the Prior Authorization of Films and Plays (the 'Film Council'). The council was established by the British Mandate-era Cinematographic Films Ordinance 1927 and had disqualified several plays before 1989, during which time its authority with regards to plays has been abolished. The Film Council is still in charge of authorizing films, mostly with respect to the minimal age restrictions. However, according to Article 4 Cinematographic Films Ordinance and Article 15 of the Films and Plays Council Regulations 1979, the Film Council is empowered to prohibit the screening of films and no film may be screened without its prior authorization. The Film Council is comprised of public representatives and civil servants and is part of the Ministry of Science, Culture and Sports. Its censorship powers have been curtailed by several decisions of the HCJ over the years.

124. In 1997, the Film Council banned the screening of the Japanese film 'L'empire de Sens' for hard core pornographic material. The HCJ overruled the decision and held that freedom of expression protects artistic expression and that the film has artistic value and that several extreme pornographic scenes should be viewed as part of the whole film.[94]

125. In 2002 the Film Council banned the screening of a drama-documentary film 'Jenin-Jenin' by actor and director Mohamed Bakri which claimed to document crimes against humanity committed by Israeli soldiers in the West Bank town of Jenin during the military operation 'Defensive Shield'.[95] The Film Council explained its decision by stating that the film contained false one sided representation of the actions of Israeli soldiers which borders with incitement and de-legitimizes the existence of the State of Israel. The HCJ overruled the decision of the Film Council and reiterated the centrality of freedom of speech to the democratic rationale. The HCJ held that those wishing to prevent the airing of a film accusing Israeli soldiers of crimes should confront the film's claims and refute them through open discourse rather than by prior restraint.[96]

126. In light of the fact that the only two cases in which the Film Council decided to entirely ban a film since 1997 have been overruled by the HCJ it is reasonable to assert that the Film Council's discretion to completely ban a film (as opposed to censoring parts thereof or classifying the appropriate viewing age) has been effectively abolished.

127. It should be noted that the Film Council's authorities apply only to cinematographic films and only insofar as they are screened in cinemas. The classification of audio-visual content (films, programmes and advertisements) broadcasted

---

94. HCJ 4804/94 *Station Film v. The Film Council*, 50(5) PD 661 [1997].
95. Defensive Shield' was a military operation in March 2002 that followed a terrorist attack on a hotel in Israel. During the operation IDF soldiers entered the town and refugee camp of Jenin. According to IDF data, in the ensuing harsh house-to-house combat 23 soldiers and 52 Palestinians were killed. Approximately half of the latter were civilians. See also Navot, *supra* n. 1, at 238–239.
96. HJC 316/03 *Bakri v. The Films and Plays Council*, 58(1) PD 249 [2003].

on television is governed by the Classification, Indication and Prohibition of Harmful Broadcasts Law 2001 (the 'Classification Law') (discussed in part II, Ch. 3 at §3) and is the responsibility of the broadcasters. Hence, a film that was not screened commercially in Israel will not bear a Film Council classification and will only be classified once it is broadcasted by one of the television broadcasters.[97] Interestingly, a television broadcaster may apply a different classification to a film broadcasted on television than the classification attached to the film earlier by the Film Council. However, such a discrepancy would be rare as it might expose the broadcaster to sanctions if the regulatory authority believes that the Film Council's classification was accurate.

97. Rule 2(1) BCL prohibits broadcasters on multichannel platforms from broadcasting films that were not approved by the Film Council. However, it seems the rule does not enjoin broadcasting films that were not submitted to Film Council at all, but rather applies to films that were banned by the Film Council.

Part II. Regulation of Print Media

Chapter 1. The Journalists' Profession

§1. Notion

128. There are no significant statutory barriers to taking up the practice of journalism by any individual. In fact, the term 'journalist' is not defined by law and no licensing or registration is required.[98] This legal situation reflects the common perception that journalism should be free from state regulation and that the mere definition of the term 'journalist' may open the gates to governmental intervention in determining who may practice the profession.

129. Although there is no permit or license required in order to practice journalism, access to some governmentally disseminated information and events arranged by the branches of the government may be restricted to holders of a Press Card which is issued by the Government Press Office ('GPO'). The GPO is a unit within the Prime Minister's Office charged with liaising between the government and the foreign media representatives working in Israel. However, the GPO issues Press Cards to both Israeli and international newspersons, production staff, technical staff and assistants. There are two types of Press Cards: a permanent card and visitor card which is issued to foreign newspersons staying in Israel for a period of less than a year (in addition, a newspersons that has less than one year of professional experience or employment contract will only be issued a visitor card).

The GPO's activities are not regulated by a specific law but as a government body it is subject to administrative law and judicial review. It has internal procedures that are available on its website. The HCJ has therefore ruled that the GPO cannot refrain from issuing the Press Card without a reasonable explanation, thereby striking down the GPO's refusal to issue press cards to journalists employed by regional and local newspapers.[99] In several cases, the GPO refused to issue press cards to Palestinian journalists working in the occupied territories. The HCJ held that the GPO's practice of collectively refusing to issue press cards to Palestinian journalists who reside in the occupied territories based on a general claim that they pose a 'security danger' is illegal due to the fact that it was collective and unfounded.

98. Furthermore, the SC notes that in the age of internet freedom of expression is amplified by the fact that 'any person may start his own "newspaper" by blogging' (author's translation). See LCiv. A. 4447/07 *Rami Mor v. Barak E.T.C* (2009).

99. HCJ 509/80 *Yones v. General Director of the Prime Minister's Office*, 35(3) PD 589 [1981].

Hence, a refusal can only be justified by an individual security check.[100] As of 2004, the GPO has an internal procedure for Palestinian journalists applying for a Press Card. The procedure which is available on the GPO website states that issuing the card is subject to the Palestinian applicant being legally employed in Israel and to a screening by the Israeli security authorities. The GPO internal rules also permit the GPO to refuse issuing a Press Card to a citizen of an enemy state unless the GPO director is satisfied that the applicant poses no danger to state security. The HCJ also struck down a petition to require the GPO to revoke the Press Card of employees in the French network 'France2' due to alleged misrepresentation of an incident in the Gaza strip that resulted in the killing of a 12 year old Palestinian child, Mohammed Al-Dura. The court held that even if the television reportage was unreliable, this does not justify revoking a Press Card.[101]

Some foreign newspersons stationed in Israel for long periods of time complained in 2006 that the renewal process of their work visas was intentionally slow in order to chill unfavourable reporting about Israel, as they were compelled to work in the country illegally with only a tourist visa in hand. However, we do not know of any documented court case dealing with such an issue.

130. The HCJ also compelled the GPO to revise its internal rules in order to enable the issuance of press cards to writers working for user generated news websites.[102]

131. Journalistic coverage of the IDF raises more complex issues due to the possible exposure of national security information to civilians. Israeli journalists covering the IDF are screened by the IDF prior to being given access to military bases, personnel and information.[103] Although it is not founded on any specific law, the HCJ has authorized this practice in 1962 and has not revisited the issue since then.[104]

§2. Subsidies to the Press

132. There are no government subsidies to the printed press. However, at the outset of the commercial television broadcasting a unique three year transitional compensation arrangement was adopted by law in order to 'balance' the private print media for losses of revenue due to the expected shift in advertising from newspapers to commercial broadcasting.

133. Articles 104–106 SATRL determined that daily newspapers and cinemas whose revenue will fall as a result of the entrance of commercial television broadcasting will receive a grant from the SATR. The funding for the grant was drawn

100. HCJ 5627/02 *Seif v. The Government Press Office*, 58(3) PD 70 [2004].
101. HCJ 10324/07 *Shurat Hadin v. The Government Press Office* (2008).
102. HCJ 7721/07 *Scoop.co.il v. The Government Press Office* (2010), interim order.
103. Negbi, *supra* n. 37, at 92-93.
104. HCJ 29/62 *Cohen v. The Minister of Defence* 16 PD 1023 [1962].

from the royalties paid by the commercial broadcasters according to their franchise, after deducting the SATR's operational costs. The SATR was authorized to determine the sum allotted each year for the grant's purpose and a committee headed by a retired judge determined the distribution of the grant. The grant was limited to a three year period starting from November 1993. However, it failed to compensate the daily printed media's actual losses. In the first year, the SATR allotted a total of NIS 1.3 million to the grant whereas the committee entrusted with apportioning the grant funds among the relevant daily newspapers and cinemas determined that the actual losses were NIS 7.2 million. In the second year the royalties allotted for compensation reached NIS 5.6 million, which still did not cover the estimated losses of NIS 7.9 million. Only the third year's royalties-based grant set at NIS 13 million covered the entire loss estimated that year at NIS 5.4 million. However, the SATR refused a request to distribute the third year's grant's surplus as an ex post compensation for the partial coverage of the grant in the previous years. The SATR's position was later affirmed by the HCJ that denied a petition by daily newspapers and cinemas and held that the definition of the unusual statutory balancing arrangement as a grant rather than a compensation scheme meant that there was no obligation on the SATR to distribute more than the annual loss estimated in each year.[105]

105. HCJ 5439/98 *Haaretz Publishing v. The SATR*, 53(5) PD 224 [1999].

Chapter 2. Journalists' Rights

§1. ROLE OF JOURNALISTS AS WATCHDOGS OF SOCIETY

134. The media are broadly perceived by the courts to be the public's representative in safeguarding the democratic nature of the state and journalists as a whole are sometimes referred to as the 'fourth estate' entrusted with checking the proper functioning of other state branches. The media are also perceived to be the guardian of freedom of speech, which is perceived to be a fundamental tenet of a democratic state.[106]

135. In accordance with this view, the SC envisions journalists as the public's agents not only in collecting and disseminating information but also in criticizing the government, in exposing negative phenomena and in acting as the 'watchdogs of democracy and of compliance with the law'.[107]

136. Consequently, it was held in CA 751/10 *Ploni v. Dr. Ilana Dayan-Orbach* that the mission of the press may justify affording it with particular rights and powers with regards to freedom of speech beyond those applicable to the ordinary public, but at the same time with regards to matters of 'the utmost social importance' the press also has a moral and legal obligation to publish information which is deemed to be of public interest.[108] On the other hand, the SC required that the press abide by principles of 'responsible journalism' as a prerequisite for enjoying a bona fide defence against a defamation lawsuit regarding a publication.[109]

137. The decision of the SC in CA 751/10 *Ploni v. Dr. Ilana Dayan-Orbach* is noteworthy for tilting the scales in favour of the press in several aspects. This pro-media approach has not always been the SC's policy. For example, in 1989 the HCJ denied a petition by Haaretz journalist Aluf Benn requesting statistical government data on police wiretapping. The HCJ held that without an express statutory duty to provide such information there is no obligation to provide the information to the press in spite of the fact that without the information the press would not be able to perform its function of providing information to the public.[110] Due to the innovative nature of the ruling in *Ploni v. Dr. Ilana Dayan-Orbach*, the President of the SC ordered another review of the main legal issues of the ruling before a wider panel of the SC. Oral arguments took place in the beginning of 2013. As of the writing of this monograph a final ruling has not yet been given.

---

106. HCJ 509/80 *Yones v. General Director of the Prime Minister's Office*, 35(3) PD 589, at 591 [1981].
107. CA 751/10 *Ploni v. Dr. Ilana Dayan-Orbach* (2012).
108. CA 751/10 *Ploni v. Dr. Ilana Dayan-Orbach* (2012).
109. CA 751/10 *Ploni v. Dr. Ilana Dayan-Orbach* (2012).
110. HCJ 414/89 *Aluf Benn v. Minister of Justice* 44(3) PD 327 [1989].

§2. JOURNALISTS' INDEPENDENCE

I. Written Press

138. The main threat to a journalist's independence in the print media is the occupational dependency on the newspaper's owner as the journalist's source of livelihood. In a clash between the journalist's freedom of speech and the owner's right to dictate the agenda of the newspaper, courts have ruled in favour of the owner. Courts have balanced the freedom of the press vis-à-vis the media owners' property rights and in the outcome of this analysis favoured the owner's right to property which is a constitutional right protected by Basic Law: Human Dignity and Liberty over the individual journalist's freedom, embodied in the freedom of the press, which is not expressly protected by any Basic Law.

139. The seminal case on the matter concerned journalist Joanna Yechiel and stemmed from the National Labour Court. The case concerned a group of journalists that resigned from the Jerusalem Post after its acquisition by a publisher that dictated a Hawkish political line. The labour court held that the owner of a newspaper, whether public or private, has the prerogative to set the political, economic and cultural line of the newspaper. The court further stated that the owner can order a journalist under his employment to write a report about a topic which the owner deems important and direct the journalist in general as to the desirable nature of the report. The journalist may not refuse to write such a report when it concerns the field which he is covering. The court underlined that an owner's refusal to publish a piece written by an employee does not constitute an obstruction of the employee's freedom of speech since the employee can find a different venue or start his own.[111]

140. The HCJ adopted a similar position and held that a publisher has the authority to suppress publications that do not adhere to his policy, and even override his own editors, in spite of a minority opinion by President Meir Shamgar who warned that there exists a concentration of ownership in the media and that media owners 'know well how to exert their powers'.[112]

---

111. Labor Court 223-3 *Palestine Post v. Joanna Yechiel* (1994). The case concerned the resignation of employees of the newspaper Jerusalem Post after the newspaper's acquisition by a publisher with a significantly different political agenda than his predecessor. The labour court held that a journalist's resignation due to her disagreement with the newspaper's new political line does not generate a right to special compensation. For a discussion of the models of freedom of speech characterizing the case law of the Israeli SC and the need to adopt a clear model in order to address the balance between the constitutional right to property and the right to freedom of speech see: Ilana Dayan-Orbach, *The Democratic Model of Freedom of Speech*, 20 Iyunei Mishpat 377 (1996).
112. HCJ 6218/93 *Dr. Shlomo Cohen v. The Israeli Bar Association* 49(2) PD 529 [1995]. In this case the publisher was the governing committee of the Israeli Bar Association, a politically elected body. The HCJ affirmed the decision of the committee to suppress an article written by a political opponent of the chairman of the bar from being published in the bar's journal in spite of an earlier authorization by the editors of the journal. See also Negbi, *supra* n. 37, at 262–263.

141. The recent protection of the journalists' right to establish a labour union could serve as a trigger to change this balance.[113] However, it is premature to estimate the outcome of a future conflict between the professional interests of an individual journalist and those of the media outlet owner.

142. It should be noted that the strong protection of the owners' interests by the courts, in conjunction with the legislature's recognition that there indeed exists a concentration of ownership in the national newspaper arena, served as one of the justifications for legislating cross ownership limitations which inhibit the ability of newspaper owners to hold controlling stakes in commercial radio or television channels thereby increasing the potential for pluralism.[114] I discuss this issue in more detail *infra* in part IV.

II. Audio-visual Media

143. The independence of journalists employed by commercial radio and television channels is not significantly more shielded from pressure by owners than that of journalists employed in print media. This reality exists in spite of the statutory structures aimed at limiting the owners' ability to intervene in content. These statutory constructions have been especially fortified in the news corporations of both commercial channels and the operation of separate news production in the cable and satellite platforms (see *infra* in part II, Chapter 3 at §1), which was originally conceived in order to ensure the commercial news corporations' independence.[115] In spite of the statutory effort, the independence of audio-visual news media remains in peril.

144. For example, in September 2011 the general manager, the editor and the anchor of the weekend edition of the commercial Channel 10 News all tendered their resignation protesting an apology forced on the news corporation. The content of the apology retracted a profile report about the Jewish American billionaire Sheldon Adelson. According to some media reports, the news corporation's board of directors did not act as a buffer against pressures, especially in view of the disagreement professed by the corporation's journalists with regards to the instructed apology.[116]

145. In addition, commercial channels are not free from political pressure. These are exerted through the government's control over statutory obligations such as

113. Regional Labor Ct. (Tel Aviv-Yafo) Case 32893-02-12 *Histadrut Haovdim v. Yediot Internet* (2012).
114. Article 41 SATRL.
115. For example, Arts 63–71 SATRL guarantee that CBF holders in the commercial channels will finance their channel's news corporation and enjoy its profits but will only control 40% of the voting power and two fifths of the representation in the board of directors while the effective control of the news corporation will be held by representatives of the public appointed by the SAC.
116. Gili Izikovich, *Channel 10 news chief quits in protest over bosses' apology for Adelson profile*. Haaretz (8 Sep. 2011).

local and original production requirements and through the ability of the government to enforce or delay the obligation to pay royalty payments.

146. For example, when financial distress caused Channel 10's failure to pay the statutory royalties in 2011, the owners of the channel appealed to the Knesset to approve an extension of the debt. According to media reports, the Knesset committee on economic affairs that rejected the plea was controlled by the Knesset coalition members who were acting in discontent with investigative reports broadcasted by Channel 10 earlier that year about the personal travel expenses of the Prime Minister.[117] Consequently, in 2012, Channel 10 was on the brink of shutting down, before American billionaire Ronald Lauder, the current dominant shareholder in Channel 10, invested NIS 80 million in the company after reaching an agreement with the government on the extension of the broadcast franchise

147. Journalists employed by the public broadcasting entities are also exposed to political pressures. The political governance structure of the IBA allows the government to exert direct or indirect political pressure on the professional employees of the IBA's radio and television channels. This pressure is wielded through the promotion of journalists whose opinions and work is viewed as favourable to the government.[118] IBA directors have also been known to promote organizational reforms in which journalists disfavoured by the government were encouraged to retire or faced pay cuts.[119]

§3. Protection of Journalistic Sources

148. Journalists are obliged to protect the confidentiality of their sources according to Article 22 of the Ethics Code of the Press which states that 'a newspaper or a newsperson shall not disclose information communicated to them under condition of confidentiality and shall not disclose the identity of a confidential source unless the source has given his consent'.[120]

149. It should be noted that the ethical obligation is absolute, and broadly encompasses not only the identity of the source but also information and documents provided by the source under the condition that they will not be disclosed even if the source's identity cannot be extracted from the additional information or documents.

117. Gili Izikovich, *Israel's Channel 10 faces Closure after Knesset Rejects Delay of Debt Repayment*, Haaretz (12 Dec. 2011).
118. HCJ 5599/11 *The Journalists' Association in Tel Aviv v. The Government of Israel* (2011).
119. A recent example involved the decision of the IBA management to impose the participation of a controversial journalist, Menachem Benn, on the anchor of the popular morning radio talk show 'Seder Yom' (Agenda), Keren Neubach, in order to 'balance' her critical opinion about the government's social and political line. See Nati Tucker, *IBA Staff Angry about Right-Wing Agenda for Leading Radio Talk Show*, Haaretz (22 Jul. 2012); Emilie Grunzweig, *Menachem Benn: "Seder Yom" Matter is over*, Haaretz (24 Jul. 2012).
120. Author's translation.

150. In contrast, no law recognizes a professional journalistic privilege against the obligation to testify in court about journalistic sources or to cooperate with a police investigation requiring such information. Proposals to enact such a law were expressly rejected by the Knesset.[121]

151. Nevertheless, the SC recognized the journalists' right to protect confidential sources in the landmark *Zitrin* decision.[122] In that case, the SC emphasized that the freedom to collect information is a fundamental tenet of democracy and includes within it the right to protect confidential sources of information. The SC further stated that a journalist has a relative privilege to refuse to testify about the identity of confidential sources but that a court has the discretion to remove this privilege. Removing the privilege is justified when three criteria are met:

(a) The information is relevant to the case;
(b) The information pertains to a material issue in the adjudicated case, but the materiality must clearly outweigh the public interest in the protection of the source, such as in cases of serious crimes and offences or of torts that have grave public implications, in which it is otherwise impossible to conduct a fair trial;[123]
(c) There are no alternative means to adjudicate the specific case save for compelling the disclosure of the journalist's sources.

152. The *Zitrin* ruling does not provide an encompassing protection of confidential sources. For example, courts have authorized search and seizure of information in media organizations and journalists' homes in spite of the *Zitrin* ruling. Unedited journalistic material is also unprotected from seizure,[124] although journalists may not be compelled to hand over to the police unedited journalistic material unless the police shows that it had exhausted all other means of obtaining evidence and that the journalist's material is crucial for the investigation.[125] Courts have obliged several police ex parte requests to receive journalists' telephone and cellular phone call logs in the years following the *Zitrin* ruling.

153. On the other hand, some case law has extended the protection of confidential sources on the basis of the *Zitrin* ruling. For example, the SC held that

---

121. The Evidence Ordinance [New Version] 1971, recognizes professional privileges for medical doctors, lawyers, psychologists, social workers and priests. Negbi, *supra* n. 37, at 148.
122. BS 298/86 *Zitrin v. The Disciplinary Tribunal of the Israeli Bar Association*, 41(2) PD 337 [1987].
123. For example, the court in the *Zitrin* case referred to a serious crime, offence or tort in which justice could not be served without the journalist's testimony about the identity of the confidential source.
124. HCJ 172/88 *Time v. Minister of Defence*, 42(3) PD 139 [1988]. In spite of the court's lack of willingness to protect journalists from search and seizure the police issued an internal guidance requiring any such search to be authorized by a high ranking officer.
125. In Case 35991-12-12 (Dist. Ct. Jerusalem) *Makor Rishon v. State of Israel* (2012) the court upheld the right of a news photographer to refuse a request by the police to hand over unpublished photographes of a violent demonstration that the photographer was invited to document by participants in the demonstration. The court held that if such requests were to be regularly allowed sources may be chilled from notifying the media about these events.

a testifying witness in trial may not be asked whether he was or was not the source of a journalistic publication.[126]

154. The protection of journalistic sources has been bolstered by a recent decision of the SC in a case concerning a police request to compel a press photographer to hand over unpublished photos documenting a riot.[127] In this case the SC clarified that the *Zitrin* privilege applies not only to the identity of the source but also to any information that may reveal the identity of the source, but not to journalistic information that cannot reveal the identity of the source. The SC declined the state's motion to compel the production of the requested photographs.

155. The unique acknowledgement given by the court to the protection of journalists' sources may also be learned from the decision of the HCJ in petitions to strike down the Criminal Procedure (Enforcement Powers – Telecommunications Data) Act, 2007. According to this law, investigative authorities are broadly empowered to compel telephony and telecommunications companies to deliver all requested data regarding the communications of subscribers with the exception of the content of the communication upon an ex parte request submitted to the court. Although the HCJ acknowledged the gross infringement of privacy embodied in the law it refused to strike the law down in the interest of combating crime. However, the HCJ particularly emphasized the potential threat to confidential journalistic sources that may be revealed when the communications data of a journalist are requested. The HCJ therefore ruled that a court shall reject a request for communications data pertaining to a journalist if the subject of the request is not himself a suspect or a victim of a crime.[128]

126. LCA 7329/96 *Hevrat Hachsharat Hayeshuv v. Reshet Schocken*, 51(1) PD 49 [1997].
127. LCri. A. 761/12 *The Sate of Israel v. The United Makor Rishon (Hazofeh) Ltd* (2012).
128. HCJ 3809/08 *Association for Civil Right in Israel v. The Israeli Police* (2012). The HCJ ruled on the matter in an expanded panel of seven justices with the majority opinion delivered by SC President Dorit Beinisch.

Chapter 3. Journalists' Liability

§1. Cascade Liability

156. There is no cascade liability system with regards to the media. To the contrary, especially with regards to civil liability, the case is often that the journalist and the editor as well as the publisher can all be found liable towards the plaintiff, with joint and severed liability.

157. Article 11 of the Prohibition of Defamation Law 1965, states that civil and criminal liability for defamatory publications applies to the journalist, the general editor of the medium, and the responsible editor. The publisher of a newspaper or the owner of an electronic medium is subject to civil liability and not to criminal liability in such cases. Only the general editor can defend himself by showing that he has taken reasonable precautions to prevent the publication of the defamatory publication and was not aware of its existence.[129]

§2. Defamation and Libel

158. Defamation is both a civil tort according to Article 6 of the Prohibition of Defamation Law 1965, and a criminal offence according to Article 7 of that law, punishable by up to one year in prison. The Israeli Prohibition of Defamation Law 1965, is founded on the recognition of the 'constant tension'[130] between a person's good name and the right to freedom of speech, and thus requires constant balancing of interests in the relevant case law.

159. According to Article 1 of the Prohibition of Defamation Law 1965, 'defamation' includes any publication that might cause the following to a person (or a corporation):[131]

- Humiliate a person in the eyes of the public or make the person a target of hate, contempt or ridicule by the public.
- Degrade a person due to attributed actions, behaviour, or qualities.
- Harm a person's job whether in public service or other, occupation, business, or profession.
- Degrade a person due to his race, origin, religion, place of residence, sex or sexual tendency.

---

129. Article 12 of the Law of Defamation extends the civil and criminal liability to printers, sellers and distributors of printed publications that appear with a frequency of more than 40 days.

130. CA 214/89 *Avneri v. Shapira* 43(3) PD 840, 859 [1989].

131. According to Art. 5 one cannot file a civil defamation lawsuit on behalf of an already deceased defamed person. Filing a criminal indictment for such defamation is possible only at the express request of the defamed person's spouse or immediate relatives. If a defamed person dies within six months of the publication without filing a civil or criminal proceedings, his immediate relatives may file a civil claim or a criminal complaints in his stead within six months of the person's death.

160. The definition of 'publication' according to Article 2 of the Prohibition of Defamation Law 1965, refers to oral statements, print, sound, movement or 'any other medium' thereby being sufficiently broad to include any additional new media.

161. Whether a publication is defamatory in the eyes of the public might depend on the relevant group to which the defamed person belongs. The court held that the defamatory nature of the publication shall be examined in light of the values of the social circle of the plaintiff even if these values differ from the values of the general society as long as the values of the social circle do not negate the existence of the general society.[132]

162. A plaintiff will not succeed in a defamation claim when the alleged defamatory publication referred to a group of which the plaintiff was a member, but could not be specifically identified as belonging to that group.[133] An attempt to bring about a judicial interpretative change of this approach has failed in the case of 'Jenin Jenin', a documentary film depicting alleged crimes by IDF soldiers during an invasion to the town of Jenin in the West Bank as part of operation 'Defensive Shield' in 2002. Soldiers participating in the military operation sued the director, Mohamed Bakri for defamation, and were rejected by the District Court. They appealed the ruling. The SC used strong words in ruling that the film included 'concrete and powerful lies' and that it was 'intentionally defamatory' and contained 'purposeful distortion of the events'. However, the court rejected the appeal on the reasoning that the individual soldiers were not identified and therefore the appellants lacked a cause in action. The Judges pointed out that while they found the result 'discomforting' in the concrete case it was justifiable from a policy consideration since in a polarized and divided society such as the Israeli society any other interpretation of Article 4 Prohibition of Defamation Law would induce endless defamation lawsuits by representatives of offended groups.[134]

Notably, in May 2013 the government decided to support an amendment to the Law of Defamation, proposed by right-wing members of the Knesset, that will allow a civil action in defamation in case of a defamatory statement about an IDF military action. The proposed amendment suggests that such an action will be treated procedurally as a class action. This would mean, for example, that filing such a claim shall be exempt from the otherwise obligatory payment of court fees. The proposal has generated public criticism and it is unclear whether it will indeed become law.

---

132. In CA 466/83 *Shaha v. Dardarian*, 39(4) PD 734 [1986] the SC rejected the claim that attributing collaboration with Israeli authorities constitutes defamation in spite of the fact that within the plaintiff's circle of Palestinians in Jerusalem this accusation was degrading and even endangered the plaintiff's safety. The issue has been central to the debate on whether a person's association with homosexual or lesbian tendencies may be defamatory. Viterbo found that at least 20 defamation lawsuits dealt with this question in the recent years. See Hedi Viterbo, *The Crisis of Heterosexuality: Constructing Sexual Identities in Israelio Defamation Law*, 33 Iyunei Mishpat 5, 7 (2010). In the most notable case a magistrate court ordered a local newspaper to pay an unusually high amount at the time of NIS 150,000 to a basketball player to whom the newspaper attributed homosexuality. Civ. Case (Tel Aviv Mag. Ct.) 20174/94 *Shimon Amsalem v. Yossef Klein* (1995).
133. Article 4 of the Law of Defamation.
134. CA 8345/08 *Ofer Ben-Natan v. Mohamed Bakri* (2011).

163. The following publications are protected from civil or criminal action according to Article 13 of the Prohibition of Defamation Law, 1965:

(a) Publication by members of the Knesset in their role as such or a fair account thereof;[135]
(b) Publication from government meetings;
(c) Publications by the government or by the government's decree or by government members in their capacity as such, or by their decree;
(d) Publication by the State Comptroller in his capacity as such;
(e) Publication by a judge, arbitrator, or member of another legally empowered tribunal with judicial or quasi-judicial authority as well as a publication by a party or a party's empowered representative or a witness, all made in the course of a hearing or included in a decision by the said court or tribunal. A fair and accurate account of the proceeding shall also be protected;[136]
(f) A fair and accurate account of a hearing in international forums or tribunals of which Israel is a member or in which it is represented;
(g) A publication obligated by law or by a legally empowered authority;
(h) A fair account reflecting the content of a database authorized or made public by law;
(i) Re-publication of the information included in (a), (c), (d), (f), (g), (h);

164. One possible defence for the media in a civil or criminal defamation proceeding is that the publication was truthful. According to Article 14 of the Prohibition of Defamation Law 1965, it is sufficient that the core of the publication is true and there is no need to prove the truthfulness of every detail. However, the truth is only a defence if the publication is in the interest of the public. The media defendant therefore bears the burden of proving both that the publication was true and that it served the public interest.

165. Until recently, the court held that false defamatory publications cannot be defended by Article 14 even if the defendant acted with utmost professional care and diligence in order to ascertain the truthfulness and accuracy of the publication. This approach has been modified by a decision concerning an investigative television reportage on the actions of an Israeli military outpost in the Gaza Strip broadcasted by the highly regarded programme '*Uvda*' (Fact). The reportage depicted the outpost commander's actions as if he had verified the killing of an unarmed schoolgirl by shooting at her body. The commander was subsequently court martialed and acquitted. He then sued Uvda's anchor and reporter, Ilana Dayan-Orbach, for defamation. The SC accepted the defendant's claim that, in spite of the commander's exoneration, the reportage was 'the truth at that time' and that it was primarily

135. Members of the Knesset are broadly protected from civil or criminal liability for any action or oral or written statement of fact or opinion made in the course of their duty. The protection does not apply to statements negating the existence or democratic or Jewish nature of the state, to incitement to racism, or in support of military or terrorist activities against the state or against Jews or Arabs. See Art. 1 of the Immunity of Members of the Knesset, Rights and Duties Law, 1951.
136. Similar protection applies to the hearings and the reports of public inquiry commissions.

meant to deal with the controversial aspects of Israeli military presence in the Gaza Strip which was an issue of high public interest. The SC further proposed that when a journalist adheres to principles of 'responsible journalism', which can be deduced also from professional journalistic rules of ethics, such behaviour can be a defence when the defamatory publication is of public importance regardless of whether it is found eventually to be incorrect.[137] As of this writing, the *Ploni v. Dr. Ilana Dayan-Orbach* ruling is being reconsidered by a wider panel of the SC.

166. Public figures are expected be more tolerant to defamatory publications. The Israeli SC specifically rejected the U.S. approach that requires a public figure to prove that a publication was false and motivated by actual malice.[138] However, the SC did point out that an individual who is active in the public sphere should be prepared to receive critical appraisals of his actions.[139]

167. The definition of a 'public figure' is rather fluid and depends on the circumstances of each case, such that plaintiffs may be identified by the court as public figures in a concrete event although they are not public figures in general.[140]

168. Another defence in accordance with Article 15 of the Prohibition of Defamation Law 1965, is that the publication was made in good faith. Article 15 contains a list of circumstances considered action in good faith, of which some are relevant to the media. These include:

(a) The publisher was unaware of the existence of the victim, or the circumstances through which the publication implies defamation to the victim;
(b) The publisher's relationship with the victim conferred a legal, moral or social obligation on the publisher to publish;[141]
(c) The publication was an opinion about the behaviour of a person in a judicial, official or public role, regarding the person's public service or a public matter, or concerning the person's character, past, actions or opinions;
(d) The publication was an opinion about the behaviour of a person who is a party, a representative, a witness in an open court hearing or before a hearing of a public inquiry commission;

137. CA 751/10 *Ploni v. Dr. Ilana Dayan-Orbach* (2012).
138. Adopted in *New York Times v. Sullivan*, 376 U.S. 254 (1964).
139. CA 751/10 *Ploni v. Dr. Ilana Dayan-Orbach* (2012), secs. 105–107. The SC acknowledged there are conflicting considerations on the matter. On one hand, public figures have better access to the media and may be better positioned to respond to criticism. On the other hand, this should be balanced against the greater potential for injury suffered by defamed public figures and the concern that individuals will refrain from taking up public positions due to weak protection against this type of defamation.
140. CA 1104/00 *Appel v. Hasson*, 56(2) PD 607, 620 [2002].
141. Note that according a narrow interpretation a complaint against a person to an individual or an authority which is legally empowered to investigate such a complaint enjoys the good faith defence, whereas other publication of the content of such a complaint or even the mere filing of it, are not protected. However, in CA 751/10 *Ploni v. Dr. Ilana Dayan-Orbach* (2012), a wider interpretation seems to confer on the journalist a good faith defence when publishing information of public interest provided that the journalist acted responsibly.

(e) The publication was a review of a public literary, artistic or scientific work including an opinion about the behaviour of the person who published the work or that person's character, past, actions or opinions as manifested in that work;
(f) The publication was a fair and true account of a public meeting or a meeting in a corporation that was open to the public, as long there exist a public interest in the publication;
(g) The publication was for the purpose of condemning or denying previous defamation;
(h) The publication was merely sharing the defamatory information with the medium's editors for the purpose of determining its public dissemination;[142]
(i) The publication occurred in the process of a live radio or television broadcast and the defendant is the editor or owner of the medium and did not know nor could have known of the intention to publish defamatory statements.

169. The burden of proving the good faith defence lies with the defendant. In addition, according to Article 16 of the Prohibition of Defamation Law 1965, there is a strong presumption that the publication was not in good faith when the publication was false and the defendant did not believe that it was true or did not take reasonable measures to ascertain whether it was true, or when the defendant meant to cause harm greater than the reasonable harm required for the protection of the values guarded by Article 15. Furthermore, the good faith defence is completely revoked when the editor or the owner of a medium refuse to appropriately publish a reasonable correction or a retraction demanded by the victim.

170. Evidently, the good faith defence is highly important for the protection of allegedly defamatory statements of opinion. However, it is for the court to decide whether a certain statement was a statement of fact or a statement of opinion. Courts make such determinations by surmising the general impression that a 'reasonable reader' will have about the nature of the publication.[143] Hence, it might be difficult to foresee the court's impression in advance and the media would thus opt to water down its critical opinions in order to reduce the risk of liability.

171. The issue of compensation receives unique attention in the Prohibition of Defamation Law 1965 due to presumption that plaintiffs may find it difficult to prove the exact monetary harm caused by a defamatory publication. A court may therefore inflict on a defendant statutory compensation of up to NIS 50,000 (circa USD 15,000) payable to the plaintiff for each defamatory publication without any proof of harm. The maximal statutory compensation is doubled if the plaintiff was

142. This is required since sharing defamatory information with more than one person is defined as a publication according to Art. 7 of the Law of Defamation.

143. CA 3199/93 *Kraus v. Yedioth Aharonot* 49(2) PD 843, at 857 [1995]. With regards to historical events the SC has taken a relatively lax approach in 323/98 *Sharon v. Benziman*, 56(3) PD 245 [2002] by granting the good faith defence to a disputed historical description. The court's reasoning was that historical descriptions are regularly disputed and the court is not the appropriate forum to ascertain historical facts and narratives.

able to prove the defendant's injurious intent in the publication.[144] The SC has noted however that a court is empowered to inflict higher damages on defamation defendants even when no monetary harm was proven if the court determines that such damages are required for deterrence purposes.[145] Conversely, good faith might be a justification to reduce the inflicted damages even when it is found to be insufficient as a defence against finding the defendant liable.

172. The criminal offence of defamation is considered almost dead letter law. The state prosecution generally refrains from indictments in matters of defamation. Although Article 8 of the Prohibition of Defamation Law 1965, allows complainants to file a private criminal indictment when the state prosecution refrains from action, it is a cumbersome alternative due to the complainant's obligation to prove the defendant's guilt beyond reasonable doubt as opposed to the significantly lighter burden of proof in the civil action alternative.

§3. Privacy

173. The right to a person's privacy is protected by the Privacy Protection Law 1981, and afforded constitutional protection pursuant to Article 7 of Basic Law: Human Dignity and Liberty. The constitutional protection provides that privacy deserves strong recognition as long as the person had not consented to such intrusion of privacy or has waived the right. The Act instructs that the consent should be 'informed' (Article 3). A breach of privacy constitutes a civil tort,[146] as well as a criminal offence, which is punishable by up to five years in prison.[147]

174. In media organizations, the dual civil and criminal liability applies to the person obtaining the information and causing its publication, the editor–in-chief and the editor responsible for the decision to publish the information, whereas the publisher or owner of the medium bears only civil liability.[148]

175. Article 2 of the Privacy Protection Law, 1981, contains a list of actions considered an intrusion of privacy, in the absence of consent:

(a) Spying on a person, including stalking;
(b) Illegal wiretapping;
(c) Photographing a person in his private domain;
(d) Publishing a person's photograph in circumstances that may be humiliating or degrading;
(e) Publishing a photograph of an identifiable person injured in a mass attack taken during or immediately after the attack in circumstances that may be

144. Statutory compensation is fixed to the Consumer's Price Index as of September 1998.
145. CA 89/04 *Nudelman v. Sheransky* (2008).
146. Article 4 of the Privacy Protection Law, 1981.
147. Article 5 of the Privacy Protection Law, 1981. The criminal sanction has not been implemented against the media to date.
148. Article 30 of the Protection of Privacy Law, 1981.

embarrassing, unless the publication is a live broadcast and is not unreasonably intrusive;[149]

(f) Copying or using the content of a letter or document unintended for the public eye without the permission of the writer or the addressee, unless the document is of historic value and created at least fifteen years prior to its use;
(g) Using a person's name, likeness, photograph or voice for profit;[150]
(h) Violating a statutory obligation of secrecy with regards to a person's private affairs;
(i) Violating an explicit or implied contractual obligation of secrecy with regards to a person's private affairs;
(j) Publishing or forwarding private information obtained in one of the methods mentioned in sections (a)-(h);
(k) Using or forwarding private information for a purpose other than the purpose for which it was collected;
(l) Publishing a matter that concerns a person's private life including his or her sexual past, health or behaviour in private domain;
(m) Publishing an identifiable corpse of a person after his death is also an intrusion of privacy unless a consent was given by the person prior to his death, or by his immediate relatives (spouse, parents or all his children or all his brothers and sisters) or by the court if the person has no immediate relatives, or if fifteen years from the person's death have elapsed.

The list is not a closed list and case law may expand the right to privacy to such matters as a person's health, financial situation, sexual tendencies, etc.[151]

176. The definition of the term 'private domain' is of special relevance to the media. Courts have held that a person may enjoy privacy in a shielded private domain even if he is in fact in a public location, thereby limiting the ability of the press to photograph grief and horror stricken terror victims unable to protect themselves against the intrusion in the midst of a terrorist attack.[152] In contrast, it is permissible to photograph and to publish the photograph of a person in the public domain as long as the photograph does not humiliate or degrade the subject. Publishing a humiliating or degrading photograph may constitute a breach of privacy by the publisher, but not by the person who took the photograph.[153]

---

149. Article 2a of the Protection of Privacy Law, 1981, as added in 2011. Mors observes that the presentation of corpses in the Israeli media tends to reflect a consideration of the dignity of Jewish victims but not that of other victims. Tal Mors, *Watching the Death of Others*, 18 Betzalel History and Theory (October 2010) at: http://bezalel.secured.co.il/zope/home/he/1286358025/1286377696.
150. Article 2(6) of the Protection of Privacy Law, 1981, seems to protect the subject's commercial interests rather than the subject's core right to privacy.
151. HCJ 6650/04 *Plonit v. The Rabbinical Court of Netanya* (2006).
152. Negbi, *supra* n. 37, at 184, noting on the other hand that a court held that a prison cell visual recording documenting the life a prisoner and broadcasted on television does not constitute and intrusion of the prisoner's right to privacy if the prisoner is aware of the fact that he is being watched and taped since a prison cell in such circumstances is not a private domain.
153. Article 2(4) of the Protection of Privacy Law, 1981.

177. In 2010 a public debate arose concerning the desirable behaviour of news-media professionals when they learn about fatal events before a formal notification reaches the family of the victim. The issue received attention after a gathering of media photographers near the home of Rona Ramon, the widow of the first Israeli astronaut Ilan Ramon, preceded the arrival of a formal officer conveying to her the news regarding the death of her son, an air force pilot, in a fighter plane crash. The Press Council reacted by adding sections to the Ethics Code stipulating that a journalist will not approach the home or contact the family of a victim of war, accident or other catastrophe, prior to verifying that the family has been notified of the event. The Ethics Code also forbids photographing family members of such victims within twenty-four hours of the fatal event without their consent.

178. The Protection of Privacy Act includes several defences relevant especially for the media:

(a) Article 18(2) of the Protection of Privacy Law 1981 adopts the protection of fair and true account with respect to publications or discussions quoted from the bodies listed in Article 13 of the Prohibition of Defamation Law 1965. An additional defence exists under this article when the publisher acted in good faith according to his legal, moral, social or professional obligation.

(b) Article 18(3) protects a true publication made for the sake of the public interest in good faith. This defence requires the defendant to prove the truthful nature of the publication. Good faith defence will be denied if the information was obtained through a criminal offence or in breach of the journalistic ethics.[154]

154. Article 20(c) of the Protection of Privacy Law, 1981.

Chapter 4. Right to Reply

179. Article 17 of the Prohibition of Defamation Law 1969, which applies to all media, indicates that refusing a demand to publish a response by the subject of a publication precludes the publisher's good faith defence in case of a defamation claim. Aside from this, there is no law obligating the right to reply in the print media. Thus, in the print media the right to reply is grounded primarily as an ethical obligation. Article 5 of the Journalists' Ethics Code establishes an obligation to check the factual basis of information with 'the most reliable source'. This often requires the newsperson to approach the subject of the information and generates an opportunity to reply ahead of the publication. However, there is no *a priori* ethical right of reply per se. Article 7 of the Ethics Code deals with 'corrections, apologies and replies'. The article stipulates that material factual corrections, omissions, and inaccuracies should be published quickly, fairly and with the appropriate saliency given the original publication. In the appropriate cases the publication of an apology is due. The article further stipulates that a person harmed by a publication will be given a fair opportunity to reply and the reply should be published expediently with the appropriate saliency as compared to the original publication. The Press Council's ethics tribunals seem to present a liberal implementation of the code. For example, they allow reporting about claims made by one party in a legal proceeding without an immediate reply from the opposing party. In addition, a pressing deadline is sometimes an acceptable reason for not publishing a reply as long as the journalist attempted to reach the subject and noted in the report that the person was unreachable or did not provide the response in due time.[155]

180. The right to reply is treated somewhat differently in the context of audio-visual media. See *infra* in part III, Chapter 3, §5.

155. Lehman, E. & Limor, Y, *The "Right to Reply" in Journalistic Ethics: The Case Study of the Ruling by the Israel Press Council*, Paper presented at the annual meeting of the International Communication Association, Dresden International Congress Centre, Dresden, Germany (2009) (hereinafter – Lehman & Limor), 13–14.

Chapter 5. Access to Public Information

181. The public's interest in a free flow of information has been recognized by the HCJ as yet another fundamental tenet of a democratic state, thereby justifying the accessibility of the press to public information.[156] Note however that the importance of access to information is attributed to the general public's interest and not merely the interest of the media. Consequently, freedom of information has been guaranteed through legislation which is not media-friendly. Namely, the process of obtaining information from the government through the freedom of information channels is lengthy, bureaucratic and cumbersome.

§1. PUBLIC DOCUMENTS

182. In an effort to increase the accessibility of the public to information and the transparency of the government, the Freedom of Information Law 1998 ('FOIL'), was enacted. Article 1 FOIL states that every citizen or person domiciled in Israel has the right to receive information from a 'public authority' and further lists the public authorities subject to the FOIA, including *inter alia* the courts, the Knesset, government and municipal corporations and any other entity which is subject to the supervision of the State Comptroller's Bureau.[157] These authorities are required to publish an annual report about their activities.

183. Applications for information according to Article 7 FOIL should be directed to the person in charge of implementing the FOIL in the relevant authority and require no explanation regarding the reason of the application or the purpose for which the information is requested. This represents the idea that information belongs to the public and not to the authority. The FOIL provides a time frame for the authority's response and also elaborates in Article 9 a list of justifications which may be raised by the authority in rejecting an application, including *inter alia*:

(a) Risk to state security, foreign relations, or public order;
(b) The requested information concerns issues specified in a decree published by the Minister of Defence;
(c) The information may constitute an invasion of privacy;
(d) The information may not be disclosed due to other laws;
(e) The information might disrupt the proper functioning of the public authority;
(f) The information concerns policy that is still being considered;
(g) The information concerns negotiations carried out with a person or entity other than the authority;

156. HCJ 243/62 *Ulpanei Hasrata v. Gerry*, 16 PD 2407 [1962] and later again in HCJ 1601/90 *Shalit v. Peres*, 44(3) PD 353 [1990], where Justice Aharon Barak stressed that the government's information is the property of the public.
157. For example, the Israeli Bar Association is an independent body entrusted with statutory authorities to license lawyers and therefore subjected to supervision by the State Comptroller. Hence, it is also subject to the FOIL.

(h) The information is a commercial or professional secret, but information about dissemination of material to the environment cannot be excluded on the basis of this justification nor can information about noise, odour or radiation measurements;
(i) The information may harm investigations or enforcement activities.

184. Additionally, Article 14 FOIL expressly excludes several authorities from the scope of the law including all bodies that deal with defence and intelligence such as the Mossad and the army intelligence, the Nuclear Energy Committee and research institutes under its supervision, and also the Commissioner for the Investigation of Public Complaints about Judges only with regard to investigations conducted into a complaint. Subject to an approval from the Knesset's legislative committee, the Minister of Justice is empowered to exclude additional entities from the scope of the FOIL for a period of up to six months.

§2. Court Hearings and Documents

185. Court proceedings are generally held in open court and they are open to public as well as media attendance. Court decisions of public interest are regularly made available online to the media and to the public by the spokesperson of the court administration.[158] Court decisions are also accessible to the public through commercial online legal databases.

The Court Administration objected to a request based on the FOIL, filed by the financial newspaper The Marker, to reveal judge caseload data on an individual name basis including the period of time each file has been with the individual judge. The Court Administration admitted that the information is accessible but that the public availability of such information would impair the proper functioning of the legal system and that the data is in itself of little value because cases differ significantly from each other in terms of complexity and the time required to resolution while there is no data that would enable a valid comparison of caseloads between judges. As of this writing, given the unique nature of the legal issues arising from this case, it is pending before a wide panel (five judges) of the SC.

186. Access to court files and documents is limited to journalists holding a permit issued by the spokesperson of the court administration. The permit is regularly issued to newspersons who are members of the Israeli Journalists Association.

187. Audio-visual recording or broadcasting of court hearings is forbidden and so is the taking of photographs during hearings. However, as a matter of practice judges allow news photographers and television cameras to document their entrance to the court in hearings that attract media attention.[159]

158. The website: www.court.gov.il.
159. Courts have been known to allow audio or audio-visual broadcasting of unique cases. For example, the trial of the Nazi war criminal Adolf Eichmann in 1961 for crimes against humanity and against

Chapter 6. Press Council

188. The Israeli Press Council was established in 1963 under the influence of the English Press Council model.[160] It is founded on a treaty agreed upon by its founding members and Articles of Association that are binding on its members. There is no legislative foundation for the Press Council's activity, which signifies the independence of the journalistic profession but is also one of the Press Council's major weaknesses.[161] The roles of the Press Council include:[162]

(a) Safeguarding freedom of information, expression and opinion;
(b) Safeguarding the commitment to the principles of journalistic ethics by all those practicing the journalistic profession in Israel and the setting of professional standards of commitment to truthful reporting, accuracy, fairness, the protection of human dignity and privacy.

189. The members of the Press Council are the National Union of Israeli Journalists, most of the Israeli daily newspapers, the IBA, the SATR, the Educational Television, the Cable television and the IDF Radio station.[163] The members have confirmed their obligation to implement the Press Council's and its institutions' decisions.[164] The treaty among the founding members states that the Press Council will strive to incorporate additional members including the local media and the electronic media. It should however be noted that the Press Council perceives itself as having the authority to regulate non-member media organizations in addition to its own members.

190. The plenum of the Press Council is comprised of 40% public representatives none of whom is paid for his contribution, 30% representatives of the publishers and editors and 30% representatives of the journalists.[165] The plenum is authorized to confirm the acceptance of a new media organization to the Press Council after the applicant has declared in writing that it accepts the Press Council's authority; Articles of Association; Rules of Ethics; and allows freedom of professional association for its employees.[166]

---

the Jewish people was taped, the trial of John Demjanjuk in 1988 for his role as a guard in the Treblinka and Sobibor death camps was broadcasted live on Israeli television. Demjanjuk was convicted and sentenced to death but later acquitted by the SC and set free. A live audio-only broadcast was allowed of the court's ruling in the highly publicized bribery trial of the ultra-Orthodox Shas party leader and Minister of Interior Arye Deri in 1999. In contrast, no such broadcast was allowed in 2011 in the trial of former President Moshe Katzav for rape and sex offences in spite of the higher official position and the wide media interest in the case.

160. Negbi, *supra* n. 37, at 51.
161. The Public Commission for Press Laws (1997) headed by former Minister of Justice Haim Tzadock recommended legislation in order to establish the role of the Press Council and the binding authority of its institutions, but the recommendations were never adopted.
162. Article 1 of the Press Council's Treaty.
163. As listed in Art. 3 of the Press Council's Articles of Association.
164. Article 6 of the Press Council's Treaty.
165. Article 9 of the Press Council's Articles of Association.
166. Article 4 of the Press Council's Articles of Association.

191. The plenum must convene at least three times a year and its additional authorities include approving the annual budget, setting the Rules of Ethics, setting the members' annual fee, appointing the managing officials of the Press Council (such as its general manager, its treasurer, etc.), and appointing the Press Council's audit committee.[167]

192. The Press Council is managed by its presiding board, comprised of seven public representatives, five representatives of the publishers and editors and five representatives of the journalists. Each member is elected for a term of three years and may serve additional three year terms.[168] The President of the Press Council and his or her alternate are public representatives proposed jointly by the plenum's constituents unless no agreement is reached, in which case any member may propose candidates. The president and alternate-president are elected by the plenum in a secret ballot. The president is the head of the Press Council and represents it in its public activities.[169] The Press Council's activities are financed by annual fees paid by its members.[170]

193. The Press Council's Articles of Association are also the source for the foundation of the Press Council's Ethics Tribunal (the 'Ethics Tribunal'), its procedures and authority, as follows:[171]

(a) The Ethics Tribunal is authorized to adjudicate complaints regarding violations of the Press Council's Ethics Rules by journalists and media organizations even if they are not members of the Press Council;
(b) Each panel of the tribunal will be comprised of a chairperson who is a public representative, a representative of the publishers and editors and a representative of the journalists. Panel members are elected by the plenum for a term of three years, which can be prolonged;
(c) The president of the Press Council has the authority to reject complaints that are evidently false and complaints filed more than twelve months after the publication;
(d) Complaints that were filed in parallel to other judicial bodies will not be reviewed by the Press Council;
(e) Legitimate complaints are forwarded to the defendant's response within forty-eight hours and the response must be produced within ten days, after which the Press Council's legal adviser has twenty-one days to decide whether the complaint shows an apparent ethics violation. If an apparent violation is found, the complaint is transferred to the chair of the Ethics Tribunal that will appoint a panel to adjudicate the case. The president of the Press Council or the panel may also try to resolve the case by agreement;

167. Articles 14–16 of the Press Council's Articles of Association.
168. Articles 17–22 of the Press Council's Articles of Association.
169. Articles 23–31 of the Press Council's Articles of Association.
170. Article 34 of the Press Council's Articles of Association. In fact, the publishers bear the main financial burden of the Press Council's activities. Negbi, *supra* n. 37, at 54, notes that this fact poses a threat to the independence of the Press Council from financial interests.
171. Articles 39–52 of the Press Council's Articles of Association.

(f) The Panel can inflict the following sanctions: warning, reprimand, publication of an apology dictated by the panel, suspension of a newspaper's membership in the Press Council;
(g) The panel can order that its decision be published by the violator in additional media. If the violator refrains from publishing the decision as required, the President of the Press Council can publish the decision in other media including a condemnation of the medium violating the decision;
(h) Panel decisions can be appealed before an appeal panel of five or seven members, which will not include members of the former panel. The chair of the appeal panel shall be a jurist. The appeal panel will not review questions of fact.

194. Due to the lack of a legislative foundation, the Press Council's institutional enforcement of its rules and decisions depends entirely on the voluntary cooperation of media organizations. This weakens the ambitious claim to enforce ethical standards on all the Israeli press.[172]

195. In fact, some media organizations have their own ethics code, alongside that of the Press Council. For example, IBA journalists are obliged to follow the IBA code of ethics (known as the 'Nakdi Document' after its drafter) and the journalists in the commercial television channels are bound by the SAEthic Rules promulgated by the SATR. The latter may sanction CBF holders for not complying with ethical obligations. The Press Council's Ethics Tribunal has ruled that it has parallel jurisdiction to adjudicate ethics complaints against such media organizations and their employees.[173]

196. The Ethics Code empowers an Ethics Tribunal to suspend a journalist from the journalistic occupation for a limited or indefinite period. To date, this authority has only been implemented after a journalist or an editor have been convicted of a criminal offence as means of purging the rows of the journalistic profession from journalists that were convicted of offences directly related to their professional role.[174]

197. The Press Ordinance bars in Article 5(1)(b)(6) a person sentenced to a term of more than three months in prison from serving as the editor of a newspaper. As Negbi notes, this is a peculiar limitation in comparison with statutes governing post-conviction restrictions on public officials where the court is granted specific authority to determine whether a conviction should prevent the convicted individual from serving in certain positions for a limited or indefinite period, regardless of the length or severity of the punishment.[175] The limitation in the Press Ordinance does not prevent convicted individuals from working as journalists nor from owning a newspaper themselves. In one such case Yaacov Nimrodi, the owner and publisher of

172. Negbi, *supra* n. 37, at 61. The Press Council's Ethics Code nevertheless may be used by the courts as an indicative measure for determining the desirable standards of professional journalism.
173. Case 33/2004 *Vardinon v. Globes Publisher* (2005); Negbi, *supra* n. 37, at 61.
174. Negbi, *supra* n. 37, at 80–86.
175. See also Negbi, *supra* n. 37, at 80.

Maariv, was convicted of obstructing justice by conspiring with his son, the previous publisher and editor of the newspaper, to use their newspaper in order to exert pressure on a witness in a criminal trial related to alleged commercial espionage between rival newspapers.[176] The Nimrodi family continued to hold a controlling stake in Maariv for several years after the conviction and later sold it, however, throughout this time Nimrodi family members no longer served as editors of the newspaper.

176. Negbi, *supra* n. 37, at 77–78.

Part III. Regulation of Audio-visual Media (Broadcasting)

Chapter 1. Public Service Broadcasting

§1. THE CONCEPT AND MISSION OF PUBLIC SERVICE BROADCASTING

I. History and Evolution

198. The IBA was established by the IBA Law 1965, as a public service. Prior to its foundation, the Voice of Israel radio was a department in the Prime Minister's Office. The Israeli Television started its operation in 1968 under the supervision of the IBA.

199. The IBA held a monopoly on broadcasting until the early 1990s, at which time the commercial television and radio broadcasting began. The competitive media market posed a challenge that the IBA has been struggling to overcome. Several professional committees have looked into the structural, organizational and financial difficulties of the IBA attributing its difficulties to high wages, inefficient workforce, inflexible employment agreements and problematic management, as well as ongoing political involvement.[177]

200. In April 2012, the Knesset passed Amendment 27 of the IBA Law ('Amendment 27') in yet another effort to reform the ailing principle public broadcaster. Amendment 27 changes the structure of management and oversight of the IBA with a view to modernize these components of the IBA Law and adopt structures that are used in other independent government authorities and government corporations such as an independent board of directors appointed by an a-political committee, an audit committee and an independent external auditor.

201. While some of the amendments included in Amendment 27 have taken immediate force (Article 40 Amendment 27), the fundamental structural reform will only take effect once the process of electing a new IBA Council will be completed,

177. Committees submitted reports in 1997, 2000, 2001, and 2005. See also The State Comptroller Report on Broadcasting Bodies 61B, 406 (2011), which notes that in 2010 the IBA employed 1766 employees.

a condition for which the government is given a period of no longer than two years to fulfil (until April 2014) (Article 38 Amendment 27).

202. Given the complexity of the appointment process which is described henceforth it is very unlikely that the structural changes will be implemented before the statutory deadline. Therefore, I will survey here the existing IBA Law alongside the changes included in Amendment 27.

II. Mission

203. Amendment 27 has changed the mission of the IBA. In the older version of Article 3 IBA Law the mission of the IBA was described as follows:

(a) To broadcast educational, entertainment and informational programmes in the subjects of policy, society, economics, culture, science and art in order to reflect the life of the state, its struggle, creation and achievements, foster good citizenship, strengthen the links to Jewish heritage and its values while deepening its recognition by the public, and reflect the lives and cultural assets of all the nation's tribes;
(b) To promote Hebrew and Israeli creative work;
(c) To broadcast in the Arabic language in order to meet the needs of the Arabic speaking population and in order to advance understating and peace with the neighbouring countries in accordance with the state's fundamental tenets.

204. After Amendment 27, Article 3 reads as follows:

> The IBA shall hold the broadcasts *inter alia* in the fields of society, education, the heritage of Israel, Zionism, economy, culture, art, science, entertainment and sports with the aim of:
>
> (a) Strengthening and deepening the Zionist identity of the State of Israel as a Jewish and Democratic state and an immigration absorbing state;
> (b) Reflecting the life of the state, the struggle for its foundation, its creation and its achievements;
> (c) Fostering good citizenship and values of equality;
> (d) Reflecting all the components of Israeli society;
> (e) Strengthening the bonds with Judaism and with the Jewish heritage and its values, and deepening the knowledge in these fields;
> (f) Broadcasting reliable information;
> (g) Broadening and disseminating knowledge;
> (h) Holding quality broadcasting with a special attention to the IBA's role as a public broadcaster;
> (i) Furthering original Israeli creation;
> (j) Fostering the knowledge of the Hebrew language and furthering its use, *inter alia* in accordance with the decision of the Academy for the Hebrew Language;

(k) Holding broadcasts in the Arabic language in order to meet the needs of the Arabic speaking population and in order to advance understating and peace with the neighbouring countries;
(l) Strengthening the values of democracy, pluralism and tolerance;
(m) Reflecting and documenting the lives and cultures of the citizens of Israel and of the Jewish people in the Diaspora, world culture and human creativity;
(n) Reflecting the Israeli experience by broadcasting outside Israel and holding broadcasts for Jews in the Diaspora;
(o) Promoting the Jewish education including all its variations and the aims of public education as stated in the Public Education Law, 1953.[178]

205. Evidently, in spite of the constant recognition of other population groups and their rights, the new objectives of the IBA strongly emphasize the Jewish and Zionist nature of the State of Israel.

§2. The Organization of Public Service Broadcasting

I. The IBA

206. The IBA is a corporation established by statute. According to the IBA Law 1965, a minister appointed by the government is charged with the implementation of the law and oversees the IBA. During the period 2000–2010, the ministerial authority had passed through the hands of ten ministers.

207. In the government elected as of 2013, the minister in charge of the IBA is the Minister of Communications. This has not always been the case. For example, the minister in charge of the IBA in the previous government was the Prime Minister.

208. According to the current regime, which will be phased out as Amendment 27 becomes operational:

(a) The minister's main authorities are the proposal of candidates to the position of General Director of the IBA ('IBA Director'), the removal of the IBA Director and the appointment of a temporary IBA Director.
(b) The IBA Assembly oversees the functioning of the IBA, instructs the Executive Committee of the IBA as to its operation and sets the IBA general agenda.

178. Author's translation. The aims of the Public Education Law, 1953, reiterate some of the general aims specified in Art. 3 IBA Law and generally emphasize the promotion of knowledge, democratic values, recognition of equal rights, critical thought, volunteering and contribution to society, deepening the values of the Declaration of Independence of the State of Israel as a Jewish Democratic state while promoting equality and recognition of human rights, etc. Additional aims include teaching the Bible, fostering loyalty to the State of Israel, deepening the memory of the Holocaust, and learning the Arabic language, culture, history and unique tradition as well as that of other population groups in the State of Israel and recognizing their equal rights.

(c) The assembly is comprised of thirty-one members appointed by the President of the State after being nominated by the government (except one member who is nominated by the Jewish Agency). The list of government nominated members to the IBA Assembly should be formed after due consultation with the representative bodies of the authors, teachers and artists in Israel as well as with academic institutions, the Academy for the Hebrew Language and other institutions with an affiliation to broadcasting. The assembly is appointed for a period of three years.

209. The purpose of the aforementioned nomination process was to form a non-political IBA Assembly. In fact, the list of nominated members was formed by the supervising minister. The minister was not bound by the recommendations of the bodies with which he was obliged to consult nor was there an express statutory obligation for the IBA Assembly to reflect the cultural, ethnic or social divides of the Israeli society. In addition, the appointment of the IBA Assembly was a long and bureaucratic process due to three main reasons:

– The obligatory consultation process had to be carried out.[179]
– The political nature of the nomination often required an (often difficult to achieve) agreement between the parties forming the coalition government on the identity of the nominees.[180]
– According to the Government Corporations Law 1975, the appointment of directors in a statutory corporation such as the IBA is subject to the approval of a committee which checks whether the nominated person has familial, political or business affiliations with any of the government's ministers and if such affiliation is found then the nominee shall only be approved when he or she has 'special qualifications' for the position.

210. Due to the aforementioned difficulties, in the last ten years at least two IBA Assemblies served for an overall term of more than five years since an assembly continued to act as an interim assembly after the completion of its three year term until a new assembly was appointed.[181]

211. According to the current regime, which will be phased out as Amendment 27 becomes operational:

(a) The government elects the Chairperson of the IBA assembly ('IBA Chairperson') and the Deputy IBA Chairperson. An IBA Assembly meeting could not be held without the presence of the IBA Chairperson or the deputy.

179. In HCJ 5933/98 *The Documentary Producers Forum v. The President of the State*, 54(3) PD 496 [2000], the court nullified the appointment of the assembly after holding that the minister did not duly weigh the nominees proposed by the bodies with which he was obliged to consult.
180. The AG and the State Comptroller have underlined the need to mitigate the increasing phenomenon of political nominees and warned against excessive political influence on the IBA. See The State Comptroller's Report 61B (2011), 421–422, 427.
181. The State Comptroller's Report 61B (2011), 414.

(b) The IBA Chairperson also chairs the Managing Committee which is comprised of seven members (including the IBA Chairperson and the deputy), elected by the government. The Managing Committee serves for a term of three years or is dispersed if the assembly is dispersed. The Managing Committee is the principle executive decision making organ of the IBA and its statutory roles and powers include making decisions with respect to the management of the IBA, preparing the IBA's budget, preparing an annual report to the assembly, preparing reports to the minister, and dictating rules for the supervision of broadcasting and efficient functioning of the Managing Committee itself.

(c) The IBA Director is nominated by the supervising minister and appointed by the government. There are four 'Media Directors' in the IBA under the authority of the IBA Director: the director of the television in Hebrew, the director of the television in Arabic, the director of the radio in Hebrew and the director of the radio in Arabic. The Media Directors are elected by a competitive tender for a term of three years.[182] In an agreement signed in 2002 by the IBA representatives of the National Journalists' Association it was agreed that the term of a media director can be prolonged for another term at the recommendation of the IBA Director and the approval of the Managing Committee without a tender process. Afterwards, a tender for the position must take place although the incumbent Media Director is not prevented from competing for the position.

212. Amendment 27 cancelled the IBA Assembly and the Managing Committee and replaced them with the IBA Council, which will receive de facto the powers granted in the IBA Law to both former bodies.

213. The process of appointing the IBA Council, as amended in Amendment 27, is stipulated in Articles 7 to 13 IBA Law and is designed to decrease the potential of political appointments.

214. Article 7 IBA Law stipulates that the government shall appoint a search committee comprised of five members of whom at least two shall be women.

(a) The search committee shall be tasked with proposing the candidates for the IBA Council. The chair of the search committee will be chosen by the minister in charge of the IBA with the agreement of the Minister of Justice and must have at least five years of experience in a one of the following roles: heading a significant business corporation, senior public position in a managerial, economics, or legal capacity, retired District Court Judge. The other members of the search committee must be a faculty member from a formally recognized academic institution specialized in the field of media, who will be chosen by the chair of the search committee after consulting with the chairperson of the Higher Education Council; a known personae in the fields of culture, education, social science or the humanities chosen by the chair of the search committee; a known personae in the fields of the heritage of Israel or Judaism chosen by the

182. Obligatory tenders apply to less senior appointments in the IBA as well.

chair of the search committee; a known personae in the fields of economics or management chosen by the chair of the search committee after consultation with the Coordination Biard of Financial Organizations.

(b) The chair of the search committee must advertise a call to the public such that individuals that wish to be considered as search committee members will be able to propose themselves. Non-profit organizations may also nominate candidates to the positions of search committee member (Article 7(c) IBA Law).

(c) Members of the search committee cannot be politically or financially affiliated with any of the government ministers nor are they allowed to be persons that have been politically active in the last three years prior to their being proposed as members of the search committee (Article 8 IBA Law).

(d) A member of the search committee will serve for a four year term and will receive remuneration for his work if he is not a civil servant or reimbursement of costs (Articles 10 and 13a IBA Law).

(e) The search committee's legal quorum is three members including the chair of the committee (Article 9(a) IBA Law).

215. As explained, the search committee's function is to propose candidates for the IBA Council. The IBA Council members are then appointed by the government following the recommendation of the minister in charge of the IBA. The IBA Council shall be comprised of thirteen members of whom, at least five must be women (Article 14(a) IBA Law).

216. The search committee must propose to the minister three candidates to the position of Chairperson of the IBA Council ('IBA Council Chair') all of whom must have an accumulated five year experience in senior managerial business position in a large corporation; senior public service position in economic, commercial, managerial or legal roles; senior managerial position in the media (Article 14(a)(1) IBA Law).

217. The rest of the IBA Council member positions shall be appointed by the government in the following process (Article 14(a)(2) to(6) IBA Law):

(a) Three public representative of stature from the field of media, one of whom will be appointed by the recommendation of the search committee and two others by the recommendation of the minister in charge of the IBA from three candidates proposed to the minister by the search committee;

(b) Three public representative of stature from the fields of culture, education, Judaism, Zionism, social science or humanities (each from a different field), two of whom will be appointed by the recommendation of the search committee and one by the recommendation of the minister in charge of the IBA from two candidates proposed to the minister by the search committee;

(c) Three public representative of stature from the fields of economics and management (one must have financial and audit experience), two of whom will be appointed by the recommendation of the search committee and one by the recommendation of the minister in charge of the IBA from two candidates proposed to the minister by the search committee;

(d) Two public representative known for their social non-profit activities for equality, democratic values and the strengthening of the heritage of Israel one of whom will be appointed by the recommendation of the search committee and the other by the recommendation of the minister in charge of the IBA from two candidates proposed by the search committee one of whom shall be a member the appointment of which represents affirmative action with regards to the population group to which he or she belongs and the other shall be from the geographical periphery of Israel;
(e) One public representative of stature from the fields television or film production from two candidates proposed to the minister by the search committee.

218. In total, the search committee must propose fourteen candidates to the minister, of whom he must recommend seven candidates to the government, one of whom must be recommended to the position of IBA Council Chair (Article 14(c) IBA Law).

219. As with the appointment of the search committee members, the chair of the search committee must advertise a call to the public such that individuals that wish to be considered as IBA Council members will be able to nominate themselves as potential candidates. Non-profit organizations may also nominate candidates to the position of IBA Council members; the search committee has the authority to approach candidates on its own initiative (Article 14(d) IBA Law).

220. The composition of the IBA Council should reflect as much as possible the range of public opinion in Israel (Article 14(e) IBA Law):

(a) Members of the IBA Council cannot be politically or financially affiliated with any of the government ministers nor are they allowed to be persons that have been politically active in the last three years prior to their being proposed as members by the search committee (Article 8 IBA Law).
(b) IBA Council members are each appointed for a four year term, and this term may be extended for another six months for the purpose of finding a replacement (Article 19 IBA Law). There are addition instruction in case the IBA Council Chair or a member of the council resign, are in absentia, or are criminally indicted (Article 20 IBA Law).
(c) IBA Council members must be impartial in their role; avoid conflicts of interest; may not partake in the broadcasts save if it is in his capacity as an expert and according to rules promulgate by the council (Articles 21f-21h IBA Law).

221. Article 17 IBA Law stipulates the roles of the IBA Council that include *inter alia*:

(a) Determining the IBA policy and the broadcast policy in accordance with the IBA budget and the purpose of the IBA as stated in Article 3 as long as the transmission methods are not altered without the permission of the minister in charge of the IBA and the number of channels or networks is not altered without the consent of the minister and the Knesset committee for economic affairs;

(b) Approving the seasonal broadcast schedules;
(c) Supervising the broadcast content in compliance with the aims set in Article 3;
(d) Appoint the IBA Director and supervise his activities;
(e) Determining the organizational structure of the IBA, the maximal number of employees and their terms of engagement;
(f) Discussing and approving the balanced budget proposal submitted by the IBA Director and submitting it to the minister in charge of the IBA and the Minister of Finance no later than thirty days before the end of the fiscal year;
(g) Discussing and approving the annual work plan submitted by the IBA Director and examining its compliance with the proposed budget;
(h) Supervising the execution of the budget;
(i) Preparing and approving the financial statements of the IBA;
(j) Determining the threshold of financial transactions that the IBA Director may approve and those that must be brought to the approval of the IBA Council;
(k) Discussing the annual report of the internal auditor;

222. According to Article 21d IBA Law, the IBA Council must appoint an audit committee comprised of at least three members excluding the IBA Council Chair and including a member with financial and audit experience; the audit committee is charged with detecting faults in the IBA activities and proposing corrective actions; the audit committee should work in conjunction with the IBA's internal auditor and it is supposed to submit an annual report to the IBA Council.

223. Article 22 IBA Law gives the government the power to disband the IBA Council after giving the IBA Council due warning that in the government's opinion the IBA Council is not performing its duties.

224. The IBA Council appoints the IBA Director with the approval of the government (Article 23 IBA Law) in the following method:

(a) A candidacy for IBA Director requires the same qualifications as the position of IBA Council Chair and the same political and financial independence from government ministers;
(b) Three candidates for the position must be proposed by a search committee formed for this purpose; the search committee shall be chaired by the IBA Council chair and will include two council members elected by the IBA Council and two members of the search committee formed according to Article 7 IBA Law also elected in this case by the IBA Council;
(c) The search committee will rank the suitability of the candidates.

225. The IBA Director is appointed for a four year term that may be prolonged only once for an additional term (Article 23a IBA Law). His roles and authorities include *inter alia* (Article 23d IBA Law):

(a) The daily management of the IBA;
(b) Preparing the budget proposal and the annual work plan as well as semi-annual progress reports for the IBA Council;

(c) Approval of broadcast schedules and acting as the chief editor of the IBA;
(d) Supervision of the Media Directors;
(e) Any residual managerial authority required for the functioning of the IBA.

226. The Media Directors are IBA employees appointed to be the editors of their medium for a term of four years which may prolonged only once for another four year term (Article 23g IBA Law). The scope of responsibility for the Media Directors is determined by the IBA Council (Article 23g(e) IBA Law).

II. Additional Public Broadcasters

227. There are three additional public broadcasters:

(a) The Knesset Channel ('KTV') broadcasts hearings of the Israeli parliament and its committees as well as related current affairs programmes. The KTV was established according to the Television Broadcasts from the Knesset Law 2003 ('KTV Law') for the purpose of increasing public accessibility to the Knesset's work and fostering democratic values (Article 1 KTV Law). Knesset plenary sessions are broadcasted live and in their entirety by the channel (Article 11 KTV Law). The broadcasting policy of the KTV including the type of programmes, the hearings that will be covered, the scope of the coverage and the length of the broadcasting time are generally determined by the Knesset committee (Article 4 KTV Law) whereas the power to execute the policy is granted to the CSBC which supervises the broadcasts of the KTV and is empowered to grant the KTV broadcast license by tender (Articles 5 and 7 KTV Law). The KTV licensee must be a non-governmental corporation based in Israel with a majority of Israeli controlling shareholders and Israeli directors and must be unaffiliated with any political party (Article 8 KTV Law). The KTV licensee cannot be any broadcaster licensed according to the SATR Law or the Communications Law or any interest holder in these entities nor can the licensee be a daily national newspaper or any of the two largest newspapers in Israel or an interest holder in the said newspapers (Article 8(e) KTV Law).
(b) The Educational Television ('ETV') is structured as a unit within the Ministry of Education and therefore it is subject to the administrative oversight of the Minister of Education and relies on the ministry for most of its budget contributions. The ETV is mentioned in the IBA Law, Communications Law and SATRL, which allocate the ETV broadcast slots within the IBA broadcasts and Channel 2 (until 2015) as well as its own channel (Channel 23) on cable and satellite television. Originally, Channel 23 was not included in the free DTT bundle transmitted by the government's DTT services in spite of the fact that the channel is a public service. This error was corrected in an amendment to the DTT Law and Channel 23 has been part of the DTT free bundle as of 2012.
(c) The army radio station, Galei Zahal ('GLZ'), which broadcasts a current affairs channel and a music and traffic reports channel is supervised by the IBA in its non-military broadcasts (Article 48b IBA Law). GLZ is a unit within the army but its commander, who acts as the editor-in-chief, is appointed by the Minister of Defence (Article 48d IBA Law). In matters that concern the army, joint

oversight is given to the Minister in charge of the IBA and the Minister of Defence, but the Minister of Defence has the authority to determine which programme shall be considered a 'military affairs programme' (Articles 48a and 48e of the IBA Law) and therefore is the more influential personae in setting the agenda of the station. GLZ is also subjected to IDF internal commands.

§3. The Financing of Public Service Broadcasting

228. The financial resources of the IBA are the television levy imposed on every owner of a television set,[183] the car radio levy which is charged as part of the annual car license fee, and revenue from the sale of PSAs, sponsorships and radio advertisements.

229. The annual television levy in 2003 was set at 515 NIS and it has been reduced every year since then (with the exception of the years 2008–2010 in which it remained stagnant) (Article 28a IBA Law).[184]

230. The structural reform of the IBA is likely to require additional investments and financial resources. Article 28a(b1) IBA Law as added in Amendment 27 foresees an agreement between the IBA and the Ministry of Finance for funding the reform, and allows the Minister of Finance to freeze the reduction of the television levy during the finance agreement period. The reform agreement has been signed in the beginning of 2013 and awaits implementation as of yet.

231. The IBA is obliged to prepare an annual budget and an annual development budget. The IBA Regulations (Budget) 1965, state that the budget shall be submitted by the Minister of Finance to the government's approval for every fiscal year. According to the IBA Law, the budget and the development budget proposals are prepared by the Executive Committee and submitted to the IBA assembly which renders its recommendations with respect to the proposals. The Executive Committee then submits the budgets and the recommendations through the Minister of Finance to the government. According to The Budget Foundations Law 1985, the Minister of Finance must approve the budget of all statutory corporations. So long as the budget is not approved by one or more of the bodies which must approve it, the IBA may only spend each month 1/12 of the annual budget approved in the previous fiscal year. As a result of its ongoing inability to present a balanced budget and its growing deficit, the IBA has not been able to obtain an approval of the budget for the fiscal years 2004–2010.[185]

183. The annual levy has been reduced by an amendment to the IBA Law, adopted in 2004. It has been changed occasionally since then but it has not increased significantly. No alternative sources of finance were named instead of the levy reduction. In addition, certain groups such as senior citizens and disabled army veterans are exempted from paying the television levy.

184. Exemptions from the television levy (Art. 28b IBA Law) were granted during the fiscal years 2012–2016 to soldiers in active service whose families do not live in Israel and during the fiscal years 2012–2013 to senior citizens.

185. The State Comptroller's Report 61B (2011), 430–431.

232. Due to its ongoing financial difficulties, Amendment 27 addressed some of the concern with regards to the restructuring of the IBA and guaranteeing its adequate financial performance. This includes:

(a) An external auditor with broad audit powers shall be appointed to the IBA, after being selected by the Government Corporations Authority (Article 23h IBA Law);
(b) The IBA shall have an internal auditor, who will be an employee of the IBA (Article 23j IBA Law);
(c) Reform agreements between the IBA and the Journalists' Association regarding the early retirement and the retirement conditions of IBA employees were implemented within Amendment 27 in order to allow the trimming down and refreshment of the IBA workforce. To date, the government has frozen further reform due to internal difficulties in the IBA.

233. Other public broadcasters rely on a variety of financial resources:

(a) The cable and satellite television providers are obliged to broadcast and offer the Knesset channel free of charge to subscribers (Article 14 KTV Law) and the Knesset reserves any intellectual property right in the broadcasts (Article 15 KTV Law). Advertisements are prohibited in the KTV but sponsorship is allowed according to the rules promulgated by the CSBC (Articles 4, 5 and 13 KTV Law) and therefore the Knesset channel's financial resources are the Knesset's budget and revenue from sponsorships (Article 19 KTV Law). In 2011 the KTV's budget was 25 Million NIS.
(b) The ETV is financed in part from the budget of the Ministry of Education and in part from advertisements and sponsorships. The ETV is subject to different advertising rules according to the platform on which it broadcasts. It may receive sponsorships for its broadcasts on IBA channels and its cable and satellite channel which are distributed free of charge, whereas it sells advertising slots during its broadcasts on the commercial channel.[186]
(c) GLZ is financed primarily from the Defence budget. However, GLZ also broadcasts PSAs and sponsorship announcements for services relevant directly to the welfare of soldiers and other defence community employees. A petition filed by private radio stations against the army (HCJ 1551/02 *Radio Kol Rega v. The Commander of Galei Zahal* (2005)) stimulated the enactment of the Galei Zahal – Broadcasts of the Israeli Defence Forces (Sponsorships and Service Advertisements)(Interim Order) Law, 2005, which authorizes the limited broadcasting of paid sponsorships and advertisements by government and non-profit entities for no longer than four and a half minutes per hour. The law, which was due to expire in 2010, is being prolonged from time to time.

186. Yizhar Tal & Dina Ivri-Omer, *Regulation of Electronic Services in Israel: The Need to Establish a Communications Authority* 127 (2009) (hereinafter – Tal & Ivri-Omer).

Chapter 2. Private Broadcasting

§1. Different Categories of Private Broadcasters

234. Although the SATRL which regulates the private radio broadcasting in Israel provides for both regional analogue radio broadcasts and national digital radio broadcasts, there are only regional private radio stations in Israel.[187] The SATRL allows private radio financing either by selling advertisements or by paid subscription or both. However, the private regional radio stations rely entirely on advertisements.

235. The following categories of private television broadcasters are distinguishable in the legislation:

(a) Private commercial national broadcasters such as the commercial channels, Channel 2 and Channel 10, both regulated by the SATRL and financed by advertisements.
(b) Private multichannel cable broadcasters and private multichannel satellite broadcasters, are both regulated primarily by the Communications Law, and they are restricted to financing their broadcasting solely by subscription fees paid directly by the subscribers to the service providers. The regulatory framework of the multichannel cable and satellite television providers in the Communications Law establishes the basis for particular channel licensing:
   - A multichannel platform broadcaster such as a cable or satellite service provider may broadcast its own internally produced channels, which require the approval of the CSBC. Multichannel television providers may not sell advertisements in their own broadcasts and therefore rely on subscription fees for their revenues.
   - A 'special license' may be granted to a channel produced independently of the multichannel platform provider. The producer of an independent channel that was granted a special license can negotiate its inclusion in the multichannel platform for a 'usage fee' which is paid by the licensee to the platform owner but if the negotiation is unsuccessful then the Communications Law enables the Minister of Communications to force the multichannel platform to carry the channel. The special channel licensee is also prohibited from selling advertisements.[188]

---

187. No competitors submitted offers to the government tender for the franchise of a national digital commercial radio broadcaster in 2008. See Tal & Ivri-Omer, *supra* n. 186, at 123. Given the ability to broadcast radio over the internet without any license or regulatory obligations, the national radio franchise seems obsolete especially in light of its cumbersome regulatory obligations.

188. The financial model supporting special channel licenses relies on subscription fees paid by the viewers to the special channel licensee. This model was not highly successful and several channels that launched on the basis of a special license were eventually shut down for financial reasons. In an effort to promote independent channel producers the CSBC now allows special licenses for film channels and considers allowing special licenses for televisions series channels. Special licensees are subject to the obligation to invest in local production (4%–12% of their revenue, as decided by

- A sub-category of the special channel license defined as a 'designated channel' license is similar to the special channel license but includes the right to sell advertisements.

§2. LICENSING REQUIREMENTS

I. Commercial Television.

236. The regulation of commercial television in Israel is undergoing a transition from a franchise-based regime to a license-based regime that anticipates the potential entrance of additional competitors to the commercial television market. The transition implies complicated legislative and regulatory discussions and is scheduled to be completed by 2014, although the date may be postponed by the Minister of Communications. However, the current commercial television broadcasters are regulated by the franchise-based regime. While the franchise- regime precludes the possibility of commercial broadcasting by non-franchised broadcasters, it is not perceived to be *a priori* censorship in the Israeli legal discourse.

237. The franchise regime envisaged a commercial television market comprised of two channels, each distributed between more than one franchisee. This structure was developed on the premise that broadcast channels are a limited public resource; that the potential revenues from advertisement may not sustain the existence of more than two channels; that under these restrictions it would be advantageous to encourage indirect competition by dividing each channel between franchisees that will broadcast on different weekdays and thus compete among themselves.

238. The SATR is empowered to distribute franchises (which will be replaced by licenses in the future) for commercial broadcasting disseminated via the airwaves, including via satellite, with the exception of encrypted broadcasting which is distributed to paying subscribers.[189]

239. The franchise term for the first commercial channel (Channel 2) was set at six years (Article 34(b) SATRL) with the possibility of prolonging the franchise for an additional term of four years and an examination of the franchisee's compliance with the franchise obligations after five years. Although the franchise term was supposed to end de facto at the entrance into force of the license regime (Articles 34(b1) and (b2) SATRL), the Knesset passed a bill to prolong the franchise until 2017, as it is unclear at the moment when the license regime will come into force.

240. The franchise term for the second commercial channel (Channel 10) was set at eight years with a compliance examination every four years (Article 34(c)

the CSBC) but the obligations apply only to special licensees with more than one licensed channel and it is deferred to the third year of the licensee's activity. See CSBC Annual Report 2010, 18–19.

189. The licensing of television broadcasts received through subscription is governed by the Minister of Communications and the CSBC according to the Communications Law.

SATRL). This franchise will terminate at the entrance into force of the license regime.[190]

241. The commercial channel franchisees are not concerned with the broadcast dissemination.[191] While the franchisees produce or acquire the content, it is the SATR which is charged with the establishment and maintenance of a terrestrial and satellite dissemination infrastructure. Hence, the franchise tender process focuses mostly on the professional and financial abilities of the potential broadcaster and the content of the proposed broadcasts. The SATR distributed the broadcast franchise through a 'beauty contest' tender process (Article 38 SATRL). The SAC acts as the tender committee and its criteria in assessing the franchise contenders include (Article 45 SATRL):

- The financial ability of the contender.
- The contender's proposed franchise fee.
- The professional knowledge and experience at the disposal of the contender.
- The contender's production capacity and proposed programme diversity.
- The contender's proposed investment in original local productions.
- Whether the contender is geared towards the general trends framed by Article 5 SATRL including among other things the promotion of Israeli creation, fostering good citizenship and democratic values, enhancing Jewish tradition, holding broadcasts in the Arabic language and manifesting the cultural diversity of Israeli society.

242. A franchise contender must (Article 41 SATRL):

- Be a corporation established and based in Israel, controlled by Israeli citizens and with at least 51% of the means of control held by Israeli citizens who are also residents of Israel.[192]
- (The contender) must not have been convicted of a criminal violation that carries 'disgrace' in the opinion of the Attorney General, nor may a director or an interest holder in the contender be convicted of such a violation.

---

190. Channel 10's initial franchise term had ended and was prolonged until January 2012 at which time the channel was in financial distress and the SAC was under political pressure to declare that the channel's franchise should not be prolonged due to its failure to comply with some of its statutory obligations. In response to this pressure, the Deputy Attorney General issued a legal opinion (dated 27 Jan. 2012), which is binding on the SAC, asserting that the legislative intent to shift the regulatory regime to a license-based regime implies that Channel 10's franchise term was automatically prolonged and the SAC did not have to make an affirmative decision to prolong it.
191. The SATR is charged with the dissemination of the broadcasts but the financial cost of setting up the dissemination network is imposed on the franchisees.
192. The limitation on foreign ownership of media in Israel can be given several explanations. See Amit Schejter, "*The People Shall Dwell Alone: The Effect of Transfrontier Broadcasting on Freedom of Speech and Information in Israel*", 31 N.C.J. Int'l L. & Com. Reg. 337, 341 (2005) (hereinafter Schejter, transfrontier). One explanation is the concern that Israeli media organizations will fall into the hands of foreign anti-Israeli owners. This concern is amplified by the fact that sensitive national security information which is not in the public domain sometimes reaches the eyes of journalists. Another concern is that non-Israeli owners applying global synergies will be ill-willing to invest in local productions and neglect the cultivation of unique Israeli and Jewish cultural values.

– (The contender) may not be an advertising agency, a performers' agency or a corporation that deals with purchasing advertising slots.

243. Additionally, the contender must produce bank guarantees (Article 41(a)(1) SATRL) and comply with monomedia and crossmedia ownership restrictions (discussed in part IV, *infra*).

244. Under the licensing regime which is expected to generate a more competitive commercial television market, it is foreseen that broadcasters may require longer periods of time to cover the costs of market entry. This can explain the fact that the commercial television license will be granted by the SAC for a term of fifteen years from the date of the first broadcast and may be prolonged for additional terms of fifteen years (Articles 34(e) and 35 SATRL). Overall compliance of the licensees with their obligations will be examined every four years and may result in the nullification of the license or its abrogation in case of in (Article 33(f) SATRL). The preconditions that apply to franchise contender will apply to license applicants once the transition to a license-based regime is completed (Article 33a(a) SATRL). The SAC may set additional terms in the license itself (Article 33a(c) SATRL).

245. The cost of news production is perceived to be a barrier to potential entrants. As with CBF holders, the commercial licensees will be obliged to broadcasts news programmes through separate news corporations. However, the barrier has been somewhat alleviated by enabling a new licensee to ask for a two year deferral of the obligation to provide news broadcast (Articles 63(a), (c) and (e) SATRL).

246. There are particular instructions with regard to license applicants that were previously CBF holders or commercial license holders, especially if the applicant has still not fulfilled his past broadcast, production and investment obligations (Article 71d(b) and 75e SATRL). A license shall not be granted to a CBF holder or commercial license holder that has violated the obligations under the SATRL, the SAC's rules or the terms of the franchise or license contract in the three years prior to the application (Article 33(a)(b) SATRL). The scope of the sanction is designed to capture a wider group of potential applicants since it applies to applicants that were interest holders in the violating entity or in the event that the violating entity is an interest holder in the new applicant or when an interest holder in the applicant was also an interest holder in the violating entity.

247. After deciding to shift from a franchise-based regime to a license-based regime in the commercial television market, the SATR published the SATR (Procedure and Conditions for Granting a Television Broadcast License) Rules 2011 ('SAPTVL Rules'). According to these rules, along with the license application, an applicant must deposit 3 million NIS to demonstrate its seriousness and financial stability, of which the SAC may deduct significant amounts if the applicant retracts the application, depending on the timing of the retraction (Rule 2 SAPTVL). The SAC will decide if the applicant is 'eligible to request a channel' within three months (Rule 8 SAPTVL) and grant the license after an additional three month period (Rule 9 SAPTVL). Milestones are shorter for existing CBF holders.

248. The requirements for granting a license include *inter alia* (Rule 10 SAPTVL):

- Compliance with the SATRL requirements.
- The CEO and the majority of the directors in the applicant are Israeli citizens domiciled in Israel.
- At least one quarter of the directors have an academic degree and academic or practical experience of minimum three years in electronic or printed mass media.
- There is at least one independent director on the applicant's board of directors if the board is comprised of up to 7 directors, two independent directors for a board of 8-12 directors and an additional independent director for every four directors above 12; the voting power of the independent directors must not be less than their relative size on the board; at least one independent director must be present in decisions on budget and appointments of significant decision making positions in the applicants.
- The applicant's rules of incorporation require the formation of an audit committee in which at least one of the members is an independent director.

249. In granting the license, the SAC shall consider (Rule 11 SAPTVL):

- The financial ability of the stakeholders in the applicant.
- The professional know-how and experience at the applicant's disposal.
- The suitability of the equipment and studios at the applicant's disposal.
- The ability of the applicant to comply with the requirement of the SATRL and the trends dictated therein.

250. The SAPTVL contains a detailed questionnaire about the applicant, its corporate structure, shareholders and their interests as well as cross media ownership information and other possible affiliations, financial ability, professional and technological facilities and a sample of the projected programme schedule, which must be submitted as the basis for the evaluation of the license application.

251. It should be noted that the shift from franchise-based regulation to license-based regulation requires a host of legal adjustments in the regulatory regime of the multichannel platform providers as well. These adjustments reflect the fact that most television viewers in Israel watch the current SATR franchised channels via the multichannel cable or satellite broadcast provider. Hence, the CRF holders invested significant amounts of money in branding Channels 22 and 10 (for Channel 2 and Channel 10) of the multichannel television platforms as their respective recognized location. The channels numbered 1 to 3 on the multichannel cable and satellite platforms are used for the multichannel providers' own purposes. Therefore on the cable and satellite platforms IBA Channel 1 is actually located on channel 11; the commercial Channel 2 is located on Channel 22; the third commercial channel was designated to be broadcasted only through multichannel and digital platforms from its outset and therefore chose its name, Channel 10, according to the available slot on the multichannel platforms that carry it.

252. The shift to a license-based regulation is expected to allow the entrance of additional commercial broadcasters. The Minister of Communications, after consulting with the SATR and the CSBC, is empowered to determine a list of five consecutive channel numbers that will be allotted by the cable and satellite providers to the new commercial broadcast licensees. The SATR and the CSBC are authorized to allot a list of five additional channels if needed, with preference to consecutive numbers, unless the councils fail to agree in which case the minister is empowered to allot the channels (Article 6(21)1(f) Communications Law).

253. The 2011 amendment of the Communications Law in Article 6(21)1 contains a unique solution to Channels 10 and 22, which is principally designed to prevent future channel broadcasters from building on the viewers' habitual tendencies to tune into Channels 10 and 22. Hence, according to the amendment, Channels 10 and 22 shall not be included in the list of consecutive channels allotted to commercial licensees for a period of three years following the termination of the current broadcasting. Additionally, a cable or satellite providers is prohibited from allotting Channels 10 or 22 to a broadcaster that is authorized to broadcast advertisements or news or any other characteristics as ordered by the Minister of Communications for the said three year period.

II. Commercial Radio

254. In 2006 the government adopted a reform intended to introduce digital radio broadcasts in order to open the commercial radio market to additional competitors. Current regional commercial radio broadcasters are subject to a franchise-based regulatory regime which will continue to exist alongside the license-based regime as a result of the reform. The introduction of a license regime is dependent on digital radio dissemination. Digitally disseminated radio stations will no longer be limited to regional reception and they will be de facto national radio stations.

255. According to the existing franchise-based regime, the SAC is empowered to grant no less than fifteen and no more than twenty CRFs (Article 72(a) SATRL). Sixteen have been granted to date. The CRF is granted by a competitive tender according to the SATR (Procedure for Granting a Radio Broadcasting Franchise) Rules 1995. The CRF is granted for a period of four years and may be prolonged for three additional four year terms (Articles 34(a) and 35(a) SATRL). The SATR (Radio Franchise Regions) Rules 1995, determine the regional distribution of broadcasts franchises and includes geographical maps delineating each region.

256. The SAC's considerations in the selection of the CBF holder reiterate the considerations specified with regards to television franchise and license holders (discussed in the previous section, *supra*), including the professional expertise, financial ability, proposed programmes, etc. (Article 72b SATRL).

257. Elaborate requirements regarding monomedia and crossmedia ownership apply to the applicants (Articles 72a(a), 72c(a) SATRL) (see *infra* part IV). Requirements with regards to the criminal background of the applicants and lack of affiliation to political parties apply as well (Article 72c(a) SATRL).

258. In 2006, the SATR promulgated the SATR (Procedure for Granting a Radio Broadcasting License) 2006 ('the SAPRL Rules') according to which commercial radio licenses will be granted by a competitive tender. The SATR is authorized to determine the term of the CRL in its rules (Articles 34(a1) and 72b SATRL). Accordingly, the CRL term was set to six years and may be extended for three consecutive four year terms (Rule 18 SAPRL). Rule 13 SAPRL empowers the SAC, as the tender committee, to require any information and disclosures from a contender for the purpose of ascertaining the contender's suitability.

259. The SAC has the authority to include in the CRL terms any obligations as it deems fit (Article 33(b) SATRL) and it has generally applied to CRL applicants similar requirements as were applicable to CRF contenders. Accordingly, the SATR (Radio Broadcasts by a License Holder) Rules 2006 ('The SARaL Rules') impose on the CRL holder similar obligations to those included in the SARaF Rules. In addition, a CRL applicant is subject to monomedia and crossmedia ownership restrictions similar to those applicable to CRF holders (Article 72(b) SATRL).

260. While the statutory regime for the distribution of digital radio commercial licenses has been established, it has not been activated due to practical reasons. As opposed to the existing terrestrial radio broadcasts dissemination system which is operated by the SATR, the digital radio transmission is supposed to be disseminated by a satellite dissemination station operated by a franchisee selected pursuant to a competitive tender (Article 72d SATRL). However, the tender for the erection and operation of a digital transmission station failed to raise interest. Hence the infrastructure for digital radio transmission is not yet in existence. As a last resort, Article 72h SATRL empowers the SATR to erect the dissemination system by itself.

III. Multichannel Television

261. Cable and satellite television broadcasting are primarily regulated by chapters B1 (Cable Television to Subscribers) and B2 (Satellite Broadcasting) of the Communications Law.

262. The CSBC is empowered to license cable television broadcasting, which encompasses television broadcasting 'disseminated via a telecommunications network' including interactive services (Article 6(7) Communications Law). There are three types of licenses distributed by the CSBC:

– A general cable broadcast license ('CBL') for multichannel television broadcasting. The holder of a general CBL can produce its own channels but must

maintain sufficient capacity to carry the broadcasts of special and designated channels;
- A 'special' channel license for broadcasting a topical television channel, which refers to channels produced for the general public by independent producers and are carried by multichannel television platforms (both cable and satellite providers);
- A sub-category of the special license is the 'Designated Channel' license which applies to independently produced channels for specific purposes and with unique characteristics (e.g., language, type of viewer population or a unique purpose such as the promotion of certain music or culture) that have been permitted to sell advertisements;[193]
- A license for the broadcast of Video on Demand (VOD).

263. The CSBC oversees the process of licensing multichannel satellite television broadcasts although the satellite broadcast license ('SBL') itself, which is defined as any type of satellite broadcasts (including encrypted or interactive broadcasts) from Israel or by an Israeli individual or an Israeli corporation received in Israel and directed at the Israeli public, is granted by the Minister of Communications (Article 6(43) Communications Law) and not by the CSBC.

264. There is a presumption that broadcasts are directed at the Israeli public if at least 50% of the contents are in Hebrew (including translation or dubbing in Hebrew); if the contents of the broadcasts during peak viewing hours are in Hebrew; if the channel broadcasts advertisements directed at the Israeli public;[194] or if the source of the broadcasts is located in Israel (Article 6(45) of the Communications Law).

265. Granting a CBL or SBL is based on considerations including *inter alia* the government policy on broadcast media, public welfare, the applicant's suitability for television broadcasting, and the contribution of the granted license to the competition, diversity and quality of cable or satellite broadcasting (Article 6(8)1 Communications Law).

---

193. There are three designated channels: the Russian language channel ('Israel Plus', Channel 9); the Music Channel ('Channel 24') designated for Israeli music; the Arabic channel ('Hala-TV', Channel 30).

194. This definition is supposed to capture cases such as the MTV Europe channel that broadcasted in English but was extremely popular among Israeli viewers to the extent that Israeli corporations chose to advertise on it thereby circumventing the limitation on advertising in the multichannel television platforms. Indeed, General CBL and SBL holders are prohibited from intervening with the content of the foreign channels. However, foreign channels may provide a platform for advertisements directed at Israeli viewers. In HCJ 10338/03 *Vash Telecanal v. Minister of Communications* (2006) the HCJ upheld the petition of the Israeli produced Russian language channel which asserted that the Russian 'RTV International' channel carried by multichannel television providers in Israel is directed at the Israeli public and therefore may not broadcast advertisements directed at the public in Israel. Consequently, RTV International stopped airing such advertisements. However, aside from banning the carriage of an infringing foreign channel there is no regulatory sanction available to prevent a foreign channel from broadcasting advertisements directed at Israeli viewers. See also Schejter, transfrontier, *supra* n. 192, at 366; Yuval Karniel, Commercial Media Law 131 (Institute for Law and Economic Research 2003) (hereinafter – Karniel).

266. Only Israeli citizens, who are also residents, or a corporation registered in Israel may be granted a CBL, and for a general CBL there is a further requirement that at least 26% of the means of control in the corporation will be held by an Israeli citizen and resident (Article 6(8)(2) Communications Law).

267. A CBL can be refused for reasons of public interest; if it poses a threat to state security; if the applicant is directly or indirectly representing a political party or may use the broadcasts to further the goals of a political party; or if the applicant is in any way held by a foreign government. However the Minister of Communications may permit granting the CBL to a corporation in which 10% of the controlling power is held by a foreign government (Article 6(8)3 Communications Law).

268. A general CBL must carry the broadcasts of the ETV free of charge (Article 6(14) Communications Law).

269. The license fees and royalties paid by CBL holders are first allocated to cover the costs of the regulatory regime including the production of community broadcasts and local productions. Surplus fees and royalties are transferred to the treasury (Article 6(36) Communications Law).[195]

270. Chapter B2 of the communications Law deals with satellite television broadcasting. Satellite television broadcasting requires a license ('SBL') granted by the Minister of Communications according to Article 6(44)(b) Communications Law. This Article provides that an Israeli citizen or an Israeli corporation are prohibited from broadcasting satellite television to the Israeli public or part thereof without the aforementioned SBL. An SBL will be granted by the Minister of Communications if the applicant fulfilled the requirements prescribed by the law or after a tender process conducted by the CSBC (Article 6(46)(a) Communications Law). An SBL is not exclusive and the Minister of Communications may grant more than one SBL but the minister may also guarantee the SBL holder exclusivity for a period of five years if the SBL was granted by way of tender (Article 6(46)(b) Communications Law).

271. An SBL may only be granted to an Israeli citizen, a person domiciled in Israel or a corporation of which the means of control at a rate determined by the Minister of Communications are held by an Israeli citizen or a person domiciled in Israel (Article 6(47)(1) Communications Law). The statute also requires that the SBL holder will not have been convicted of a crime which according to the opinion of the Attorney General should prevent the granting of an SBL (Article 6(47)(2) Communications Law).

272. The Minister of Communications is broadly authorized after consulting with the CSBC to set the conditions of the SBL in regulations or in the terms of the tender (Article 6(48) Communications Law) including limitations on the transfer of

195. As of 2013 CBL holders are exempt from royalty payments. There are no annual license fees imposed on CBL holders and therefore the CSBC is funded only from the budget of the MOC.

ownership or control in the SBL, the financial ability of the SBL holder, experience and know-how, the programming diversity, broadcast technology, and the scope of broadcasts in the Hebrew language.

273. The Minister of Communications is also authorized after consulting with the CSBC to include terms in the SBL concerning the length of the SBL period and the conditions that must be met in order to prolong it, technology standards, must carry obligations regarding terrestrial radio and television channels and with regards to independent channels, the maximal fees that may be imposed on subscribers and guarantees required from the SBL holder (Article 6(49) Communications Law).

274. The Minister of Communications is also authorized after consulting with the CSBC to allow an SBL holder to offer its subscribers VOD services, in the scope and framework used by general CBL holders (Article 6(50) Communications Law).

Chapter 3. Programme Standards

§1. Impartiality

275. Impartiality in the Israeli media law focuses primarily on two types of bias. The first is the concern that broadcasters will be politically imbalanced in terms of content. The second concern regards intervention by owners and stakeholders in furtherance of their own interests rather than the public interest in programming or programme content. Hence, the rules governing impartiality could be categorized in two categories. On the one hand we find the 'institutional' rules that aim to ensure the political impartiality of the broadcasting entities, e.g., the ownership structure of the broadcasters, the nomination of officers, etc. These can be referred to as objective impartiality rules. On the other hand we find the rules governing the broadcasters' behaviour in terms of content, e.g., representation of different opinions, controversial topics, advertising, etc. These can be termed subjective impartiality rules.

276. It is often noted that broadcast media regulation in Israel aspires to enshrine an across-the-board requirement for political impartiality.[196] The three main laws regulating broadcast media require the public and private broadcasters to provide a fair representation of the various opinions in Israeli society.

277. Commercial television and radio broadcasters are obliged to objectivity and impartiality in their broadcasts and must not abuse their powers.

278. The commercial broadcasters (or their interest holders) are prohibited from expressing their personal opinion or suppressing other opinions directly or indirectly in the broadcasts (Articles 46(c) and (d) SATRL). They are expected to heed not to promote the personal, financial or public interests of any of their stakeholders (Rules 5 and 6 SAEthic). Rule 2 SAEthic obliges CBF and CRF holders to respect freedom of speech, including that of unpopular and unorthodox views and opinions.

279. In the commercial radio, a CRF holder is obliged to guarantee that advertiser interests will not influence the content or the scheduling of a programme (Rule 6 SARaAD) and that advertisements are clearly separated from the rest of the broadcasts (Rule 7 SARaAD). Similar rules apply to commercial television (discussed in Chapter 5, *infra*).

280. In the multichannel television platforms, a CBL or SBL application may be refused if the applicant is directly or indirectly representing a political party or may

196. Amit Schejter, *'The Stranger That Dwelleth with You Shall Be unto You as One Born among You' – Israeli Media Law and the Cultural Rights of the "Palestinian-Israeli" Minority*, 1 Middle East J. Culture & Communication 156, 160 (2008) (hereinafter – Schejter, stranger); Amit Schejter & Moran Yemini, *"Eyes Have They, But They See Not": Israeli Election Laws, Freedom of Expression and the Need for Transparent Speech*, 14 Comm. L. & Pol'y 411, 418 (2009) (hereinafter – Schejter & Yemini) noting that the model of impartiality has been inspired by the British doctrine.

use the broadcasts to further the goals of a political party (Article 6(8)3(3) Communications Law). In addition, Article 10 BCL Rules which applies to broadcasters on multichannel platforms requires broadcasters to grant 'due balance of popular public opinions' in programmes with content of public significance, echoing the fairness doctrine. The article expressly stipulates that in such cases the broadcaster should *inter alia*:

- In a matter in which there are several public opinions the broadcaster should present at least two central opinions without preferring one opinion over the other in terms of the method of presentation and the time allocated to the presentation.
- If it is impossible to present two opinions in the initial programme the broadcaster should inform the viewers on the matter and arrange the presentation of another opinion in another programme soon after the initial broadcast.

281. In the commercial channels, impartiality concerns focus on news broadcasts. Article 64 SATRL obliges the commercial news corporations to be 'accurate, reliable and balanced' an avoid reflecting the opinions of its owners. The impartiality of the commercial news corporations is guaranteed by complex ownership structures that aim to separate the bodies producing news content from their financial stakeholders (discussed in the following sections). Some observers claim that the complex regulatory structure of the news corporations of the commercial channels reflects a deep distrust by the legislators regarding the ability of private owners to refrain from intervening in the production of the news.[197] On the other hand, the structure may reflect the desire of the government to maintain some political influence over the news in the commercial channels as it relinquished its IBA monopoly over supply of broadcast news.

282. The impartiality guarantees (which also strive to provide professional independence) of the commercial news corporation rely on a statutory separation between the ownership and obligatory financing of the news corporation which is imposed on the CBF holders, and the control of the corporations which is dispersed between the CBF holders and the SATR. The SATR retains a significant share of the voting power in the governing organs of the corporations thereby creating a mixed public-private supervising board of directors.

283. The news corporations of each commercial channel are established as separate corporate entities from the CBF holders according to Article 63A SATRL. The shareholders of Channel 2 news corporation are the SATR and the CBF holders (or the commercial license holder after the license regime will be launched) (Article 66 SATRL). The CBF holders were issued pro rata 60% of the voting shares and all the shares that guarantee the right to dividends and to the assets of the corporation in case of dissolution, whereas the SATR was only issued 40% of the voting shares (Article 66 SATRL). The same ratio of 60%–40% is maintained in the board of directors in which the SATR is represented by public representatives qualified to be chairpersons of a board of directors according to the Government Corporations Law

197. Karniel, *supra* n. 194, at 62.

1975 (Article 67 SATRL). The general director of the news corporation is proposed by the CBF holders and elected by the board of directors by a required majority of 75% of the votes which gives the SATR representatives a potential veto right (Article 68 SATRL). This regime applies *mutatis mutandis* to the news corporation of Channel 10 (Article 63A(b)(1) SATRL). The SAC determines the time slots and length of the news broadcasts for both commercial channels (Article 63(b) SATRL).

284. With regards to commercial radio, a CRF holder may integrate local and national news and current affairs programmes in its broadcasts. Local news programmes must be self-produced, whereas national news can be self-produced or produced in cooperation with other CRF holders and with another entity that deals exclusively with news production (Rule 4a(a) and 4a(b) SARaF). Some degree of impartiality, professionalism and accountability is assured by the requirement that the appointment of the chief editor of the national news programmes, regardless of the production arrangement, will be subject to prior written consent by the SATR director (Rule 4a(d) SARaF).

285. A general CBL holder must broadcast regional news broadcasts (concerned only with local and not with national news) produced internally or by an external producer (Article 14 BCL Rules). The BCL Rules contain specific stipulations imposed on the CBL holder designed to guarantee the impartiality of these news broadcasts, such as the obligations (Rule 14(c) BCL):

(a) to conduct accurate and reliable news broadcasts;
(b) to guarantee independent collection, verification and editing of news;
(c) to refrain from employing news staff in commercial activities;
(d) to avoid basing investigative reports on sources reflecting only one point of view (Rule 16b(2) BCL).

286. CBL and SBL holders may not broadcast their own national newscasts. In a 2001 amendment to the Communications Law the CSBC was empowered to license a designated national cable news channel as well as to allow general CBL holders to broadcast newscasts concerning national affairs provided that both were produced by an external independent producer approved by a majority of the members of the CSBC including at least half of the public representatives of the CSBC and after giving the public an opportunity to render an opinion on the engagement of the independent news producer and its terms (Article 6(20)2 Communications Law).[198] So far the attempts to launch such a channel have failed.

198. The original intention of the Communications Law was to limit CBL holders to local news broadcasting. In Amendment 25 of the Communications Law CBL and SBL holders were allowed to broadcast national news but only by carrying an independently produced news channel. Prior to Amendment 25 of the Communications Law, there were several cable companies and each served a different geographical region of the country. Under that regime broadcasting national news made little sense. While the legislator recognized that broadcasting national news would be more sensible once the regional cable broadcasting has been abolished and the cable providers merged into a single corporation, the separation between ownership and news production policy that can be

287. Impartiality of the designated news channel (should one come into existence) is guaranteed at the licensing stage. The CSBC is authorized to refuse an application for a news channel license by an independent producer if the applicant represents a political party or if the applicant represents any other entity directly or indirectly and the CSBC has reason to believe that the applicant might use the news broadcasts to further the goals of the party or the entity (Article 6(20)2(d) Communications Law). The CSBC's authority to refuse an application in this case is broader than its authority with respect to the general CBL or SBL application as it applies to any entity and not just political parties.

288. Article 6(20)2(e) of the Communications Law requires the independent cable news producer to broadcast 'accurate, reliable and balanced' newscasts that shall not reflect the opinions of the managers, employees or shareholders of the producer or the licensee.

289. An independent news producer is prohibited from receiving any benefits other than the payments from the CBL holder. The news producer may supply news to other licensees including SBL holders but it is prohibited from price discriminating among licensees.

290. Independence of the designated news channel from physical intervention in its content is also guaranteed. The general CBL holder may not intervene, cut, edit or delay the independent news producer's newscasts (Article 6(20)2(b)(5) Communications Law).

§2. Cultural Diversity

I. Access to Airtime for Cultural Groupings

291. The legislation in the first two decades of the State of Israel was highly influenced by a government-driven cultural 'melting pot' policy designed to create a new Israeli-Jewish culture. This policy aimed to erase cultural and ethnic divides caused by waves of immigration from post-World War II Europe, North African countries, Yemen, Iraq, Syria, etc.[199]

---

observed in the commercial channels was adopted in this case as well by enjoining the general CBL or SBL holders from producing their own newscasts.

199. It is often the case that the melting pot policy meant the imposition of cultural and social values held by the hegemonic socio-ethnic groups on the weaker groups. A representative example in this case is the ruling in HCJ 1/81 *Shiran v. The IBA*, 35(3) PD 365 [1981]. In this case, activists defending the representation of Mizrachi Jews petitioned the HCJ to ban the screening of a documentary television series produced by the IBA (which was the only television channel in Israel at the time) depicting the evolution of the Zionist movement and the events leading to the foundation of the state of Israel according to geographical diasporas. The petitioners claimed that the series emphasized the role of European-Ashkenazi Jews and grossly reduced the role of Mizrachi Jews coming from Arab countries. The HCJ denied the petition and stated that any such intervention would constitute censorship. The HCJ also noted that Mizrachi and Ashkenazi Jews are 'parts of the same body' and therefore rejected the claim that Mizrachi Jews could be offended by their portrayal in

292. Schejter argues that broadcasting in Israel, both public and commercial, has been assigned a role in advancing the social melting pot policy in which the Jewish culture is dominant.[200] According to his contention, the regulation of media in Israel is still aimed at controlling the diversity of news and cultural programmes available to certain groups of the Israeli society – namely, Palestinian-Israelis and Russian immigrants – for the purpose of promoting social unity.[201] At least with regard to legislative declaratory actions, there has been an attempt to bring about a change in this policy. For example, Article 5(b)(1) SATRL counts the promotion of Hebrew Israeli creation among the principle objectives of the SATR but Article 5(b)(5) SATRL includes among these objectives the promotion of Arabic language broadcasts to 'meet the needs of the Arabic speaking population' and Article 5(b)(6) SATRL expressly charges the SATR with expressing the 'cultural pluralism of the Israeli society'.

293. Regulators and the government seem to react, albeit slowly, to the needs of minority groups. Some of these regulatory efforts are attempts to counter illegal activities such as minority communities setting up illegal local cable networks or illegal radio stations. In other events, the regulatory efforts are a reaction to the reliance of cultural minorities on foreign and potentially anti-Israeli media.[202]

294. In fact, cultural groupings have been granted increasing access to multi-channel broadcast platforms in recent legislative activities (discussed in the following section). Indeed, the general aims of the recent legislation governing broadcast media emphasizes both the need to promote Israeli social values and the need to recognize and manifest the plurality of Israeli society. Naturally, these interests occasionally conflict, given that the Israeli society is persistently conflicted and polarized. Such conflicts are mostly resolved through a political or a practical compromise rather than by a forced imposition of social values on a cultural group or vice-versa. Nevertheless, there are cases in which legal intervention is called for, as discussed in the following paragraph.

---

the series. Compare to the approach voiced by Justice Aharon Barak in CA 105/92 *Re'em Engineers and Contractors v. Upper Nazareth Municipality* 47(5) PD 189, 212 [1993], who stated that '[W]e are a pluralistic society, aspiring to ingather exiles, and to absorb them in a melting pot, while preserving their uniqueness, their customs, and origin'.

200. Schejter, transfrontier, *supra* n. 192, at 343.

201. And he is critical of this policy even at the formative stage of a democratic state, as it tends to persist long after the formative stage. Schejter, transfrontier, *supra* n. 192, at 367–368.

202. Katz notes that the development of regional cable television providers was a reaction to the unofficial private local cable networks which were widespread in Israeli cities and neighbourhoods in the 1980s as a substitute for the limited supply of content provided by the IBA; regional radio and particularly radio stations directed at the religious and ultra-Orthodox public were offered as a substitute to the phenomenon of illegal radio stations estimated at more than 100 during the 1990s; the designated cable channels in Russian language and the various broadcasts in Arabic are intended to counteract the reliance of Russian immigrants and of the Arab population on foreign channels received via satellite as their principle source of information. Yaron Katz, *The "Other Media" – Alternative Communications in Israel*, 10 Int'l J. Cultural Stud. 383 (2007).

295. This tension can be illustrated by the implementation of CRF holders' obligation to direct their radio broadcasts, and reflect in them, the characteristics of the population in the franchise region (Rule 2(a) SARaF). Some CRF holders serve a unique cultural grouping, such as Orthodox Jews. These radio stations may be required to comply with religious diktats of rabbinical authorities, either because the employees or the owners of the radio station abide by the rulings of these rabbinical authorities or because the listeners of the station abide by them. In fact, the SATR recognizes the religious nature of these radio stations by including a requirement in the franchise or license terms giving the 'spiritual committee' an influential position in the station's decision making process. Some strict Orthodox Rabbis interpret the Jewish religious edicts as prohibiting listening to the voice of women in radio or public performance. This issue has been the focus of a heated debate at the CSBC concerning the obligation of radio station 'Kol Barama', a CRF holder serving an audience of Sepharadi-Orthodox listeners in the central region of Israel. For a while, the station refrained completely from broadcasting female voices. It does not employee women broadcasters to date and its editors regularly cut out female voices from newscasts; refused women callers in talk shows, etc. After some negotiations with the SATR, the station did agree to dedicate several broadcast hours to programmes where the voices of women would be heard. In April 2012 the matter reached the CSBC which agreed to a four-hour per week of women inclusive broadcasts on 'Kol Barama'. The CSBC was split on the matter and approved the agreement only after the CSBC Chairperson casted a double vote according to his powers in case of a deadlock. The decision reflects the strengthening of ultra-Orthodox trends within the Israeli religious population as well as the tendency to accommodate the demands of such populations, mostly for political reasons. In May 2013, a report by a team appointed by the AG published a review of the legal implications of religion-based discrimination against women. With respect to 'Kol Barama', the report indicated that the current arrangement is still discriminatory and that the purposeful policy against hiring women broadcasters, which was not eliminated in the current agreement, is also discriminatory and illegal. The report noted that the discrimination is founded on an extreme interpretation of the religious diktats. The station's argument that broadcasting female voices will result in listeners abandoning the station and subsequent financial losses was rejected by the committee's report, which noted that no such effect was documented after the station started including female voices in its broadcasts in 2012. The AG adopted the committee's recommendation to allow the SATR a period of six months to negotiate with the station but clarified that the negotiations must result in the discriminatory policies of the station being abolished.[203]

296. In 2012 the CSBC published a tender for a designated channel on Jewish heritage. The license will enable the licensee to broadcast a cable and satellite channel focused on Jewish tradition for a term of ten years with the option of extending the license for an additional term of six years. The tender terms oblige the licensee to invest in local production and require a quota of 33% original programmes.

---

203. The Report of the Committee for the Examination of the Phenomenon of Excluding Women from the Public Domain (2013), 51–59.

297. Considering the dominance of Jewish culture in Israel and the political influence that religious parties have on government policies, it is surprising that a Jewish heritage channel has not materialized thus far. Previous tenders have been unsuccessful.

298. The most comprehensive access arrangement for cultural groupings can be found in the BCL Rules and applies to multichannel platforms. Rule 29 BCL promotes broadcasts produced by a host of recognized educational and non-profit community-oriented organization engaged in public and social non-political activities and provides financial support for these the productions from the CSBC budget ('Community Broadcasts'). Recognized producers of community broadcasts may also receive funding in return for sponsorship announcements (Rule 33b BCL). Rule 23 requires CBL or SBL holders to broadcast every month five 30 minute programmes on topics related to the region's community but an exemption from this obligation is given for multichannel providers that carry community broadcasts, which are costless to produce from the multichannel platform provider's perspective.

299. In conclusion, there are some statutory and financial efforts to encourage the access of cultural and other groupings to airtime. However, the Jewish-Israeli group continues to dominate mainstream audio-visual broadcasts.[204]

II. Content Obligations (Quota)

300. The IBA is obliged to invest no less than 15% of its annual income on the purchase of local productions and no less than 10% of its annual income on 'elite genre' local productions (Article 44c IBA Law), defined in the addendum to the IBA Law as documentary and drama programmes or special original programmes of unique value. The minister in charge of the IBA has the authority to reduce the IBA's statutory obligations, and has done so often in the recent years.[205]

301. A unique phenomenon in Israeli media regulation is the broad quota requirements imposed on private broadcasters. These obligations, which impose a

204. The general issue of access to the media is insufficiently addressed in the case law. For a critical assessment see: Daphne Barak, *The Freedom of Access to the Media: A Balance of Interests within the Right to Freedom of Speech*, 12 Iyunei Mishpat 183 (1987).

205. The State Comptroller's Report 61B (2011), 436–437. However, at the time the quota was higher and it was reduced in Amendment 27 due the IBA's financial distress. In 2012, the reduction in the quota of external local productions has been justified by the IBA's need to invest significant financial resources in reforming the ailing organization. Independent television producers criticize the IBA for lack of transparency with regard to the actual amounts invested in external local production and the actual distribution of this amount between types of genres. A petition by the organization of documentary film producers against the IBA filed on October 2012 is pending before the HCJ. The petitioners allege that the IBA invested only 19% of the required amount in external productions. See also: Shuki Sadeh & Nati Tucker, *The IBA: Scandals and Small Politics in a Public Entity that Controls a Billion Shekel Budget*, The Marker (27 Jul. 2012) (Hebrew) at: http://www.themarker.com/markerweek/1.1787188.

significant financial burden on private broadcasters, are explained by the unique market failures that characterize a small media market with relatively high productions costs, and relatively low potential revenue from local productions which are seldom marketable outside Israel.

302. I turn first to private radio stations. The content of local radio broadcasts by CRF holders is regulated by the SATR (Radio Broadcasts by a Franchise Holder) Rules 1999 ('the SARaF Rules'). As CRFs are distributed to geographical regions, the CRF holders are obliged to direct their broadcasts to the unique population within the franchise's geographical region and to reflect the characteristics of the regional population in the broadcasts (Rule 2(a) SARaF). The CRF holder is obliged to offer diversified programmes (Rule 2(b) SARaF) and schedule them appropriately, giving special attention to minors and to religious holidays (Rule 3 SARaF).

303. Turning to television broadcasters, the SATR applies a hefty quota regime to CBF holders with obligations to broadcast original programmes produced in Israel. The intent behind the quota regime is twofold. First of all, it is supposed to generate diversified high quality television content which represents the unique Israeli social and cultural fabric. Second, it aims to promote the local television production industry. The regime is the result of the fact that less stringent regulation has proved to be inefficient and enabled broadcasters to backslide to the production of low quality programmes.[206]

304. Consequently, Article 59 SATRL obliges that at least 40% of the broadcast content of the commercial broadcasters will consist of local Israeli productions and that 65% of the local productions will be acquired from independent producers other than the broadcaster itself. These requirements apply to both commercial channels (Channel 2 and Channel 10), but the SAC has the power to reduce the quota up to half of the statutory requirement during the first two years of the broadcaster's franchise.[207]

305. The SATRL stipulates that 'local production' includes a programme produced entirely or mostly in Israel except for newscasts, current affairs programmes and sportscasts. However, there is no reference regarding the required language of the programme nor is there a requirement for originality. Thus the law does not preclude the inclusion of local productions of international programme formats in the required quota.[208] The SATRL further contains an addendum stipulating an elaborate list of content requirements such as 180 hour minimum quota of 'elite genre'

206. Karniel, *supra* n. 194, at 82–83.

207. The required local production quota for Channel 2 was 45% in 2010 and for Channel 10 it was 40%. See SATR Annual Report 2010, at 16 and 82. Given the close scrutiny of the SATR, franchisees usually meet or at least come close to meeting their general investment obligations. However, the internal division of different types of productions within the quota, e.g., elite genre programmes of various types, is often not met as required.

208. Karniel, *supra* n. 194, at 60, notes that the law's focus is on the financial aspect of the quota although its original intention was both to support local production firms but also to encourage original Israeli creative programmes.

programmes which includes 'documentary programmes, drama programmes, docu-drama programmes' and so on.

306. The SATR (Television Broadcasts by a Franchise Holder) Rules 2009 ('the SAFraB Rules') provide the intricate basis for regulating the commercial broadcasters' content. CBF holders are expected to broadcast a wide variety of programmes reflecting the 'Israeli experience', the Jewish-Israeli discourse and the cultural diversity of the state including the Arab and immigrants population (Rule 6 SAFraB). During religious holidays and memorial days the CBF holder must broadcast an 'adequate' amount of half-hour programmes produced locally and aimed at increasing public knowledge and awareness of the relevant occasion (Rule 6(b) SAFraB).

307. The SAFraB Rules dedicate a chapter to guaranteeing broadcast content quality. Rule 20 SAFraB stipulates that the criteria for judging the quality of broadcasts shall include:

- The appropriateness of the conditions, time and place allocated to the production, including the time for post-production.
- The appropriateness of the means and equipment used for the production.
- The professional experience of the production team, the technical team, performers, and creators.
- The financial investment in the production.
- Globally accepted professional standards for the appreciation of similar programmes around the world.
- The appropriateness of employment terms of all individuals involved in the production.
- Language eloquence of the production, when appropriate.
- The respect of intellectual property rights.
- The promotion of SATR trends as mentioned in Article 5 SATRL.

308. The quota mechanism outlines an overall mandatory minimal investment threshold for programmes. A CBF holder must expend 60% or 220 million NIS (whichever is higher) of its annual revenue after deducting the contribution to the news corporation on the production and purchase of programmes (Rule 21(c) SAFraB). The expenditure amount is determined after the SATR Director projects the annual revenue for the following year in the 1st of August, based on the CBF holder's revenues in the preceding twelve months, and reports the projection the CBF holder (Rule 21(b) SAFraB). The rule further stipulates that revenue projection and the ensuing expenditure on programmes will be updated with additional revenue data at the 1st of January and 1st of July of the relevant year.

309. Rule 21(d) SAFraB specifies that a CBF holder that exceeds the required expenditure may deduct the excess amount from the following year's expenditure, whereas a CBF holder that did not meet the expenditure ceiling given the final annual revenue data must complete the expenditure by investing in programmes that will be broadcasted within the following two years or transfer the funds at the behest of the SATR Director to a fund set up by the SATR for financing SATR productions. The SATR Director has the authority to forfeit collateral guarantees of the CBF holder to guarantee the implementations of these obligations.

310. The quota mechanism proceeds to outline the minimal investment in Israeli productions. 80% of all expenditures must be expended on Israeli productions (Rule 21(f) SAFraB), of which the CBF holders together must expend, in equal parts, 8 million NIS on Israeli films (Rule 21(g) SAFraB). An investment equal to at least 1% of the expenditure on non-elite genres must be directed towards research and development of elite genre content (Rule 23 SAFraB).

311. The investment of a CBF holder in local productions is determined according to its projected annual revenue, but at any case it must be no less than a minimum of 40% and up to a minimum of 50% at the highest scale (Rule 11 SAFraB).

312. Within the quota requirements, certain types of 'preferred programmes' (as defined in the following paragraph) must be broadcasted. The minimal quota applies to a projected annual revenue of up to 500 Million NIS and includes 150 hours of which 100 hours must be aired between 17:00 and 24:00 and these distributed to 25 hours of knowledge and culture programmes, 30 hours of periphery programmes, 30 hours of Jewish heritage and culture programmes and 15 hours of public discourse programmes (Rule 7(b)(1) SAFraB). The maximal quota applies to a projected annual revenue of 690 million NIS or more and includes 316 hours of which 216 hours must be aired between 17:00 and 24:00 and these distributed to 60 hours of knowledge and culture programmes, 60 hours of periphery programmes, 48 hours of Jewish heritage and culture programmes and 48 hours of public discourse programmes (Rule 7(b)(5) SAFraB). If the annual revenue exceeds projections then the CBF holder must complete the balance between the fulfilled quota and the adjusted quota in the two following years, whereas if the annual revenue falls below projections the CBF holder may reduce the following year's quota accordingly (Rule 7(d) SAFraB).

313. The SAFraB Rules define four types of 'preferred programmes' which include:

(a) 'Culture and knowledge programme', defined as a locally produced programme aimed to enrich the viewer and is not an entertainment or leisure programme; the SAC may indicate the topics that should be the focus of culture and knowledge programmes from time to time (Rule 7(a) SAFraB);
(b) 'Periphery programme', defined as a locally produced programme focusing on groups with ethnic, national, tribal, religious, social, or geographical characteristics which do not have access to the public, economic, social or cultural pivots of public influence and enjoy a limited access to Israeli media;
(c) 'Jewish heritage and culture programme', also locally produced, on historic as well as contemporary Jewish cultural issues;
(d) 'Public Discourse programme' defined as a locally produced programme including in-depth reportages filmed on location outside the studio and commentary

and debates relating to and increasing the knowledge of current public events in Israel and worldwide.

314. In order to be recognized as a local production, the programme must be produced uniquely for the CBF holder for that purpose and never broadcasted in a national television channel prior to its initial broadcast by the CBF holder (Rule 12(a) SAFraB). An exceptional recognition of a programme as part of the local production quota can be allowed by the SATR Director for programmes that have been aired once by another national channel if the CBF holder has reached the minimum 40% and is obliged to broadcast a higher quota (Rule 12(b) SAFraB).

315. The CBF holder may cooperate in producing local programmes with the IBA; foundations relying on budgets granted according to the Cinema Law 1999; a CBL or SBL holder or other channel licensees according to the Communications Law; a radio broadcaster; a government ministry; a non-profit organization without commercial or political interests (Rule 13 SAFraB). In case of cooperative productions in which the CBF holder invested less than 51% of the cost, only the CBF holder's relative investment will be recognized for the purpose of measuring the fulfilment of local productions quota (Rule 12(b)(3) SAFraB) and the SATR Director may also decide not to recognize it at all if the investment is too low (Rule 13(b) SAFraB).

316. At least 65% of the local productions broadcasted by the CBF holder must be purchased from external producers (Rule 14(a) SAFraB), of which 65% of the elite genre productions must be purchased externally at an investment equal to the average investment in internally produced elite genre programmes (Rule 14(c) SAFraB). 15% of the local programmes purchased from external producers must be produced in the country's periphery areas (Rule 14(e) SAFraB). Only a maximum of 20% of the local productions broadcasted annually may be purchased from the same producer (Rule 14(f) SAFraB), but an exception can be made for the external producer of a daily morning current affairs programme (Rule 14(g) SAFraB).

317. A programme will not be recognized as a purchased local production if the producers used employees of the CBF holder or its production facilities, or invested more than 15% of the production budget in means of production of which the CBF holder holds more than 20% directly or indirectly (Rule 14(h) SAFraB), but certain leniencies may apply when the production belongs to a non-elite genre.

318. The SATR Director may recognize part of a production in cooperation with a non-Israeli entity as a local production, based on the relative Israeli share of the production (Rule 15(c) SAFraB). An animation programme dubbed in Hebrew by a professional team of Israeli actors can be recognized as a local production for up to 50% of its length (Rule 15(d) SAFraB). A purchased Israeli film will be considered as purchased local production but not as elite genre, whereas a film in which the CBF holder invested at least 30% of the production cost (but no less than 811000 NIS) will be recognized at a rate of 150% of its length, but not as elite genre (Rule

15(e) SAFraB). Re-runs are recognized for up to 12% of the local production quota (Rule 15(f) SAFraB).

319. In addition to the elaborate local production quota, the SATR implements a regime directed at guaranteeing programme quality. CBF holders must broadcast a quota of preferred programmes (each programme at least 24 minute long) according to a scale of revenue (Rule 7(b) SAFraB).

320. According to Rule 16(a) SAFraB, CBF holders are obliged to broadcast 180 hours of 'elite genre' – a definition explained forthwith – programmes annually (of which at least 15% must be 'preferred programmes' according to Rule 16(e) SAFraB) at an investment of at least 50 million NIS in the following distribution:

(a) 40 hours of drama programmes including at least 3 different drama programmes at an investment of no less than 20 million NIS in total;
(b) 22 hours of special documentary programmes at an investment of no less than 8 million NIS;
(c) 55 hours of documentary programmes of which at least 12 hours will be investigative reportage programmes at a total investment of no less than 8 million NIS;
(d) 63 hours of special programmes or documentary programmes at a total investment of no less than 14 million NIS.

321. The elite genre quota is increased proportionally if 60% of the CBF holder's annual projected revenue multiplied by 17% exceeds a 50 million NIS threshold (Rule 16(b) SAFraB). If the CBF holder's investment in elite genre programmes turns out to be lower than the required quota due to higher revenues at the end of the year compared to the projected revenues, then the CBF holder must complete the quota in the following two years but the SATR Director may instruct the CBF holder to transfer the money instead to a special fund set up by the SATR to finance its own productions (Rule 16(d) SAFraB).

322. The detailed hours and budgets in Rule 16(a) create a minimal hourly genre budget which is the result of distributing the minimal budget per genre by the minimal quota of hours required for that genre. Individual programmes are recognized by the SATR for the purpose of calculating the fulfilment of the quota only if they comply with the minimal hourly genre budget (see for example, Rule 16(h) SAFraB). Co-productions may also be recognized if the investment of the CBF holders meets the hourly genre budget threshold (Rule 17 SAFraB).

323. As part of the elite genre obligations, the CBF holder must broadcast at least 12 hours of a 'historic series' with a budget of 110% of the hourly genre budget (Rule 18 SAFraB). Reality shows and leisure programs cannot be recognized as elite genre, but the SATR Director has some discretion with regards to tourism, travel and food programmes (Rule 16(k) SAFraB).

324. The originality of broadcasted content is also guaranteed by limitations on re-runs. For example, re-runs must be indicated for the viewers and may not exceed 20% of the broadcaster unit's time (Rules 19(a) and 19(f) SAFraB). A programme that assembles parts of other programmes is not considered a re-run but may not be aired more than twice in every quarter (Rule 19(c) SAFraB). Rebroadcasting an Israeli film for the second time shall not be considered a re-run nor rebroadcasting the film after another four years have elapsed (Rule 19(d) SAFraB). For a foreign series to be rebroadcasted without being considered a re-run, eight years must elapse from the first broadcast (Rule 19(e) SAFraB).

325. The legal structure supporting content regulation in cable and satellite television is more flexible than the one provided by the SATRL, thereby granting the CSBC greater latitude in shaping content requirements. According to the Communications Law (Article 6(20)) the CSBC has to power to set rules regarding the content of the broadcasts. With respect to the general programming of the cable and satellite television providers, the CSBC published rules regarding the local production quotas, quality and topics.

326. With regards to designated channels, the Communications Law (Article 6(34)1(d)) requires a minimum of 20% local production. This is significantly lower than the burden on CBF holders. However, the CSBC compensates for this lenient statutory requirement by setting stringent requirements in the tender terms or in the franchise agreement.[209] For instance, the tender for a CNN-like Israeli cable news channel contained a requirement obliging the licensee to produce 60% of the programmes in Israel, to dedicate 15% of the programmes to foreign affairs and to refrain from broadcasting entertainment or sports programmes of any kind except brief news reports on such events.[210]

327. The content obligations of the cable and satellite broadcasters are distributed between the CBL and SBL holders themselves and the external channel producers. General CBL holders (this applies to SBL holders as well) are obliged to allocate 10% of their broadcasting to original local productions, of which 50% must be purchased and not internally produced (Article 6(5)1 Communications Law). A production entity in which a CBL or SBL holder controls 10% of the means of control directly or indirectly is considered 'internal local production' and is not considered part of the required quota of purchased local productions (Article 6i Communications Law).

328. The CSBC has the authority to set rules regarding the minimum quota of local productions (expressed by a minimum number of hours that must be broadcasted), their types, genres, the times in which they are broadcasted and their distribution between the various channels of a general CBL or SBL holder as well as the manner in which the general CBL or SBL holder's investment in local production should be reported (Article 6(5)1(b) and (c) of the Communications Law).

---

209. Article 6(34)(d) Communications Law. See Karniel, *supra* n. 194, at 125.
210. Karniel, *supra* n. 194, at 127. Note that to date there is no Israeli cable news channel.

329. The CSBC requires that 8% to 12% of the CBL or SBL holder's annual revenues from subscription fees will be allocated to the production or purchase of local productions (Article 6(5)1(a1) Communications Law).[211]

330. Additional stipulations with regards to production quotas in the multichannel television platforms' own channels are detailed in the BCL Rules. A CBL or SBL holder are obliged *inter alia* (Rules 17a-17h BCL):

(a) to direct 50% of the 'investment amount' (as defined by Article 6(5)1(a1) Communications Law) to external local productions (Rule 17a(b) BCL);
(b) to direct 27.5% of the investment amount to programmes for children and youth; but 2.5% of this amount can be directed to science programmes even if they are not for youth or children; but no less than 3% of the investment amount or NIS 3.5 Million (attached to the consumer price index as of 2006) shall be invested in local productions for channels directed at infants.
(c) to direct at least 18.75% of the investment amount to children's programmes that are broadcasted in channels which are part of the basic bundle;
(d) to direct no more than 20% of the entire investment amount to a single channel but if the channel is part of the basic bundle (a minimal mandatory bundle of channels) the investment in local productions can be up to 50%;
(e) to invest no less than 50% of the investment amount in 'complex' genres;[212] 16% of this amount should be directed into drama programmes and half of this amount shall be invested in drama with productions costs of at least NIS 350,000 per hour; another 16% of the said amount shall be directed to documentary programmes;
(f) to invest no less than 8% if the remainder of the investment amount in science, music and arts programs.

331. A CBL or SBL holder may invest up to NIS 1.3 million in a film and Rule 17i BCL stipulates the length of the film that will be recognized as a local production as a function of the ratio of the investment relative to the total cost of the film's production. This is also conditional of the broadcasting of the film no later than eighteen months after its initial screening in cinemas (Rule 17i(c) BCL).

332. A CBL and SBL must report their expected investments in local productions three months before the beginning of each year to the CSNC (Rule 17k BCL).

333. Rules 18(a)(b1) and (b2) BCL stipulate that the appropriate classification of local productions to the respective genres shall be examined according to the conditions and means of the productions and that the CSBC shall have the power to

211. Since 2009 the obligation was set to 8% but de facto, HOT and YES invest higher amounts. CSBC Annual Report 2010, 27.
212. Complex genres are defined as local productions that are not entertainment, satire, talk show, quiz show or other competitive programmes (Rule 17(c)(f) BCL).

add a production to the broadcaster's obligations in the following year if the CSBC found that a production did not comply with the appropriate standards.

334. In order to expand the external production market, the CSBC is authorized to compel a CBL or SBL holder to avoid concentrating its external acquisitions in a small number of external producers (Rule 20(b) BCL).

335. A general CBL holder must also broadcast daily regional news broadcasts with the minimal average length of 25 minutes (Rule 22 BCL). The CBL holder HOT has been de facto relieved of the financial cost of this obligation and the cost of producing regional news broadcasts was shifted to the state, which means that the future existence of the regional newscasts is subjected to political whims.[213]

336. The CSBC may additionally require:

- An investment of up to 12% of the revenue in local productions as a condition for granting a 'special license' (Article 6(5)1(a2) Communications Law).
- An investment of up to 4% of the revenue from VOD services in local productions as a condition for granting a license for VOD services (Article 6(5)1(a3) Communications Law).

337. The CSBC may inflict monetary sanctions on a CBL or SBL holder for violating the local production quota requirement or impose on the violator a penalty of a doubled quota in the following year (Article 6(6) Communications Law).

III. Language Requirements

338. The Hebrew and the Arabic languages are the formal language of the state of Israel.[214] While Hebrew is spoken by most of the Israeli population including most of the Arab-Israeli minority, the HCJ acknowledged that the Arabic language

213. Currently HOT broadcasts five daily regional news programmes in Hebrew and one national news programme in Arabic. See CSBC Annual Report 2010, 4. The general CBL holder (HOT) has contracted out the production of regional news. The regional news had been produced by external production companies and for a while they were produced for HOT by the IBA. Due to the high cost of producing the regional news, the CSBC and the Ministry of Finance agreed to deduct the cost, estimated at NIS 25 million from the royalties paid by the CBL holder to the state and transfer this amount directly to the independent regional news producer, thereby relieving the CBL holder of the burden of financing the regional news. This has been done through a temporary order which was due to expire in the end of 2011. The Ministry of Finance refused to prolong the temporary order and suggested to consider the regional news as local production. The leader of the Labor Party in the Knesset warned against the dismissal of 150 employees of the regional news in the event that the regional news broadcasts are shut down and also proposed a bill for the reduction of the cost of the regional news from the CBL's required investment amount in local productions. As of yet, an intermediate solution guarantees the continued production of local newscasts only until the end of 2013.
214. Article 82 of the King's Order-in-Council (Palestine), 1922, enacted during the British mandate government in Palestine, stipulated that English, Arabic and Hebrew shall be the languages of the government. Art. 15(b) of the Governance Procedures Ordinance enacted by the Interim Council

has a unique status as the language of the state's largest minority group.[215] In addition, Russian is spoken by almost one million immigrants and descendants of immigrants from former-Soviet Union countries and Amharic and Tigrinya are spoken by a significantly smaller ethnic minority of immigrants and descendants of immigrants from Ethiopia.

339. The regulation of language usage in the Israeli media cannot be explained without understanding the unique historic bond between the Hebrew language and the Jewish people. Although Hebrew is an ancient language, it has not been used as an every-day language until its so-called revival in the nineteenth century. The revival of the language is intertwined with the Zionist movement in Europe which was a dominant force in the immigration of European Jews to Palestine and in the political processes that led to the international recognition of the right of the Jews to self-determination in the territory now known as the State of Israel. One element of self-determination was the dramatic and swift adoption of the Hebrew language as the every-day language of all immigrating European Jews within a timeframe of one generation.

340. No statute gives Hebrew priority over Arabic but in practice Hebrew functions as the dominant language in the public sphere. However, with the increasing reliance on internationally produced broadcast content, Hebrew is in itself now threatened in the broadcast context. The Hebrew language has regenerated itself as the native national language of Israelis in a unique process that motivates the legislative efforts to promote and defend the use of Hebrew in the electronic media. All three media laws generally require the broadcasters to promote creation in the Hebrew language. For example, the IBA is obliged to ensure that at least 50% of the songs broadcasted on the public radio will be in the Hebrew language (Article 44d IBA Law). The CSBC has authorized a designated channel for Hebrew music.

341. Broadcasts in the Arabic language have been historically motivated by propaganda concerns rather than public service perceptions of the media. In fact, one of the reasons for initiating television broadcasts in Israel in 1968 was the desire to broadcast propaganda in Arabic and to communicate with the occupied Palestinian population after Israel had occupied the West Bank and Gaza during the 1967 so-called six day war.[216]

342. In 1993 the IBA initiated a satellite channel broadcasting in Hebrew and Arabic which later developed into what is now known as 'Channel 33' which is transmitted only by cable and satellite television providers but is also available free of charge through the 'Idan Plus' DTT system. Channel 33 intends to target the Palestinian population in Israel and the Arab population in surrounding countries by

---

with the establishment of the state of Israel in 1948 adopted the British mandatory legislation but abolished the status of the English language, leaving only Hebrew and Arabic as the formal languages.

215. HCJ 4112/99 *Adalah v. Tel Aviv-Yaffo Municipality* (1999), sec. 25.

216. Amit Schejter, *The Cultural Obligations of Broadcast Television in Israel* 56 Gazette 183, 187 (2000).

broadcasting programmes in Arabic produced by the IBA. In conjunction with the initial development of Channel 33, the IBA abandoned its Arabic language broadcasting on its main broadcast channel, Channel 1.[217]

343. In the commercial channels, CBF holders are obliged to dedicate 5% of the weekly broadcast time to programmes in Arabic. An additional 5% of the programmes must be in Russian. However, most of these quotas are fulfilled also when the programmes are dubbed in these languages or when they include subtitles in the required language (Rule 8(a) SAFraB), which allows the broadcasters to meet their obligation by integrating subtitles in their regular programming. In comparison, a CBF holder must translate all programmes in foreign languages to Hebrew and offer dubbing when the programmes are directed at minors under the age of 7 (Rule 24 SAFraB).

344. Language requirements are closely linked to minority representation requirements (discussed *infra* in the following section). For example, CBF holders are obliged to broadcast one locally produced half-hour programme (or one hour programme if the CBF holder broadcasts four days a week) in Arabic dealing with issues that concern Arab-Israeli society (Rule 8(b) SAFraB). This programme must be produced by a team consisting in its majority of Arab-Israeli employees. This quota can be filled with re-runs up to 12%.

345. The MOC identified the need to license designated channels in Arabic and Russian.

346. A license for a designated channel in Russian was granted and a Russian language channel is broadcasted as 'Channel 9' on cable and satellite platforms. The designated Russian language channel was conceived as a substitute for international Russian language channels viewed by Russian immigrants, and was charged with programming obligations aimed at promoting the integration of Russian speaking immigrants into the Israeli 'melting pot' such as a quota for programmes on issues concerning Russian immigrants in Israel and a quota for programmes concerning the general public in Israel.[218]

347. The launching of an Arabic language channel encountered difficulties concerning the financial viability of such a channel and the financial backing of the investors in the channel. After a long process, involving three tenders, an Arabic language channel was launched in 2012 by the independent channel producer 'Hala TV' and it is carried on Channel 30 of the cable and satellite platform providers. As

217. Schejter, transfrontier, *supra* n. 192, at 354–355, noting that before the inception of DTT, the decision to stop Arabic language broadcasts in terrestrial channels was challenged in the HCJ in the case of HCJ 375/03 *Musawa centre for the Right s of Arab Citizens of Israel v. The Prime Minister* (2004) which eventually forced the government to offer several hours of Arabic broadcasts in terrestrial broadcasting although paradoxically these broadcasts were in essence propaganda broadcasts directed at the Arab enemy countries surrounding the state of Israel.

218. Schejter, transfrontier, *supra* n. 192, at 364–365, criticizing the intention of the government to promote a vision of ethnic uniformity by creating controlled ethnic media.

was the case with other designated channels, as of 2013, Hala TV is still struggling to meet its regulatory obligations.

348. In 2011, the government amended the Communications Law to include a 4.8 million NIS budget allocated to finance the production of programmes in the languages Amharic and Tigrinya spoken by the Jews who immigrated to Israel from Ethiopia (Article 6(6)2 Communications Law). The amendment stipulates that funds will be distributed to programmes in these languages provided that 75% of the personnel working on the production were either born in Ethiopia or descendants thereof and that the programmes will be aired on channels that offer at least 50% of their broadcasts and no less than 6 hours in the aforementioned languages. In 2012 the CSBC published a call for productions in the Amharic and Tigrinya following the government's decision.

349. The language of internally produced channels by CBL and SBL holders is subject to Rule 16g BCL which stipulates that the broadcasts will be in Hebrew unless they are for the purpose of teaching a foreign language; directed at Arabic speaking population or immigrant population; directed at tourists. Broadcasts in a foreign language must be appropriately translated into Hebrew or dubbed in Hebrew (Rule 16g(c) BCL).

350. A general CBL holder is also obliged to broadcast regional news in the Arabic language for the relevant Arabic speaking population (Rule 25 BCL) (*supra*, paragraph 338).

IV. Representation of Minorities on the Screen

351. With respect to representation of minorities on the screen, both public and private broadcasters are legally obliged to reflect the ethno-cultural diversity of Israeli society.[219] However, there are only few laws or regulations giving concrete meaning to this obligation in terms of actual representation of minorities on the screen, as opposed to their integration in other production activities.

352. Focusing on the representation of minorities in professional broadcast functions such as news presenters, reporters, programme hosts and participants it is evident that minorities are represented in broadcasts directed at their own minority groups but they are under-represented outside this setting. For example, the IBA broadcasts in Arabic language are often presented by Arab-Israeli IBA employees. The same is true for Arabic, Russian and Amharic language programmes or channels in the commercial television and in the designated channels on multichannel platforms. It should be noted that there is no concrete legal obligation to integrate

219. Due to the nature of the competitive tender for the CBF, bidders voluntarily committed to culturally diversify their broadcasts to reflect the 'other'. However, the SATR notes that CBF holders failed to fully comply with their own commitments in programmes and in the integration of minority groups in professional positions on the screen. See SATR Annual Report 2010, 32.

minority professional in on-screen functions in these broadcasts and the representation in these cases is often a natural outcome of individual professional suitability for the professional function.

353. On the other hand, the representation of Arabs or immigrant minorities in professional media functions on mainstream Hebrew language programmes is extremely low and by no means reflects or even comes close to reflecting their share in the general population.[220] The same is true with regards to the representation of population of Mizrachi origin Jews and of Orthodox Jews. Despite anti-discrimination and equal employment legislation, Israeli television is dominated by Ashkenazi secular Jewish men.

354. In terms of the appropriateness of the representation, content analysis of commercial media broadcasts shows that minority groups are often represented in stereotypical and offensive ways.[221] Analysis of the impact of legal obligations regarding the representation of minority groups has shown that the representation of religious Jews and of immigrants has improved; that the representation of women, Arabs and ultra-Orthodox Jews has remained unaltered; and that the representation of minority groups in the roles of reporters and hosts was unaffected.[222]

§3. Protection of Minors

355. Protection of minors is a cross-cutting issue regulated principally by the Classification, Indication and Prohibition of Harmful Broadcasts Law 2001 ('Classification Law'). The Classification Law stipulates (Article 2) that any broadcast in Israel that contains visual, verbal or audio expressions of violence, sex, or cruelty or that there is a reasonable concern that it may lead to criminal behaviour or to the usage of dangerous drugs, must carry an indication or information as prescribed by rules enacted by the Minister of Communications regarding the minimum viewing age for which the broadcast is appropriate. The law applies to promos and advertisements as well (Article 4A Classification Law).

356. According to the Classification, Indication and Prohibition of Harmful Broadcasts Regulations 2002 there are three levels of classification: up to 8 years of age, up to 14 years and up to 18. The Minister of Communications is empowered (Article 2(b) and 3 Classification Law) to set in regulations the type of the indication and the frequency with which it must appear during a broadcast. The regulations

220. According to research conducted in 2007 by 'Agenda', a non-governmental organization dedicated to promoting social issues in the media, the representation of Israeli Arabs in both print and broadcast media organizations in Israel is less than 1%. See http://agenda.org.il/researches/share-of-voice/.

221. Nechama Laor et al., *The Present and the Missing in Prime Time* (SATR 2004, 2006) (Hebrew) available at http://www.rashut2.org.il/editor/uploadfiles/final%20134.pdf.

222. Eli Avrahami & Anat First, *Can a Regulator Change Representation of Minority Groups and Fair Reflection of Cultural Diversity in National Media Programs? Lessons From Israel*, 54 J. Broadcasting & Electronic Media 136, 145 (2010).

stipulate that the indication must appear at the corner of the screen at the beginning of the broadcast for a period of 30 seconds; it must appear again after each advertisement break and every 30 minutes.

357. It is the responsibility of the broadcaster to determine the classification of the programme (Article 4 Classification Law). If a programme falls into more than one classification with different severity of restriction, then it must eventually carry an indication according to the strictest classification.

358. The different regulating authorities may use their general supervision powers to sanction a broadcaster, ex post, in case of an inappropriate classification of a harmful programme. Incompliance with the Classification Law may constitute a criminal offence punishable by a fine (Article 5). Enforcement is mostly affected through complaints submitted by viewers to the relevant regulators.[223]

359. The power to set the appropriate time for broadcasting classified programmes belongs to the regulating authorities. The SATR has included such limitations in an addendum to the broadcast franchise. The CSBC enacted specific regulations on the matter,[224] whereas the IBA has no formal regulation on the matter to date.[225]

360. The CSBC compels the multichannel platform providers to enable subscribers to block channels, thereby effecting parental control.[226] Pay-per-view Adult content channels may only broadcast between 22:00 and 06:00; require encoded access; and are initially blocked unless the subscribers contacts the multichannel service providers and requests to subscribe to the service.

§4. Human Dignity (Prohibition of Hate Speech)

361. The publication of hate speech, particularly incitement to racism, is prohibited by Article 144B of the Penal Law 1977. This prohibition is the result of the ascent of the extreme right political Kach movement in the 1980s espousing a Jewish state free from non-Jews.[227] In two seminal cases, the SC adopted and reiterated a majority opinion according to which incitement to racism falls within the ambit of

223. Report by the Knesset Research and Information Center, 19 May 2009, 12–14.
224. For example, Rule 13(a) BCL requires CBL or SBL holders to indicate content which is unsuitable for minors in such a manner that will enable parental control over the viewing of such programmes; in the event that the programmes may induce minors to imitate dangerous behaviour a visual or audio warning must be broadcasted against such imitation (Rule 13(b) BCL); a minor may not be interviewed about family matters without the consent of both parents (Rule 16(a) BCL); sponsorship announcements regarding products unsuitable for minors shall not be broadcasted before 22:00 (Rules 53i and 53j BCL).
225. Report by the Knesset Research and Information Center, 19 May 2009, 11.
226. CSBC Annual Report 2010, 30–31. In addition in 2008 the CSBC initiated a voluntary forum on ethics in children's programmes. The forum developed ethics rules for the relevant channels and continues to hold annual supervisory meetings.
227. Navot, *supra* n. 1, at 240.

the freedom of expression and therefore may only be curtailed or penalized when there exists a 'near certainty' of harm.[228]

362. One of these decisions, the *Kahane* case, concerned the decision of the IBA to cover only 'newsworthy' activities of Meir Kahane, the leader of the racist Kach movement, and ban him from live interviews and current affairs programmes. Kahane was at the time a member of the Knesset. The HCJ allowed Kahane's petition and overturned the decision of the IBA by holding that it may not categorically *a priori* refuse to broadcast the views of Kahane, abhorring as they may be. This decision may reflect the fact that the Kach movement has been allowed at the time to participate in the elections to the Knesset in spite of its racial agenda. It may also reflect the fact that the IBA was a monopoly television broadcaster at the time and thus banning Kahane would have deprived him of any exposure in broadcast media.[229] Kach was later banned from participating in the elections for the Knesset and the IBA no longer has a monopoly on news broadcasts, however, the *Kahane* decision remains the main authority not only with respect to broadcasting hate speech by the IBA but also by private broadcasters.

363. The particular legislation and rules concerning the broadcasting of hate speech and racial incitement should be interpreted restrictively in light of the *Kahane* ruling. For the commercial broadcasters, Article 46(a)(2) SATRL prohibits the broadcasting of racial incitement or any other discrimination on the basis of faith, race, gender, nationality, ethnic grouping, etc. Rule 15 SAEthic further stipulates that as long as such indications may cause harm to an individual, it is prohibited to mention an individual's origin, race, religion, ethnicity, nationality, sex or sexual preferences, social status, political views, and organizational belonging, unless they are strictly related to the content of the matter and it is not forbidden by law. At the same time, Rule 2 SAEthic obliges CBF and CRF holders to respect freedom of speech, including that of unpopular and unorthodox views and opinions.

364. A cable or satellite broadcast licensee is prohibited from broadcasting racial or nationalistic incitement (Article 6(25)(4) Communications Law).

365. Additional ethical duties applicable to commercial broadcasters reflect the recognition of other human dignity principles. Given the ongoing military confrontation between Israel and some of its neighbouring countries as well as the terror events within Israel, media is often required to report on the reactions of families and relatives to events of death and injury. Many of the ethics rules deal with the tension between the media's ambition to reflect the personal suffering of victims and their family vis-à-vis the desire to allow individuals to guard their dignity and their privacy. Relevant rules include, *inter alia*:

228. HCJ 399/85 *Kahane v. The Managing Committee of the Israeli Broadcasting Authority*, 41(3) PD 255 [1987]; Cr. A 2831/95 *Rabbi Iddo Alba v. The State of Israel*, 50(5) PD 221 [1996].

229. Navot, *supra* n. 1, at 241.

- Rule 16 SAEthic forbids broadcasting violence or extreme human suffering unless it is relevant to the topic and tolerable to the 'reasonable viewer or listener';
- Rule 17 SAEthic requires that information about victims in 'catastrophes', applicable to terror attacks as well, will rely only on reliable medical sources;
- KTV Ethics Rule 24 also stipulates that reporting on occasions such as terror attacks must respect the right to privacy of the concerned individuals.

366. Similar restrictions apply to multichannel platforms with regards to local productions. For example, Rule 6(b)(10) BCL particularly requires to avoid mentioning private matters concerning an individual which are not essential and conflict with the principles of Basic Law: Human Dignity and Freedom; Rule 6(b)(9) BCL prohibits mentioning an individual's origin, nationality, religion, race, political affiliation or sexual tendency unless it is essential for the broadcast.

367. Religious feelings are also regarded. Rule 18 SAEthic requires that franchise holders avoid recording or broadcasting private funerals without the prior consent of the relatives of the deceased person; Rule 18a SAEthic requires the franchise holders to respect the requests of individuals that appear in a programme to refrain from broadcasting the programme on Saturday (the Jewish 'Shabbat') usually due to religious observance and the franchise holders must also notify participants in a recorded programme if it is intended to be broadcasted on a Saturday.[230]

§5. Right of Reply

368. Broadcasters are subject to the general legal obligations with regards to the right to reply (*supra*, in part I, Chapter 4). In the audio-visual context it is tightly related to the fairness doctrine that has been adopted by the HCJ from the American case law and survived to date in Israel in spite of its repeal in the United States.[231] The fairness doctrine focuses on television and radio broadcasting and implies a right to reply and a broader obligation to present multiple opinions on controversial issues. The HCJ first applied the right to reply with respect to the IBA. This was an extension of the IBA's obligation under the IBA Law 1965, to ensure 'reliable information' and 'an appropriate expression of the views and opinions of the public'. The HCJ decided that a right to reply exists either before a broadcast or following it.[232]

230. In HCJ 1514/01 *Gur-Arye v. The SATR* 55(4) PD 267 [2001] the court denied the petition of a religious Jew who was recorded for a programme on a weekday to ban the broadcast of the programme on *Shabbat*, which was the only broadcast time slot available to the producer (which was the SATR itself) at the time. The court held that freedom of expression outweighs the offence to religious feelings and that it would be sufficient if the SATR would add a subtitle in the broadcast stating that it was recorded on a weekday.

231. According to the fairness doctrine, which was adopted by the American Federal Communications Commission in 1949, a broadcaster is obliged to present matters of public controversy but must also ensure that the coverage of such matters will include all sides of the controversy. See *Red Lion Broadcasting v. FCC*, 395 U.S. 367 (1969); HCJ 6218/93 *Dr. Shlomo Cohen v. The Israeli Bar Association* 49(2) PD 529 [1995].

232. HCJ 259/84 *MILAN v. The Israeli Broadcasting Authority*, 38(2) PD 673[1984]; HCJ 146/89 *Aldori v. The Israeli Broadcasting Authority*, 44(1) 798 [1990].

Following the example of the IBA, commercial radio and television broadcasts in Israel are also subject to statutory regulation which includes the right to reply, as supervised by the SATR.[233] The HCJ reiterated that the fairness doctrine and its implications are now an ingrained obligation of any broadcasting body in Israel.[234] The right to reply is also regulated by particular ethics rules for each type of broadcaster, as we elaborate henceforth.

369. Rule 2 of the IBA (Right of Reply) Rules 1997 requires the IBA to take reasonable steps in order to obtain the response of an individual that may be harmed, prima facie, by a broadcast and subsequently air the reply as the IBA deems fit unless it is inappropriate. Rule 3 thereof indicates that if the individual refused to respond or could not be obtained, the IBA is obliged to note that fact in its broadcast and if a reply is provided after the fact it should be aired as soon as possible. Rule 4 enables an injured party claiming that a response should have been sought, but was not, to submit a complaint with the Ombudsman of the IBA. The Ombudsman has the power to instruct the IBA Director to broadcast a reply if the complaint is found to be justified.

370. With regards to commercial broadcasting, Article 5(b)(6) SATRL requires the SAC to set rules guaranteeing that the broadcasters will offer the right to reply given the relevant circumstances to any person or entity that has been or may be directly offended by a broadcast. The SAC has implemented this requirement as part of the SAEthic Rules.

371. Commercial television and radio broadcasters are thus obligated to broadcast accurate and true information and therefore must check the facts with the most reliable sources (Rule 8(b) SAEthic). Chapter D SAEthic contains detailed instructions with respect to the right to reply obliging franchise holders to receive prior to a broadcast the response of an individual that may be offended by the broadcast and subsequently air the response in the same programme (Rule 10(a) SAEthic). If a response was not included in the programme, the franchise holder must air as soon as possible and in the most appropriate programme a concisely worded reply by the injured party (Rules 10(b)-(d) SAEthic). In severe cases the injured party may request and the franchise holder may consider allocating the injured party an opportunity to respond in person by allocating an appropriate broadcast time (Rules 10(e)-(f) SAEthic). Only serious considerations such as the fact that the injurious information is mostly accurate and correct may justify refusing a demand for reply (Rule 10(h)-(i) SAEthic).

372. In the multichannel television platforms, a slightly different regime applies. The relevant BCL Rules are directed at the individual demanding the reply. Rule 11(a) BCL stipulates that an individual that wishes to contradict factual information or demand the inclusion of facts that would shed a different light on a factual matter should address the broadcaster and the broadcaster is then obliged to broadcast the

233. Lehman & Limor, *supra* n. 155, at 4–5.

234. HCJ 10203/03 *Hamifkad Haleumi Ltd v. The Attorney General* (2008).

information as soon as possible in a similar programme. The broadcaster may refuse to broadcast the reply if it is an abuse of the broadcast or if there is clear basis to believe that the information included in the reply is false (Rule 11(b) BCL).

373. The KTV Ethics Rules surpass other ethics rules by requiring that KTV will not only correct but also apologize for false, inaccurate or incorrect information as soon as possible after learning about the mistake (Rule 6 KTV Ethics Rules). KTV Ethics Rule 12 requires KTV to use reasonable means to seek an *a priori* response from any person that may be injured by a broadcast and air the response in the relevant programme or as soon as possible thereafter.

Chapter 4. Political Broadcasting

§1. Rules on Political Independence of Broadcasters

374. There are legal provisions designed to guarantee the political independence of the public and the private television and radio broadcasters. These provisions fall within the category of objective impartiality regulation (discussed *supra*, in paragraph 275). In many cases however these provisions are weak or inconclusive at best.

375. The independence of the IBA is supposedly guaranteed by its status as a non-political statutory corporation. The means by which political influence is exerted on such entities are primarily the government appointment of like-minded officials to management positions. Although there are mechanisms designed to stifle such politicization of the civil service, they are not entirely effective. This is exemplified by the recent legal challenge to the appointment of the IBA Director, discussed forthwith.

376. One of the checks and balances against political appoints is the senior officials approval process, which applies to the appointment of the IBA Director. According to this process, the appointment of the IBA Director is subject to the approval of the Committee for the Approval of Senior Appointments in Government Corporations (Article 60A Government Corporations Law 1975), which is empowered by Article 16A Government Corporations Law 1975 to disqualify a candidate that is politically affiliated with the appointing government (e.g., a member of a political party represented in the government; a personal relation to a political figure; a financial relation to a political person, etc.) unless the candidate presents unique skills that justify disregarding his or her political affiliation.[235] While this procedure is useful for disqualifying candidates with overt political affiliation it may be circumvented by appointing non-political candidates who display loyalty to their political patrons.

377. In the case of the appointment of the IBA Director, the latter concern has been addressed by an instruction of the Attorney General to the Minister in charge of the IBA to ensure that the position of the IBA Director will be filled by a candidate selected by a search committee procedure applied to senior government appointments. According to the procedure (which is founded on government decisions), search committees are regularly comprised of five members, chaired by the General Director of the relevant government ministry (who is customarily an official appointed personally by the minister and thus is often himself a professional with political loyalty to the minister), the Civil Service Commissioner and three public representatives with relevant expertise elected by the minister.

235. Note that following Amendment 27 this process applies also to the appointment of the chair of the search committee for the appointment of the IBA Council and to the appointment of the IBA Council Chair.

378. In the *Ben-Menachem* case, the Journalists' Association in Tel Aviv petitioned the HCJ to nullify the appointment of the IBA Director who was recommended by a search committee chaired by the chairperson of the IBA and approved by the Committee for the Approval of Senior Appointments in Government Corporations.[236] The petitioners claimed that the Chairperson of the IBA has formerly worked as the public relations advisor to the Prime Minister, who was at the time also the minister in charge of the IBA. The petitioners also claimed that two other members of the search committee had ties to the Prime Minister thereby guaranteeing that the recommended candidate will be one favourable to the Prime Minister's views. The HCJ denied the petition due to the fact that the candidate had been duly screened and found to be without political affiliation. The HCJ did not reject the possibility that the composition of the search committee may be pre-arranged to guarantee a politically favourable recommendation. However, the HCJ found that intervening in this case would be unmerited since the search committee had concluded its work and a petition attacking its composition should have been filed at the outset of the committee's work rather than after its conclusion.

379. Since the HCJ grants the government de facto broad discretion in its appointments and intervenes only in 'extremely unreasonable'[237] appointments, it is doubtful whether the IBA could be said to be politically independent.

380. In private broadcasting, the legislative efforts seem to have been concerned with provisions guaranteeing against the involvement of partisan and political entities in the composition of franchise or license applicants at the tender stage.

381. There are legislative measures designed to guarantee that the broadcast franchise or license shall not be granted to or controlled by political parties, directly or indirectly. Article 42(a)(3) SATRL obliges the SATR commercial television franchise tender committee to disqualify any applicant that may utilize the broadcast franchise in order to promote partisan goals. This requirement is also extended to any future granting of a television broadcast license after the franchise regime will be phased out (Article 33a(b)(3) SATRL). The same applies to commercial radio franchises and licenses (Articles 72c(a), 72d(e) SATRL) and to the licensing of broadcasters on multichannel platforms (Article 6(8)3(d) Communications Law; Article 11(a)(7) SBLReg).

382. Once the franchise or license have been granted, the legislation is more concerned with the potential distorting influence of private ownership on broadcasters, and especially on news broadcasts, than the possibility of political dependence. Thus the regulatory regime governing the provision of broadcast news and preventing possible government influence on broadcasters leaves windows of opportunity for political influence and pressure.

236. HCJ 5599/11 *The Journalists' Association in Tel Aviv v. The Government of Israel* (2011).
237. *Ibid.*

383. Indeed, broadcasting news in Israel is particularly regulated and supervised with a view to insulate the news broadcasters from the possible influence of the financial interests of the owners. The SATRL goes a great length in order to ensure that the influence granted to broadcasters in general will be dispersed among a wide group of interest holders rather than concentrated in the hands of a single controller or a dominant group.[238] With regards to news broadcasting the 'Chinese walls' between the broadcasters and the owners are even stronger.

384. Legislation dispersing the private ownership and control over the commercial channels has subsequently increased the power that politicians can rein over the decisions of commercial news broadcasters. In fact, the government's supervisory powers increase at an inverse relation to the decreasing influence of the private owners. There are few barriers against the exertion of indirect political influence through the implementation of the legal obligations of the broadcasters. The problem is especially intense in the face of the financial difficulties of CRF holders in the commercial channels.

385. For example, due to its financial distress in 2012, the CRF holder of Channel 10 appealed to the Knesset for a deferral of the royalties owed to the SATR. According to some media reports, the Knesset committee for economic affairs which is dominated by the governing Likud party rejected the request and brought the CRF holder to the brink of bankruptcy as a retaliation to an investigative report broadcasted in the channel about the Prime Minister and Likud party leader Benjamin Netanyahu's alleged financial ties with wealthy American businessmen and about his travel expenses.[239]

386. The decision to shift from a franchise regime to a license regime in regulating commercial broadcasting may also reflect the intention of the government to exert political pressure on the current CBF holders. At the very least, the shift creates an opportunity to exert such pressure on CBL holders that are in financial distress. By stating that any CBL applicant that has been a CBF holder in the previous three years may be refused in the event of any significant incompliance with the CBF holder's obligations under SATRL (Article 33A(b)(1) SATRL) the SAC as a government proxy may terminate the activity of current broadcasters, especially those who fail to fully comply with the quota obligation or royalty payments due to financial distress. Since the SAC has broad discretion in the final decision, a distressed CBF holder may assume it would be wise to take this fact into account in its broadcast content.

---

238. Karniel, *supra* n. 194, at 36-37.

239. At the same time the Prime Minister was willing to waive a larger debt owed to the state by the IBA. See Jonathan Lis, *Knesset: PM May Forgive Debt of Israel's State Television Station*, Haaretz.com (11 Dec. 2011) At http://www.haaretz.com/news/national/knesset-pm-may-forgive-debt-of-israel-s-state-television-station-1.403901.

§2. FAIR REPRESENTATION IN ELECTION PERIODS

387. Elections laws in Israel call for tightening the rules during election campaign periods in order to assure fair representation. This is supposedly done by prohibiting political propaganda in the period before elections day.

388. The election process is supervised, according to the Knesset Elections Law (Consolidated Version) 1969, by a Central Elections Committee ('CEC') whose members are representatives of the political parties proportionate to the party size in the sitting Knesset.[240] The committee is chaired by an acting Supreme Court justice. The Election Law (Means of Electioneering) 1959, strictly forbids the broadcasting of 'election propaganda' during the sixty day period prior to the election, and until the ballots close.

389. The Election Law allocates radio and television airtime for the partisan propaganda in the IBA radio and television. The obligation was extended by law to the commercial channels as well. None of the broadcasters are allowed to charge fees for the propaganda broadcasts.[241]

390. The statutory propaganda broadcasts take place during a period of fourteen days prior to the elections (Articles 15(a)(1) and 15a(a) Elections Law). The chair of the CEC determines how and when the propaganda broadcasts will be integrated into the broadcasters' programming schedule.[242]

391. Each party and each list of candidates in the election is allotted 25 minutes of radio propaganda and 10 minutes of television propaganda. Incumbent parties are allotted six additional radio minutes and three additional television minutes for each serving member of the Knesset. The law thus ensures formal equality among parties yet it allocates significantly less time to new and small parties as compared to existing and large parties.[243]

392. Municipal elections are subject to a different regime. Local radio stations franchised by the SATR may broadcast paid advertisements regarding the municipal elections in the radio franchise's locality, during the thirty day period prior to the elections according to Article 16 Election Law (Means of Electioneering) 1959. The total political advertisements must not exceed 10% of the maximal allowed

---

240. For a historical survey of the development of electioneering laws in Israel see generally Schejter & Yemini, *supra* n. 196.

241. The significance attributed to the propaganda can be understood from the HCJ decision in HCJ 372/84 *Klopfer-Naveh v. The Minister of Education and Culture*, 38(3) PD 233 [1984] to enforce the airing of the propaganda broadcasts on the IBA in spite of an ongoing television 'blackout' strike by the IBA employees. The court held that the interest of a democracy in free and informed elections overrides the relevant employees' right to strike.

242. Since the launch of the commercial channels, the chairperson of the CEC has opted to air the elections broadcasts in peak viewing hours but not simultaneously in spite of expert opinions indicating that simultaneous broadcasts on all channels would yield maximal exposure. Schejter & Yemini, *supra* n. 196, at 425.

243. Schejter & Yemini, *supra* n. 196, at 423–424.

daily commercial time and 15% of the maximal hourly allowed commercial time. The broadcaster must set the advertisements' fees ten days prior to the beginning of election advertisements and may not discriminate between advertisers or offer discounts of any kind. The maximal fee for a 30 second commercial is set by law. If requests for commercial propaganda exceed the maximal time allowed for such advertisements the broadcaster must allot the maximal time to the applicants pro rata.

§3. News and Current Affairs Programmes

393. The prohibition on political propaganda in the Election Law (Means of Electioneering) 1959 applies to news and current affairs programmes, as well as any other programme. The limitations apply to the period starting sixty days prior to the elections day (Article 5(a)(1) Elections Law). Violating the law is a criminal offence sanctionable by up to six months in prison or a fine. For example, politicians may be interviewed in a television programme during the election period but they may not engage in political propaganda during such an interview. The term propaganda is not defined by law. Naturally, the enforcement of this prohibition is left to the media itself and is very difficult to achieve. Due to ongoing circumventions of the Elections Law, all the chairpersons of the CEC in recent years called to change or eliminate the prohibition on election-time political propaganda. However, several bills to that effect have failed in the Knesset.[244]

394. The Elections Law prohibits the publication of polls in the 24 hours prior to the elections day (Article 16e(h) Elections Law). The prohibition applies to all types of media. Article 16e Elections Law also requires that detailed statistical data on all elections polls published in the media will be sent to the CEC within twenty days of the publication and that a publication of a poll will include information about the person or entity that conducted the poll and the person or entity that financed the poll.

§4. Political Advertising

395. The audio-visual media in Israel are generally prohibited from broadcasting paid partisan or political advertisements. The IBA's ban on Public Service Announcements containing political or controversial content is founded on internal regulations. The Broadcasting Authority (Advertisements and Messages on the Radio) Rules 1993, prohibit in Article 7(b) the broadcasting of advertisements containing propaganda or dealing with political or ideological controversies, including encouragement to change the legislation in such matters. In the commercial channels the same ban applies through Article 81 SATRL.

244. Schejter & Yemini, *supra* n. 196, at 441.

396. The prohibition on political and partisan advertisements has been upheld by the HCJ as a barrier against the concern that public opinion will be dominated by individuals with superior financial means which will render the fairness doctrine worthless (see the discussion on the fairness doctrine *supra*, in paragraph 368).[245] However, in some views the HCJ application of the law has been erratic.[246] At times the HCJ was willing to confirm the broadcast of a commercial containing a prima facie uncontroversial message even if the message concerned a broader context that was in controversy,[247] whereas in another case, the HCJ was willing to look beyond the content of the advertisement in assessing whether it was political or partisan and examined the context of a seemingly innocent advertisement which was due to be broadcasted during an election campaign within the labour union.[248]

245. HCJ 10203/03 *Hamifkad Haleumi Ltd v. The Attorney General* (2008). The fairness doctrine implies not only that a broad range of opinions ought to be reflected in matters of political controversy but also that these opinions or beliefs ought to be given fair representation, e.g., in terms of airtime, in a manner that reflects their public pervasiveness. For example, views that reflect the opinion of the majority of the public should be accorded more airtime, whereas extreme or minority views may not be disregarded but should be given lesser exposure. Allowing paid political advertising would create the potential for an in imbalanced presentation of political opinions, thereby stifling the fairness doctrine.

246. Schejter & Yemini, *supra* n. 196, at 420.

247. HCJ 1893/92 *Reshef v. IBA*, 46(4) PD 816 [1992], approving a public service announcement for apartments in the occupied territories.

248. HCJ 7012/93 *shamai v. The SATR*, 48(3) PD 25 [1994], disqualifying a commercial supporting a strong labour union because of the approaching internal elections.

Chapter 5. Advertising Rules

§1. Different Forms of Commercial Communications

397. The main platform for commercial advertisements is supposed to be the commercial television and radio channels. However, some competition on advertising exists between the public and the private broadcasters. This competition is especially dominant in radio broadcasting but exists also in television.[249]

398. IBA radio channels are permitted to broadcast advertisements (Article 25a(a)(1) IBA Law) and therefore pose direct competition to the private commercial radio broadcasters.

399. The IBA also broadcasts sponsorships and Public Service Announcements ('PSA'). The legal source permitting sponsorships and PSAs on IBA television broadcasts was a matter of legal controversy until recently although the practice has been condoned by the HCJ.[250] In Amendment 27, Articles 25c and 25d were added to the IBA Law and they anchor the IBA's authority to broadcast PSAs and sponsorships, respectively.

400. The ETV, also a public broadcaster, is subject to the regimes governing the channels in which it broadcasts and therefore the ETV is permitted to broadcast advertisements in the franchised slots allotted to it on Channel 2 and sponsorship slides in the time slots allotted to it in the IBA channels but it is prohibited from broadcasting advertisements on its cable and satellite television channel.[251]

401. Indeed, CBL and SBL holders are prohibited from broadcasting advertisements (Article 6(24)(a) Communications Law; Rule 4 BCL).

402. As of 2006 the Minister of Communications may permit CBL and SBL holders to broadcast advertisements after consulting with the CSBC and with the approval of the government and the relevant Knesset committee (Article 6(24)(b) Communications Law). However, to date the general prohibitive policy has not changed, with the exception of designated channels that have been permitted to broadcast advertisements by the Minister of Communications according to his authority in Article 6(34)(a3) Communications Law).

403. Due to the dispersed legislation regulating audio-visual media there is particular legislation with respect to each segment of the commercial and non-commercial media applicable to the various forms of commercial content including

249. Karniel, *supra* n. 194, at 163.
250. HCJ 6032/94 *Reshet Communications and Productions Company v. The IBA*, 51(2) 790 [1997] was the fourth and last petition challenging the IBA's authority to broadcast PSA's and sponsorship announcements, all of which were rejected. See also Karniel, *supra* n. 194, at 163.
251. Karniel, *supra* n. 194, at 164.

television and radio advertisements, sponsorship slides, product placement, concealed advertisements, etc.

§2. Restrictions on Content

404. Commercial content is subject to general legal restrictions on freedom of speech which apply equally to advertisements in all broadcast media. Observers note that the case law handed down by the HCJ concerning freedom of commercial speech is inconsistent. Nevertheless, the general observation one can draw is that the strong protection of freedom of speech is guaranteed by the HCJ with regards to commercial speech but not as vehemently as it is guaranteed with regards to non-commercial speech.[252]

405. The most notable across-the-board restrictions that concern advertisements, that can be drawn from the general legislation include *inter alia*:

- Misleading advertisements are prohibited by Article 2 of the Consumer Protection Law, 1981 and constitute a criminal offence.
- Misleading advertisements are also a civil tort by the distributor of the advertisement under Article 2 of the Commercial Torts Act, 1999, if he or she knew that the advertisement included false representation.
- The advertising of prostitution is banned by Article 205c of the Penal Law, 1977.
- The Consumer Protection (Advertising and Marketing to Minors) Regulations, 1991, apply to all minor-related advertising on radio and television, requiring that such advertisements will not abuse the level of maturity, knowledge, trust and intelligence of minors in the presentation of the products or services and that the advertisers refrain from using violence, nudity, sexual insinuations, feelings of social acceptability, suggestion that the product generates qualities beyond the obtainability of a minor; advertising alcohol, smoking or gambling is also prohibited.
- The Law on Limitations on Advertising Tobacco Products for Smoking Law, 1982, prohibits television advertisements for cigarettes or smoking.

406. Article 4A Classification Law prohibits television advertisements and promos encouraging violence or the use of drugs but allows advertisements containing violence, sex, cruelty on the condition that they are not aired close to programmes

252. Most notable is the decision allowing a radio commercial with sexual insinuations in HCJ 606/93 *Kidum Yazamut U-Molut v. The Israeli Broadcasting Authority*, 48(2) PD 1 [1994]. See also Karniel, *supra* n. 194, at 305. In his detailed review of the issue of freedom of speech in commercial advertisements Karniel notes that the SC is willing to restrain the freedom of commercial speech when the public's health, safety and consumer rights are at stake but not when good taste, public feelings or style are in question. Indeed, following the *Kidum* ruling the court has persistently overturned decisions of the SATR disqualifying advertisements with sexist, demeaning and sexually offensive content by ruling that the near certainty of a severe harm test to public feelings has not been proven. See for example HCJ 5118/95 *Maio Simon Advertising v. The SATR*, 49(5) PD 751 [1998]; HCJ 226/04 *Neto v. The SATR* 51(5) PD 519 [2004].

directed at minors or on peak family viewing hours (14:30 to 21:00 on weekdays and 6:00 to 21:00 on weekends). As it might not be possible to prevent the broadcasting of such advertisements on foreign channels transmitted via cable or satellite television, Article 4a(d)(3) Classification Law empowers the relevant regulator to exempt these channels from the prohibition.

407. Additionally, the three main laws governing the broadcast media and the rules stemming from them each have particular restrictions on advertisements, some of which emulate the general legislation but not all of which are identical, thereby posing a risk of regulatory arbitrage by advertisers.

408. On the basis of its general authority to set rules for the activity of the IBA, the IBA Managing Committee has formulated the IBA (Commercial Broadcasts Notifications on the Radio) Rules 1993 ('IBA RADR'). Advertisements on IBA radio channels require the prior authorization of the IBA Director (Rule 3 IBA RADR). Advertisement are prohibited if the IBA Director maintains that they:

- Include elements contrary to state laws;
- Include partisan propaganda or a matter that is in a public political or ideological controversy;
- Pose harm to religion, nationhood, ethnic group or gender including religious feelings or the feelings of minority groups in Israel;
- Refer to names of persons or corporations with the permission of the referred person or entity;
- Include curses, abominations, verbal violence or slander;
- Include elements contrary to the Consumer Protection Law 1981 and especially misrepresentations such as exaggerating the qualities of a product, attributing qualities that cannot be proven, misleading comparisons with other products or services;
- Include statements that may cause public panic or fear or abuse superstitions;
- Promote missionary activity or sects;
- Include the opinion of a medical doctor or a nurse about the qualities of a product regardless of whether they are real or fictional figures;
- Promote a medication unless authorized by the Ministry of Health, with the exception of medication produced by a well-known producer for cold, headache, toothache or similar problems;
- Stereotype persons including sexual objectification and gender-biasing;
- Promote tobacco and smoking;
- Promote professions that are prohibited from advertising such as lawyers, medical doctors, dentists, as well as services such as fortune-tellers, astrologists, escort services, matchmakers, sexual services, but not the use of birth controls.

409. Advertisements on IBA radio broadcasts are prohibited from using texts such as 'this is an important notification' or 'we interrupt our broadcasts' or 'help' (Rule 9 IBA RADR) and are expected to comply with the customary IBA grammar and accent requirements (Rule 15(3) IBA RADR).

410. Advertisements in the commercial radio and television channels, as well as in the multichannel television, are governed by a multilayer set of statutory restrictions, rules and ethics rules (both the rules and the ethics rules have a binding force and the principle difference between them is that the ethics rules are often characterized by a high degree of detail). While they bear some similarities, they are not identical. Furthermore, in some cases specific statutes, rules and ethics rules echo other pre-existing legislation but use different language and therefore create potential interpretative collisions.

411. The general prohibitions on broadcast content included in Article 46(a) SATRL are applied to advertisements through Article 86(a) SATRL. This implies a prohibition on radio and television advertisements that include:

– A criminal offence or a civil tort according to any law.
– Incitement to racism or discrimination of any person on the basis of religion, race, nationality, gender, ethnic grouping, origin or way of life.
– Partisan propaganda except as permitted by the electioneering laws.
– Any other prohibition set by the SAC rules.

412. Article 86(b) SATRL prohibits advertisements by entities whose purposes are related to the abovementioned issues and by labour unions and labour organizations, regardless of the content of the advertisement.

413. According to Article 88 SATRL, the SAC has a broad authority to set rules regarding the content of the advertisements, prohibition of advertisements of certain products and services, restriction of advertisements directed at children and restrictions on the participation of children in advertisements.

414. The SATR may set rules requiring prior approval of advertisements including the authority to disqualify an advertisement or oblige the advertiser to omit or change the content of the advertisement (Article 89 SATRL). The SATR published the relevant rules in 1994, authorizing the SATR Director to determine a list of advertisement subjects requiring prior approval and obliging the broadcasters to submit the scripts of such advertisements to the prior approval of the SATR.

415. In its capacity as regulator of advertisements in designated channels, the CSBC has powers similar to those of the SATR to promulgate rules on the following issues (Article 6(34)1(g) Communications Law):

– Prohibited advertisements and prohibited content including broadcasts offending good taste or public feelings;
– Limitations on concealed advertisements;
– Limitations on advertisement regarding products and services and price comparisons with the objective of ensuring trustworthy information and fair competition;
– Limitations on children-oriented advertisements and on the participation of children in advertisements;
– Limitations on broadcasting non-Israeli produced advertisements;

- Limitations on the use of the human body and the preservation of human dignity in advertisements;
- Prior approval of advertisements.

416. Radio advertisements in the commercial radio stations operated by CRF holders are regulated by the SATR (Integrating Advertisements and Commercial References in Radio Broadcasts) Rules 1999 ('The SARaAD Rules') which apply to any form of commercial reference on radio broadcasts by CRF holders (Rule 2 SARaAD).

417. The SARaAD rules entrust some discretion in the hands of the CRF holders. Rule 8 SARaAD requires the CRF holder to act with care and discretion in the integration of advertisement into the broadcast schedule, including special care with respect to integrating advertisement during current affairs programmes and special attention to the listening habits of minors (Rule 8 SARaAD). The CRF holder is obliged to guarantee that the interests of advertisers will not influence the content or the scheduling of a programme (Rule 6 SARaAD) and that advertisements will be clearly separated from the rest of the broadcasts (Rule 7 SARaAD). Rule 9 SARaAD stipulates that advertisements should be avoided completely in programmes during which advertisements may hurt 'public feelings', but leaves the particular implementation of this rule to the CRF holder. Rule 5 SARaAD prohibits advertisements on memorial days.

418. The SATR (Ethics in Radio Advertisements) Rules 1999 ('The SAERAD Rules') echo some of the restrictions in the general legislation but add additional restrictions on CRF holders. The SAERAD Rules thus include obligations:

- To comply with the general law (Rule 2 SAERAD).
- To avoid advertisements with incitement to racism, violence or inappropriate behaviour (Rule 3 SAERAD).
- To avoid distasteful advertisements or such that harm public feelings or individual privacy (Rule 4 SAERAD).
- To avoid matters of public controversy (Rule 5 SAERAD).
- To avoid untrue, false or misleading advertisements (Rules 6 and 7 SAERAD).
- To avoid incidental advertisements in programmes, but mentioning brand names or commercial names is allowed when it is done within reasonable limits (Rule 8 SAERAD).
- To take into account when determining the broadcast timing the question of whether the advertisement is appropriate for minors or mentions minors or produced with the participation of minors (Rule 9 SAERAD).
- To avoid advertising beverages containing more than 1.2% alcohol to minors (Rule 10(a) SAERAD).
- To avoid encouraging behaviour that is hazardous to health and to 'especially ensure' the reliability of advertisements dealing with health or medicaments and that any possible negative effects are properly revealed (Rule 11 SAERAD).

- To avoid completely the advertising of tobacco and its products, products intended for avoiding legal examination, arms and guns, and sex services (Rule 12 SAERAD).

419. Advertising in the commercial television channels is regulated by the SATR (Integrating Advertisements in Television Broadcasts) Rules 1992 ('The SAAD Rules'). A prior screening mechanism is effected through Rule 2a of the SATR (Prior Approval of Advertisements) Rules 1994 that empowers the SATR Director to require the submission of certain types of advertisements for prior approval either through the submission of the script or the entire Advertisement.

420. The Communications (Telecommunications and Broadcasting) (Advertisements, Public Service Announcements and Sponsorship Announcements in Designated Channels) 2004 ('CommAD Rules'), promulgated by the CSBC govern all aspects of advertising in designated cable channels.

421. Cable and satellite broadcasters are generally advised to use discretion in the integration of advertisements in programmes in order to avoid harm to 'public feelings' (Rule 14 CommAD). The same is expected from CBF holders in commercial television (Rule 37 SAAD).

422. Advertisements in the commercial channels are subject to the SATR (Ethics in Television Advertisements) Rules 1994 ('the SAEthAD Rules') obliging the CBF holder to ensure the compliance of advertisements with the general law and the applicable rules (Rule 2 SAEthAD). The SAEthAD Rules stipulate *inter alia* that advertisements shall:

- Respect human dignity, good taste and public feelings (Rule 3);
- Refrain from untrue information, exaggerations or misrepresentations (Rule 4);
- Refrain from incitement to racism (Rule 5);
- Refrain from invading individual privacy (Rule 6);
- Refrain from excessive violence or appealing to feelings of fear unless there is clear public interest in doing so (Rule 7);
- Refrain from encouraging criminality or the use of drugs (Rule 7a).

423. For the multichannel television broadcasters, Chapter D CommAD Rules entitled 'Ethics in Advertising' subjects the cable and satellite broadcasters to ethics rules similar to SAEthAD including the obligations to avoid broadcasting advertisements that harm human dignity or good taste (Rule 31 CommAD); privacy (Rule 33 CommAD); false information (Rule 32 CommAD).

424. The ethical obligations included in the CommAD Rules also include prohibitions on the following in advertisements:

- Preachings of religious messages (Rule 35 CommAD).
- Advertising matters in political, social, public or economic controversy (Rule 36 CommAD).

- Including excerpts from Knesset hearings (Rule 37 CommAD).
- Showing figures in uniforms used by one the state's authorities (Rule 38 CommAD).
- Reference to a programme or relating a product or a service to a certain programme (Rule 39 CommAD).
- Tobacco and smoking, mysticism and the occult, ammunitions, arms and shooting clubs, escort services and sex services (Rule 40 CommAD).
- Sexual relations, sexual insinuations, sexual violence, all unless there exists clear public interest in presenting such content and it is done at a reasonable degree and subject to all other legal prohibitions (Rule 41 CommAD).
- Violence or content instilling fear, unless there exists clear public interest in presenting such content and it is done at a reasonable degree and subject to all other legal prohibitions (Rule 42 CommAD).
- Behaviour harmful to health, encouraging the use of drugs or dangerous driving (Rule 43 CommAD), which is amplified by a prohibition to link alcohol advertisements to driving (Rule 47 CommAD).
- Illegal lotteries (Rule 44 CommAD).

425. Consumer protection is addressed in the CommAD Rules by restricting the following:

- Promotion of purchases through the post, telephone, fax or internet unless the advertiser made a declaration to the broadcaster regarding its ability to respond to all purchase requests and provide the product or the service accordingly (Rule 45 CommAD).
- Advertising a service provided by telephone unless the advertisements contains the per-minute cost of the telephone call and if the service requires a call lasting more than 5 minutes an indication of the length of the service must also be included (Rule 46 CommAD).
- Content which may appear as a broadcast that is not an advertisement, especially including identifiable media personae (Rule 48 CommAD).
- Recommendation by persons that only appear to be qualified to recommend the product or service (Rule 49 CommAD).
- Content abusing prejudices or popular false beliefs (Rule 50 CommAD).
- Comparative content that falsely or unfairly demeans other products or entities (Rule 51 CommAD), further requirements stipulate that comparisons should be between similar and comparable products, and will refrain from claiming superiority of the one product over others using a limited basis of comparison (Rule 25 CommAD).
- Prices must be shown inclusive of VAT, sale periods must include the dates during which reduced prices apply and instalment prices must include the applicable interest rates (Rule 53 CommAD).
- The term 'new' may only be applied to products or services initially offered during the last six months and the product has been first advertised no earlier than three months ago (Rule 54 CommAD).

- Warranties or guarantees to products or services may only be advertised after the advertiser has given a written and signed confirmation that the warranty or the guarantee is provided (Rule 55 CommAD).
- Products or services given for a free trial periods may be described as 'given for free' even if the consumer must bear the cost of returning the product at the end of the trial period provided that the return procedure is described and its costs are reasonable (Rule 56 CommAD).
- Products or services given as an addition to purchasers of another product or service may not be described as 'free' (Rule 57 CommAD).

426. In comparison, chapter C of the SAEthAD Rules lists prohibitions on advertising including restrictions on the inclusion of religious messages (Rule 10); controversial messages (Rule 11); tobacco products (Rule 12(1)); products used to avoid law enforcement (Rule 12(2)); mysticism and the occult, although the SATR Director can allow advertising printed material on these topics for public interest reasons (Rule 12(3)); abusing or degrading the human body (Rule 13); sexual relations (rule 14); encouraging behaviour that is harmful to health, safety, environment or animals or the excessive use of products that cause such harm (Rule 15); devaluating other products or services (Rule 16); illegal contests or lotteries (Rule 17); an advertisement requiring payment or deposit for additional information (Rule 18); courses or studies that guarantee future employment (Rule 19); substances containing more than 2% alcohol directed at minors or suggesting that alcohol contributes to success, health, quality of life or improved mental or sexual performance (Rule 23).

427. The restrictions contained in chapter D SAEthAD Rules regarding consumer protection, misrepresentation, and marketing products via post and telephone are identical to the abovementioned CommAd Rules.

428. Specific attention is dedicated to advertisements on health, medication and lifestyle. In advertisements concerning matters of health the SATR Director may impose a stricter prior approval procedure by requiring a medical opinion from an objective medical expert or an authorized government agency (Rule 42 SAEthAD). The general prohibitions in SAEthAD are similar to the CSBC limitations, but SAEthAD Rules prohibit advertising medicaments against hair loss (Rule 43(a)(4)) but permit natural food supplements (Rule 43(c)). Insinuating that vitamins and minerals are vital for dieting is prohibited (Rule 46 SAEthAD). A CBF holder may broadcast advertisements for diets and weight loss products and treatment if the advertiser supplied a medical opinion reasonably proving that the product or the treatment is effective and harmless and the advertisement is not directed at minors (Rule 47 SAEthAD).

429. In comparison, the CommAD Rules, include:

- An obligation to receive a medical expert opinion from the advertiser on the reliability of the advertisement and the Ministry of Health's authorization for any advertised medicament (Rule 60 CommAD);

- Prohibition on advertising prescription medicaments, medicaments unauthorized by the Ministry of Health, hypnosis, psychoanalysis, psychiatric treatments, unscientifically tested treatments, an offer for medical advice or treatment given by correspondence; however the chairperson of the CSBC may approve the advertisement notwithstanding the prohibition if the advertisement has been approved by the SATR Director (Rule 61 CommAD);
- Asserting that certain foods are healthy can only be allowed if there is medical basis for the assertion (Rule 62(a)) and the same applies to vitamin and nutrition supplements (Rule 63 CommAD); claiming that certain foods have dietetic advantages is forbidden if it creates a false general impression of the product (Rule 62 CommAD);
- Advertisement of weight reducing or body altering treatments require the advertiser to supply a medical expert opinion confirming that the treatment is efficient and not hazardous (Rule 64 CommAD).

430. Some restrictions aim at preventing confusion between the programme and the advertisement. For example, Rule 35 SAAD bars broadcasting a parody-style advertisement during the programme depicted in the parody. Restrictions of this type are characteristic of advertisements during programmes directed at minors.

431. The CommAD and SAEthAD Rules do not make significant additions to the general consumer protection regulations with regards to advertisements directed at minors.

432. Most notably, Rules 16 and 17 CommAD forbid the advertising of certain products or matters during programmes aimed at children, including: fireworks, lighters, matches, medicaments, vitamin or mineral nutrition additives, condoms or other means of birth control, matters that may cause anxiety to children, sexual content or adult programmes, alcoholic substances, diets, treatments aimed at changing one's physical appearance.

433. Chapter E SAEthAD and Rules 27 and 28 SAAD contain very similar restrictions. However, Rules 29 to 33 SAAD contains an additional restriction on the promotion of merchandising products and the use of television characters in advertisements broadcasted during or in temporal proximity to their related programmes.

434. Rule 59 CommAD requires cable and satellite broadcasters to receive all legally required confirmations before allowing the broadcast of advertisements in which minors are participants.

435. Advertising containing explicit sexual or violent content may not be integrated during programmes directed at minors; between 14:00 and 21:00 on weekdays and between 06:00 and 21:00 on weekends (Rule 36 SAAD). Similar restrictions apply to multichannel television. For example, alcoholic drinks may only be advertised after 21:00 (Rule 17(c) CommAD)

436. Special restrictions apply to charity-related advertisements. Only non-profit public organizations incorporated for a public cause may advertise charity-related advertisements, but the CSBC may authorize other advertisers at the request of the broadcast licensee (Rule 66 CommAD). In order to broadcast a charity-related advertisement the licensee must demand from the advertiser information about its identity, objectives, activities, directors, and any other information guaranteeing that the advertisement is not misleading and is indeed intended for a public cause, as well as documents proving the use of the charities received (Rule 67 CommAD). Charity-related advertisements must be restrained; matter of fact; avoid extreme and unrepresentative examples; refrain from suggesting that not answering the advertisement's call for a donation will result in physical or spiritual harm (Rule 68 CommAD). Identical restrictions apply in chapter G SAEthAD.

437. Advertisements concerning financial, banking, investment or insurance matters are restricted to advertisers that are authorized or licensed by the relevant regulator (Rule 69 CommAD; Chapter H SAEthAD).

438. Additional restrictions reflect the respect for those deceased. Rule 9 SAAD and Rule 8 CommAD prohibit advertisements on memorial days. Memorials, funerals and programmes on genocide may not be interrupted by advertisements (Rule 25 SAAD; Rule 12 CommAD).

439. The CSBC can require that in designated channel licensees whose broadcasts are primarily in languages other than Hebrew (namely, the Arabic and Russian language channels) the advertisements will also be entirely in the channel's language or dubbed or subtitled accordingly (Article 6(34)1(e)(1) Communications Law).

§3. TIME AND FREQUENCY RESTRICTIONS

440. In the IBA broadcasts, advertisements must be separated from regular IBA programmes but the exact time slots are determined by internal IBA guidelines according to a general planning scheme (Rules 10 and 11 IBA RADR). The IBA Director has the authority to determine the span of time during which the advertisement will continue to be broadcasted, after consulting with the corporation providing advertisement distribution and production services to the IBA (Rule 16 IBA RADR).

441. The commercial broadcasters are permitted to include paid advertisements before and after programmes (Article 81 SATRL) or during programme breaks as long as the advertisements are clearly separated from the programmes (Article 82(b) SATRL). Integrating paid advertisements within the broadcasts of commercial broadcasters is forbidden with few exceptions (Article 83 SATRL).

442. Commercial broadcasters may sell up to 6 minutes of advertisements per hour on television and 9 minutes per hour on the radio (Article 85(a) SATRL). The SAC may permit increasing the time allotted to advertisements in certain hours of the day provided that the total time devoted to advertisements shall not exceed 10% of the broadcast time on television and 15% of the broadcast time on the radio (Article 85(b) SATRL and Rule 5b SARaAD). Rule 3 of the SATR (Allotting Advertisements in Television Broadcasts) 1992 ('SATR TV Allotment Rules') extended the maximal advertisement time per hour to 10 minutes, provided that the total 10% quota is not exceeded.

443. The SAC has the authority to set additional rules on such matters as the timing of advertisements within the programmes themselves, the length of advertisements, and the types of programmes that may or may not be interrupted for advertisements (Article 88 SATRL). Accordingly, the SATR TV Allotment Rules determine *inter alia*:

- A limit of 90 seconds per advertisement.
- Advertisements for a single product or service will not exceed 5% of the annual advertisement time, 8% of the monthly advertising time and 12% of the weekly advertising time.
- 75% of the advertisements will be produced in Israel.
- Advertisements must be separated from the programme by a 3 seconds break using a signal or a 'fade to black'.
- During the broadcasting of advertisements a signal indicating that the content is an advertisement must be shown in one of the corners of the screen.
- Advertisements are prohibited on the Holocaust Memorial Day, The Memorial Day for the IDF Soldiers and the religious fast of 'Ninth of Av' (a Jewish date marking the destruction of the Temple in Jerusalem).
- Advertisements are also prohibited in broadcasts concerning memorial events, funerals or programmes concerning genocide.

444. With regards to designated channels, the CSBC has the authority to include in the tender or license terms or in particular rules, instructions regarding the separation between advertisements and broadcasts, the slots and the manner in which advertisements may be introduced, the length of every advertisement slot, time between advertisement slots with the aim of broadcasting the advertisements in a condensed form, the types of programmes that may be interrupted for advertisements, and limitations on the sale of advertisement time to one buyer (Article 6(34)1(g) Communications Law).

445. According to Rule 10 CommAD, the maximal number of commercial breaks per hour is ten, but if the main programme during the broadcasted hour is a drama or a film then the maximal number of breaks is reduced to eight. An advertisement is limited to a maximum of 90 seconds and the same product or service may not be advertised more than four times in one hour (Rules 4 and 5 CommAD).

446. A 2008 amendment across all broadcast media regulating laws prohibits broadcasters from unilaterally increasing the volume of the broadcast during advertisements and promos above the average sound level of the rest of the broadcasts, thus banning a practice common until that time among television and radio broadcasters.

§4. SPONSORSHIP

447. The regulation of sponsorships is often similar to that of other advertisement types, but some differences tackle unique concerns.

448. Sponsorships in IBA programmes are prohibited in case of potential personal or commercial conflict of interest or if the sponsor has a political-partisan interest in the programme (Rule 8 IBA RADR), although prize shows may consult the sponsor with regards to the content of questions posed to the competitors.

449. In the commercial radio, sponsorships are governed by the SARaAD Rules, which state sponsorships may not be given to news, current affairs and consumer-related programmes although weather reports within news programmes may be sponsored (Rule 10 SARaAD). The length of the sponsorship announcement is limited to 10 seconds and may increase to a maximum of 20 seconds if there is more than one sponsor (Rule 10(d) SARaAD). The maximal number of sponsorship announcements per hour is six (Rule 10(e) SARaAD). Credit may be given in the beginning and the end of programmes to commercial entities that supported the programme or parts thereof, subject to the rules applicable to sponsorships (Rule 11 SARaAD).

450. In the commercial television, the SATR has the authority to require preliminary review of sponsorship announcements. The SATR (Sponsorships) Rules 2009 ('SASpon Rules') provide that the SATR Director may require the prior submission for approval of certain types of sponsorships (Rule 2 SASpon). The SATR Director may require any information from the franchisee with regards to the sponsorship; disqualify a sponsorship announcement or pose conditions for its broadcasting (Rules 9 and 10 SASpon). The regulation of sponsorship announcements includes time and content limitations such as:

- A single sponsorship announcement may not exceed 6 seconds, a group of announcements may not exceed 18 seconds and the maximum time for announcements per hour is 54 seconds (Rule 5 SASpon).
- The general limitations on advertisements apply to sponsorships as well, with special emphasis on the prohibition of political sponsorships (Rule 3(b) SASpon).
- News programmes may not be sponsored, with the exception of the weather forecasts (Rule 3(a) SASpon).
- Investigative programmes or programmes on finance or consumer affairs may not be sponsored by entities dealt with in the programme (Rule 3(d) SASpon).

451. Rule 23 CommAD stipulates that sponsorship slides in cable and satellite broadcasts must be accompanied by a text read by an announcer and may not exceed 10 seconds in length. Rule 23 further stipulates that the sponsorship announcements can be broadcasted before and after the programme or at the beginning and at the end of commercial breaks. The rule instructs that sponsorship announcements may include the sponsor's name, the sponsor's products, a short phrase or slogan, a trademark or a logo, and the sponsor's telephone number or website. During live broadcasts or sports broadcast the sponsor's name may be shown on the lower third of the screen no more than four times per hour (Rule 24 CommAD). Sport and local music events may also include the sponsor's name in the programme's name (Rule 26 CommAD).

452. The rules applicable to the integration of advertisements in programmes broadcasted by cable and satellite television apply to sponsorships as well (Rule 27 CommAD). In addition, Rule 20 CommAD prohibits sponsorships when:

– The sponsor has a personal, commercial, political or partisan interest in the broadcast.
– The sponsor is a political or partisan entity.
– The sponsorship exceeds 40% of the sponsored broadcasts during a given week unless the CSBC confirmed that other sponsors are not deprived of sponsorship opportunities.
– The sponsorship is conditional upon intervention in or influence on the programme's content, but the sponsor may condition the contribution on the programme not being filmed or broadcasted during days of rest as defined by law (namely, the Jewish observed Saturday).
– According to CommAD Rules, advertising the sponsored product is prohibited if the sponsor is the producer of a product which may not be advertised.
– In addition, sponsorship may not be given to news, current affairs or consumer affairs programmes (Rule 21 CommAD).

§5. Product Placement

453. One of the most challenging issues for commercial regulation is advertising efforts through product placement.

454. One technique of product placement in radio stations is combining the product's name in the name of the radio station. The name of a radio station may include the commercial name of a product, service or brand (the 'name-entity') subject to the approval of the SAC after the commercial entity declared that it has no means of control in any other CRF holder; it will report the contribution made in return for the inclusion of its name; it is committed to a contract of no less than six months (Rule 12a and 12b SARaAD). Rule 12c SARaAD limits the scope of advertisements by the name-entity to no more than 10% of the total advertisement time. The references to the name-entity during the programmes may not exceed fifteen references per hour.

455. For the commercial television channels, product placement is governed by a general prohibition on broadcasters to include advertising in their programmes

(Article 83 SATRL), except where it is allowed by the SAEthAD Rules. The prohibition applies to commercial content and 'inadvertent advertisements' (defined as advertisements that seem to be incidental).

456. Rule 9 SAEthAD reiterates the prohibition against the inclusion of commercial content in programmes but specifies exceptions in case of:

- Inadvertent inclusion of products or advertisements during programmes.
- Broadcasting an event produced by a producer that is not the broadcaster, as long as no more than ten commercial sponsors or their products are mentioned (each not more than three times) and at least five of which are related to the content of the programme.
- During fund-raising programmes for public causes commercial contributors may be mentioned, with certain limitations, and with the prior approval of the SATR Director and the chairperson of the SAC.
- In programmes in which prizes, monetary or other, are being distributed the names of commercial contributors or products may be mentioned but the contributing entity may not be mentioned more than three times and shall not sponsor more than three prizes (Rule 9a SAEthAD); the participants in the programme are prohibited from praising the nature or quality of the products.

457. A CBL or SBL may mention commercial entities who contributed prizes in prize-awarding programmes but restrictions apply, e.g., mentioning the entity may not exceed 6 seconds and it must not be mentioned in the programme's promo (Rule 4a BCL). It is permissible to thank commercial entities that supported a programme within the slides at the end of the broadcast (Rule 4b BCL).

458. The CSBC introduced a highly developed regime concerning the integration of commercial content in programmes in 2006. However, doubts were raised as to whether the CSBC has the authority to regulate the issue and consequently the rules were defunct after six months. It is worthwhile to survey the rules for comparative purposes:

(a) 'Commercial content' was defined as content relating to a product or promoting it in any way as well as the integration in the programme of a participant, a consultant, a competitor in an entertainment programme; all in exchange for consideration by the financer of the programme (Rule 27a CommAD).
(b) Integrating commercial content in programmes was allowed provided that the integration had reasonable editorial justification (Rule 27g CommAD) and that the broadcaster informed the viewers about the involvement of an external financer in the programme in a written announcement shown before the programme (Rule 27i CommAD). If the programme was longer than 30 minutes, the written announcement about the existence of commercial content was due to appear every 30 minutes.
(c) The general prohibitions that applied to advertisements were also applicable to commercial content (Rules 27e and 27f CommAD) including the prohibitions on products and services that may not be advertised.

(d) Commercial content was prohibited in certain types of programmes, such as (Rule 27c CommAD): news, current affairs, drama unless it is broadcasted daily or includes more than 60 episodes, documentary, social or political satire, programmes for minors under 14 years of age unless approved by the CSBC, programmes shorter than 5 minutes and programmes in which sponsorships are prohibited according to Rule 12 CommAD.
(e) Additional restrictions on commercial content include (Rule 27 CommAD): The product could not be shown for an unreasonable time or frequency or in a manner that is unjustified compared to other items in the programme; the visual design of the programme ('Look & Feel') could not be similar to the product unless the similarity is inadvertent and random; the programme could not recommend the product; product placement in programmes for children under 14 years of age required the prior authorization of the CSBC.
(f) Rule 27 CommAD stated that the CSBC could waive some or all of the restrictions, by way of prior authorization, with regards to reality, entertainment and musical programmes.

Chapter 6. Right to Information

§1. Access to Major Events

459. The right of broadcasters to access major events received scant attention in Israeli law.

460. In the *Tele Event* case, the SC held that public events in and of themselves cannot be the subject of intellectual property rights such as copyright, however the edited live or recorded broadcast of such events is protected by copyright.[253]

461. The CSBC recognizes the importance of enabling public access to certain sport events and obligates the licensees to offer them free of charge. This is done either through CSBC policy decisions,[254] or by conditioning the approval of subscription-based sports channels upon the broadcasting of certain attractive sports events in the sports channel which is included in the basic channels bundle.

462. Article 14 of the Copyright Law 2007 forbids the transmission to the public of a broadcast without the permission of the owner of the broadcast's copyright. This relatively recent statutory formulation incorporates some of the preceding case law on the matter.

463. The issue of rebroadcasting major events was raised when foreign sports channels that were rebroadcasted in Israel by cable and satellite television providers included sports events to which other broadcasters purchased exclusive national broadcasting rights. Article 6(25)(5) Communications Law prohibits CBL and SBL holders from broadcasting any broadcast that constitutes an infringement of copyright. The SC addressed the issue (prior to the enactment of the current copyright law) with respect to 'secondary broadcasts'. The term 'secondary broadcast' referred to a broadcast by a foreign channel received by an Israeli CBL or SBL holder and subsequently rebroadcasted by the latter in Israel. The SC held that secondary broadcasts infringe the copyright of the holder of an exclusive broadcast permission.[255]

464. The issue has been revisited by the courts with respect to secondary broadcasts of sports events by internet websites, after the enactment of the new copyright law. In 2008, an Israeli district court reached the apparently mistaken conclusion

253. CA 2173/94 *Tele Event v. Arutzey Zahav*, 55(5) PD 529, 540 [2011]. The SC held that multichannel television providers that transmit foreign satellite channels may not broadcast sports events (in this case it was the Wimbeldon tennis tournament) which they are not authorized to broadcast by the owner of the broadcasting right in Israel. As a result general CBLs and SBLs are obliged to stop the transmission of foreign channels during the broadcasting of events over which they do not have broadcasting rights. The court grounded its protection of the rights of the producer of the event on the doctrine of unjust enrichment.

254. For example, the CSBC resolved that international games of Israeli football teams shall be broadcasted in subscription free sports channels. CSBC Annual Report 2010, 32

255. CSBC Annual Report 2010, 32.

that the recently enacted copyright law provided no protection against the live secondary 'streaming' of television broadcasts of football games (by capturing the television broadcast and then rebroadcasting it online) by an Israeli website that was unauthorized to do so by the claimant, the Premier League Football Association in the United Kingdom.[256] The decision received public attention but was reversed by the SC in 2012.[257] The SC declared that the unauthorized secondary streaming of sports events is not protected by the 'fair use' exception in the copyright law because it severely damages the business interests of the original broadcaster and the social interest in promoting sports events. Note that football matches are not copyrighted in and of themselves but the video broadcast of a match is protected under copyright law. The SC added that the fact that the state obliges CBL and SBL holders to provide certain sports broadcasts free of charge to the subscribers does not derogate from the broadcasters' intellectual property rights in the broadcasts vis-à-vis unauthorized broadcasters. Nevertheless, the claimant in the latter case did not prevail. This was due to the fact that the website's operator was anonymous. To date, Israeli procedural law precludes filing a lawsuit against an unknown defendant. It is also currently impossible to compel the host of the website to supply identifying information about the anonymous operator. Consequently, it is impossible to recover compensation from an infringing website when the operator thereof successfully cloaks his or her identity.

§2. Short News Reporting

465. Broadcasting short reports that include audio-visual content from major events is not regulated in Israel. It seems that broadcasting material from major events, even in short excerpts, would constitute an infringement of the broadcasting right. Hence, unjust enrichment. In practice, there are bilateral agreements between broadcasters in Israel for the exchange and broadcast of short footage from major sports events.[258]

466. Factual reporting about major events on radio or on television without screening audio-visual content does not constitute an infringement of the broadcaster's rights and therefore is allowed.[259]

256. CA 011646/08 (Dist. Ct. Tel Aviv) *Football Association Premier League Ltd. v. Netvision* 013 Barack Ltd. (2008).
257. CA 9183/09 *Football Association Premier League Limited v. Anonymous* (2012).
258. These agreements normally require the receiving broadcaster to note the owner of the broadcasting right during the broadcast of the footage.
259. Civ. Case (Dist, Ct. Tel Aviv) 1101/01 *Radio Lelo Hafsaka v. The IBA* (2002). In this case the IBA radio stations were prohibited from broadcasting live coverage of the national football after the exclusive license to broadcast the games was tendered by the national league to a regional radio station. The court held that the license does not prevent factual reporting about the games.

Chapter 7. Access to Networks and Platforms

§1. Introduction

467. Must carry obligations, per se, can be found only in the Communications Law and they are primarily designed to guarantee two principles. The first principle is that subscription fee based multichannel television platforms will provide a bundle of public and commercial channels without charging their subscribers additional fees on top of the basic subscription fee. The second principle is that independent channel producer licensed by the relevant regulator will be able to apply to the Minister of Communications to force a multichannel television provider to carry the channel in the event that the platform owner and the channel producer could not reach an agreement with regards to the carriage terms.

§2. Must-Carry Rules

468. Due to the fact that only two television channels were broadcasted terrestrially (Channel 1 by the IBA and until recently Channel 2), a digital terrestrial transmission service was established by the SATR in order to supply public channels to viewers who do not wish to subscribe to multichannel television services. The DTT service can be received by purchasing a receiver which is sold for a modest price or by television sets with integrated receivers.

469. The DTT service entitled 'Idan Plus' currently carries six television channels: two IBA channels, the two commercial channels, ETV and KTV.

470. On 15 July 2010 the government instructed a joint team of the MOC, the treasury, the SATR and the CSBC to recommend ways to broaden DTT services. The team proposed to expand the range of channels included in the free DTT service to include all designated channels (all of which are currently available only on the cable and satellite platforms), the ETV (which was not initially included in the bundle but was added in 2012), IBA HD channels, national and regional radio stations and additional channels as determined by the Minister of Communications. Channels carried by the DTT system are obliged to pay a transmission fee to the SATR. Transmission fees vary according to whether the carried channel is a radio channel or television channel.

471. The Transmission of Broadcasts via DTT Law 2012 ('DTT Law'), which implements the government's team's recommendations also proposes that broadcasters will be able to receive a license to broadcast a topical channel through the DTT services provided that the channels will focus on topics listed in a list of topics published by the Minister of Communications. Topical channels will have to devote 75% of the broadcast time to the approved topic and 90% of the broadcasts in peek viewing hours (defined as 19:00 to 23:00) and licenses for topical channels will not be granted to broadcasters whose broadcasts are currently transmitted by the DTT services.

472. In view of the small number of competitors in the multichannel platform market in Israel, the MOC has been considering the possibility of privatizing the DTT system so that it would act as a third competitor in this arena (in addition to HOT and YES). However, to date, there is no formal government proposal on the matter.

§3. Obligations for Conditional Access Providers

473. Cable and satellite multichannel television in Israel are both services provided via encrypted broadcasts and received by purchasing a receiver and paying subscription fees. The subscription fee covers a basic bundle of channels which includes channels that the service provider is obliged to carry by law, designated channels and additional channels as stipulated by the CSBC or the Minister of Communications, depending on the applicable regulatory regime. While the regimes governing must carry obligations of the cable television provider and of the satellite television provider have similar goals, they are not identical. One reason for the discrepancies is that the CBL holder is a monopoly whereas the regulator envisaged, at least theoretically, the possibility of more than one SBL holder.[260]

474. Hence, a CBL holder must carry in full, real time, and without cutting or editing all television and radio channels that are broadcasted in Israel according to any law and is exempt from paying any royalties to the channel broadcasters as a result of this obligation (Article 6(21)(a) and (b) Communications Law; Rules 40-41 BCL). These channels are part of the basic bundle of channels provided to subscribers.

475. The CSBC may set rules with regards to must-carry obligations for non-Israeli channels as well (Article 6(21)(c) Communications Law). Rules 45-48 BCL stipulate that a non-compulsory channel will be carried only after the approval of the CSBC. The CSBC has the authority intervene in the allocation of channel numbers (Article 6(21)(1)(b) Communications Law).

476. A CBL holder must also carry any independent channel that was granted a special license by the CSBC (Article 6(34)(a) Communications Law) however the CBL holder is not obliged to include these channels in the basic bundle. These channels may be sold separately to subscribers. The CBL holder may charge independent channel producers (except designated channels) a transmission fee. This fee should be agreed upon between the independent channel producer and the CBL holder but if a mutual agreement is not reached then the Minister of Communications will set within one year a fee that will reflect a 'reasonable profit' (Article

260. Article 6(46)(b) Communications Law states that an SBL holder shall not be granted an exclusive right to provide satellite broadcasts unless the SBL was granted by tender and the Minister of Communications decided to grant such exclusivity, which shall be then granted for a period that will not exceed five years.

6(34)(b) Communications Law). The ETV channel must be carried by a CBL holder free of charge (Article 6(34)(c) Communications Law).

477. The CBL holder may – but it is not obliged to – carry an independent Israeli news channel provided that the channel has been licensed by the CSBC (Article 6(20)2 Communications Law). The same applies to SBL holders (Article 6(51)1(b) Communications Law).

478. For SBL holders, the must carry obligations are effected through the license terms. The Minister of Communications is authorized to include in the license terms must carry obligations regarding national television and radio channels (Article 6(49)(4) Communications Law). In addition, the Minister of Communications may include in the license terms obligations to carry independent channels, designated channels the ETV channel (Articles 6(49)(5) and 6(49)1 Communications Law). The SBL holder is not required to pay royalties to channels that must be carried (Article 6(49)(1)(a) Communications Law).

479. The SBL holder may carry national broadcasters that were not required by the Minister of Communications and regional radio broadcasters, in which case the SBL holder may charge transmission fees (except designated channels) (Article 6(54) Communications Law). Nevertheless, if an SBL holder cannot reach an agreement with an independent channel producer then the Minister of Communications after consulting with the CSBC and weighing the interests of the public, the SBL holder, the source and designation of the channel and the local productions offered by the channel, may oblige the SBL holder to carry the channel. The Minister of Communications may in such case determine the terms under which the channel will be provided (Article 6(55)(a) Communications Law).

§4. Other Access Obligations for Network Operators

480. In light of the view that commercial channels use public resources and provide a public service the regulator found the need to ensure that some of the broadcasts provided by the commercial broadcasters will contain news and educational content. This is done by quasi-must carry obligations (de facto these are 'must broadcast' obligations) enforcing the commercial broadcasters to provide news, educational programmes and television productions produced by the regulatory authority, the SATR. There is no equivalent measure with respect to multichannel platforms.

481. Commercial channels are thus obliged to transmit their respective news corporation's broadcasts as prescribed by the SAC (Rule 4 SAFraB). The rule is also warranted due to the quasi- 'Chinese walls' between the ownership and control of the commercial channel and the channel's news corporation. As it might be in the interest of the commercial channel owners to downplay the prominence of the news corporation, the SAC obliges the channels to broadcast the news corporation's broadcasts and regulates the timing of the broadcasts, their length and the restrictions on the ability of the CBF holder to intervene in the broadcasts.

482. The SAC prescribes the terms by which a time slot is allocated to the broadcasts of the ETV in the commercial channels until 2015 (Rule 5 SAFraB).

483. Additionally, CBF holders must broadcast programmes produced by the SATR itself, of which at least 26 hours a year must be aired between 17:00 and 24:00 (Rule 6(e) SAFraB).

Chapter 8. Standards and Interoperability

484. There are very few instructions concerning standards and interoperability in primary or secondary legislation. These issues are either regulated in tender or license terms or left completely unattended. For example, Article 6(49)(2) Communications Law authorizes the Minister of Communications to include standards regarding broadcast and end-user-reception equipment in the license terms of SBL holders. For CBL holders such terms may be included in the license by the CSBC through its broad authority to set license terms.

485. In October 2010, with the phasing out of terrestrial broadcasting and the initiation of DTT, the SATR published an online manual detailing the minimal standards required from set-top boxes, digital receivers and integrated digital television in order to receive the free DTT channels. According to the manual a digital receiver must support DVB-T standard with MPEG-4 compression and SDTV resolution. The SATR recommended compliance with standards that were expected to be operational, e.g., compliance with HDTV resolution. Nevertheless it remains up to the consumers to ensure the compliance of the reception equipment with the broadcast standards.

Chapter 9. National Emergency

486. Given the importance of controlling mass media platforms during times of emergency and threats to national security, the laws governing broadcasting all contain provisions that enable the relevant authorities to take over the broadcast for security reasons, e.g., in the event of a military attack on civilian population. For example, Article 6(22) Communications Law requires multichannel broadcasters in such circumstances to transmit any announcement by the government, the police, the army or the Civilian Defence Command.[261] The HCJ held that this power must be construed narrowly and that it does not justify interrupting all of the channels provided by a general CBL or an SBL holder simultaneously even for the purpose of instructing civil population during a rocket attack launched at cities in Israel.[262]

487. Commercial television and radio broadcasters must keep a stock of programmes to be used in the event of unexpected intervention in the broadcasts which includes malfunctions or programme disqualification but also applies to an unexpected shift to 'memorial day programming', which occurs following major terror events (Rule 6 SARaF; Rule 6 SARaL). Identical stipulations can be found with regards to all private and public broadcasters.

261. Similar stipulations can be found in Art. 46 IBA law; Art. 50 SATRL and Art. 6(57) Communications Law (for the SBL holder).
262. HCJ 2753/03 *Kirsh v. The Chief of Staff*, 57(6) PD 359 [2003].

Part IV. Cross-Ownership Regulation

§1. Introduction

488. The need for cross media ownership regulation is a constantly debated issue in the Israeli public arena, even after such regulation has been introduced. On one hand, the Israeli media market is relatively small and due to its limited economies of scale (e.g., the difficulty is selling Hebrew language productions outside Israel) cross media ownership restrictions may weaken the financial independence of media organizations. On the other hand, the limited number of Hebrew sources of information requires that a minimal level of plurality would be guaranteed through some dispersion of the media ownership.

489. The requirements of financial stability and cross media ownership restrictions create a barrier which is insurmountable for most corporations in the Israeli market, allowing only a small group of competitors to belong to the broadcasters club. Some critics maintain that the Israeli regulator has not yet internalized the fact that the internet offers the possibility to broadcast to mass audiences at a low cost.[263]

490. It is worthwhile to note that the Israeli Competition Authority does play a significant role in addressing some of the fundamental concerns that underlie the discussion about cross and monomedia ownership. The Restrictive Business Practices Law 1988 is the main law dealing with general competition law issues in Israel and it focuses on mergers, monopolies and restrictive business behaviour in the markets. However, issues such as pluralism in media venues are neglected in the law and therefore must be addressed through media-specific regulation outside the context of competition law issues. The latter issue was raised by a the Committee for Increasing Competitiveness in Israel in 2011. The committee discussed the concentration of ownership in the financial and real businesses in the private sector and the unusually large pyramidal conglomerates. As this was not in the direct subject matter of the committee, it made a relatively peripheral comment suggesting the need to evaluate the impact of media ownership by major conglomerates.

263. Karniel, *supra* n. 194, at 103.

§2. MONOMEDIA OWNERSHIP RESTRICTIONS

491. The SATRL intended to ensure that the influence granted to the CBF holders will be dispersed among a wide group of stakeholders rather than concentrated in the hands of a single controller or a dominant group.[264]

492. The distribution of commercial broadcast franchises was based on competitive tenders. According to the SATR (Procedures for Granting a Television CBF) Rules 1992 ('The SAPFra Rules'), the SAC was empowered as a tender committee to choose up to three CBF holders in Channel 2 and up to two CBF holders in Channel 10 (Rules 14(e) and 14(e1) SAPFra). Every CBF holder in the commercial channels must be comprised of several partners (three in Channel 10 compared to four in Channel 2).

493. In practice the idea was only partially successful. The SATRL initially dispersed the control of the first commercial channel, Channel 2, by distributing the channel between three franchisees (*Reshet*, *Keshet* and *Telad*). In addition, the franchise was initially limited in time and could be prolonged only once. The SATRL was later amended to distribute Channel 2 between two rather than three franchisees (only *Reshet* and *Keshet* remained). The second commercial channel, Channel 10, was dispersed between two franchisees from its inception but not too long after its launch the two merged into a single franchisee, 'Israel 10', that took control of the channel.

494. The monomedia radio ownership restrictions in the regional commercial radio are primarily concerned with the monopolization of local radio stations by dominant owners in the same geographical broadcast region. Article 72A SATRL therefore stipulate that the SATR shall not grant a regional radio broadcast franchise to an existing franchisee in the same region or to any related entity in the same region or to a corporation that already holds 20% of the existing franchises or to a franchisee or corporation that controls 24% or more of a franchisee in the cities Jerusalem, Tel Aviv or Haifa (but the Minister of Communications is authorized to approve exceptions).

495. In the digital radio license regime the license requirements preclude *inter alia* applicants that are already holders of a broadcast license or franchise (Article 41(c) SATRL).

496. The SATRL monomedia and crossmedia ownership restrictions are intertwined in Article 41(b2). With regards to monomedia Article 41(b2) SATRL prohibits granting a broadcast license or allowing participation in a tender for a broadcast franchise in the following cases:

(a) the applicant is the holder of another broadcast franchise or any of its shares are held by another broadcast franchise holder;

264. Karniel, *supra* n. 194, at 36–37.

(b) the applicant holds any share of the means of control in another broadcast franchise holder;
(c) in the event that there is a single license or franchise holder in the channel: the holder of at least 15% of the means of control in the applicant holds at least 15% of the means of control in another single broadcast franchise holder; two holders of the means of control in the franchise or license holder will not hold together more than 24% of the means of control or its control;
(d) in the event that there are two franchise holders in the channel: the holder of at least 24% of the means of control or the control in the applicant holds at least 15% of the means of control or the control in another broadcast franchise holder; two holders of the means of control in the franchise or license holder will not hold together more than 30% of the means of control or its control.

497. The principle objective of the introduction of Channel 10 was to increase the competition in the market for advertising in television broadcasts.[265] Monomedia ownership limitations in Channel 10 are somewhat harsher than in Channel 2. An amendment from 2000 to the SATRL concerning monomedia ownership limitations in the third commercial channel, Channel 10 (Article 41(b1) SATRL), applied stricter limitations than those applicable to Channel 2 and guaranteed that none of the existing participants in the broadcast market may be able to partake in the broadcast franchise.

498. In the multichannel broadcast platforms, the Communications Law (Article 6(8)4) prohibits granting a CBL to applicants in the following events:

- If the applicant already holds a television license according to the SATRL, a general CBL, a VOD broadcast license or an SBL (all referred to together as 'another license holder').
- If the applicant is a corporation that holds the means of control in another license holder or is controlled by another license holder.
- If the applicant is a corporation in which a holder of more than 5% of the means of control also holds more than 5% of the means of control in another general cable or VOD license holder or if the holder of more than 24% of the means of control in the applicant also holds more than 24% of any means of control in an SBL holder, unless the Minister of Communications determined with the consent of the CSBC that granting the license advances the competition and diversity in broadcasting.

499. Monomedia ownership restrictions on the independent cable news producer require that any person or corporation controlling one of the following shall not have a controlling stake or more than 5% of the means of control in the applicant (Article 6(20)2(c)(5) Communications Law):

- A general cable broadcast licensee including its controlling stakeholder or the holder of more than 5% of the means of control;

265. Karniel, *supra* n. 194, at 81–82.

- A general satellite broadcast licensee including its controlling stakeholder or the holder of more than 5% of the means of control;
- A broadcaster licensed by the SATR including its controlling stakeholder or the holder of more than 5% of the means of control; although a corporation of which an interest holder is also an interest holder in a broadcaster licensed by the SATR may hold up to 24% of the applicant as long as this holding as well as the corporation's holding in other broadcast licensees does not constitute control over these entities;
- A legally authorized entity broadcasting news on radio or television but the CSBC may approve such a news broadcaster that is not one of the two news broadcasters with the highest ratings and as long as it does not control the applicant.

500. With regards to SBL holders, the Minister of Communications retains the authority to set mono- and crossmedia ownership restrictions in rules or in the terms of the tender. This authority has been implemented in Article 11 of the Telecommunications (Procedures and Terms for the Granting of a Satellite Broadcasting License) Regulations 1998, which stipulates that an SBL application will be denied in the following cases:

- the applicant is a CBL holder, a subsidiary or owner thereof or affiliated with a CBL holder; the applicant is a CBF holder; the applicant is an officer in any of the aforementioned entities or a corporation controlled by such a person or a corporation in which such a person serves as an officer or has any right whatsoever;
- the applicant is a corporation in which a channel producer holds at least 75% of any means of control;
- the holder of 25% or more of any of the means of control in the applicant is held by an entity which holds a CBF, or is the parent of an entity which holds a CBF or is an entity controlled by a CBF holder; in addition, the SBL shall be denied when the applicant is an entity in which a total of 45% or more of the means of control are held by entities which are held by a CBF holder or controlled by a CBF holder;
- an excess of 50% of any means of control in the applicant is held by an entity affiliated with a CBF holder or by a group of entities affiliated with a CBF holder.

§3. Crossmedia Ownership Restrictions

I. Commercial Television

501. At the outset of commercial television broadcasting in Israel, the focus of concern with regards to ownership was the possibility of commercial audio-visual media being taken over by the dominant participants in the print media market, which was financially robust at the time and sought to fortify its dominance in anticipation of the crossmedia competition over advertisers. In contrast, cross media ownership regulation envisaged a dispersion of ownership as means of preventing the concentration of media venues in the hands of a small and powerful group of media tycoons.

502. The SATR Law cross media ownership restrictions prohibit granting a broadcast license or allowing participation in a tender for a broadcast franchise in the following cases (Article 41(b2) SATRL):

(a) the applicant is a corporation which is a newspaper or a person controlling any of the means of control in a newspaper;
(b) if there is only one licensee or franchisee, a newspaper or a person that holds any of the means of control in a newspaper or controls a newspaper holds at least 8% of the means of control in the applicant;
(c) if there are two or more franchisees in the channel, a newspaper or a person that holds any of the means of control in a newspaper or controls a newspaper holds at least 16% of the means of control in the applicant;
(d) the applicant is a corporation in which a newspaper or the holder of 5% or more of the means of control in a newspaper holds any of the means of control;
(e) the applicant is a corporation in which two or more of the holders of the means of control above the rates specified in subsections (b) and (c) are newspapers or hold together 10% of any kind of the means of control in a newspaper;
(f) if there is only one licensee or franchisee, and the applicant is a corporation in which two or more of the holders are limited by monomedia restrictions and by the restrictions in subsections (b) and (c) herein and they hold 24% or more of the means of control in the applicant or the control in the applicant; or if there are two or more franchisees, and the applicant is a corporation in which two or more of the holders are limited as described above by monomedia restrictions and by the restrictions in subsections (b) and (c) herein and they hold 30% or more of the means of control in the applicant or the control in the applicant.

503. Karniel notes that the cross-ownership limitations with respect to Channel 2 (24%) were only slightly below the threshold for monomedia ownership (30%) determined in the SATRL and were insufficient to prevent major actors in the newspaper market and the cable corporations from obtaining stakes in the channel's franchisees. Consequently, Channel 2 franchisees played a minor role in legal proceedings that were initiated against the cable television franchisees move to collaborate in the acquisition of foreign programmes which eventually led to their merger into a single cable television company.[266]

504. In commercial radio broadcasting, cross media ownership restrictions similarly aim mainly at restricting the dominance of the print media. Therefore a license or franchise will not be granted if the applicant is *inter alia* (Article 41(c) SATRL):

– A newspaper or at least 24% of any of the means of control in the applicant are held directly or indirectly by a person or a corporation that holds or controls a newspaper unless the tender is for a license or franchise in an area in which there already exists one radio franchise and the applicant is not related to that franchise

266. Karniel, *supra* n. 194, at 145–146.

or unless the applicant is not a daily newspaper or is a newspaper in a language other than the language of the radio broadcasts.

- The applicant is any other entity which disseminates broadcasts to the public or the applicant is 'Bezeq', the former state telecommunications corporation or a subsidiary thereof.

II. Cable and Satellite Television

505. In the multichannel television platforms too, the cross media ownership limitations were drafted to reflect the concern that corporations dominating the print media will dominate cable television broadcasting, thereby strengthening their market dominance and decreasing competition and content diversity. The current cross media ownership limitations on cable and satellite licensees are the result of the 2001 reform of the Communications Law (also known as 'Amendment 25'). Amendment 25 increased cross media ownership restrictions by stipulating that a CBL will not be granted to any holder of a television, cable or satellite broadcast license or a newspaper (Article 6(8)4 Communications Law). But The new regime included an eight year grace period for existing cable franchisees and the possibility of prolonging the grace period dependent on the market share of cable television broadcasts at the end of the grace period (Article 6(12)8 Communications Law).[267] The exemption enabled the owners of the two main newspapers in Israel at the time, Yediot Ahronot and Maariv, along with the financial newspaper Globes, to retain stakes in the cable corporations for a long period of time.[268]

506. In more detail, the Communications Law (Article 6(8)4) prohibits granting a CBL to applicants in the following events:

- If the applicant is a newspaper.
- If the applicant is a corporation controlled by a newspaper, or that a newspaper holds more than 24% of any means of control in it; or if the holder of more than 24% of any means of control in the applicant corporation also holds more than 24% of any means of control or otherwise controls a newspaper.
- In the event that two persons or more hold a combined stake of more than 24% in any means of control in a newspaper, they shall not have control of the applicant corporation nor shall they be allowed to hold more than 24% of any means of control in the applicant, combined.
- In the event that two persons or more hold a combined stake of more than 24% in any means of control in different newspapers, they shall not have control of the applicant corporation nor shall they be allowed to hold, combined, more than a third of any means of control in the applicant; however if one of the persons holds more than 24% of the means of control in a newspaper then the 24% limit on the means of control in the applicant will apply.

267. Karniel, *supra* n. 194, at 105.
268. Karniel, *supra* n. 194, at 108–109. Yediot Ahronot later sold its share.

507. The cable news channel producer is subject to more stringent mono- and crossmedia ownership restrictions which incorporate the restrictions included in the SATRL (Article 41(a)(2) to (4) SATRL) as well as additional limitations which exclude ownership by major existing broadcasters and by the two major national newspapers.

508. In particular, crossmedia ownership restrictions on the independent cable news producer require that any person or corporation controlling a national newspaper or the corporation publishing a national newspaper or their controlling shareholder or any of their interest holder shall not have a controlling stake or more than 5% of the means of control in the applicant (Article 6(20)2(c)(5) Communications Law), but the CSBC may approve a newspaper that is not one of the two most widespread national daily newspapers and as long as it does not control the applicant.;

509. There are no particular cross media restrictions on the ownership of special or designated channel licenses, but the CSBC can include such restrictions in rules or within the tender terms (Article 6(34)1(b) Communications Law). The CSBC has included only mild restrictions in such tenders.

510. With regards to SBL holders, Article 11 of the Telecommunications (Procedures and Terms for the Granting of a Satellite Broadcasting License) Regulations 1998, stipulates that an SBL application will be denied if the applicant is affiliated (e.g., controls or holds more than 25% of any means of control) with a national daily newspaper of the publisher thereof.

511. Article 12 SBLReg gives the Minister of Communications the authority to override the mono- and crossmedia ownership limitations in Article 11 in specific cases where the restrictions apply but only because of one entity with a relatively small interest in the applicant and provided that the lenient approach would not severely impair the competition in the multichannel television market. However, this exception shall not apply if the entity is a national daily newspaper.

§4. Restrictions of Board Member Positions

512. Setting aside obligations that may apply due to non-competition clauses or corporate law limitations on multiple memberships of directors and other corporate officers, there are very few specific media-related limitations on board member positions in the media laws.

513. There are two particular exceptions. The first is Article 63 SATRL which stipulates that a person may not hold a position in the news corporations of both commercial channels simultaneously, and seems to apply also to board members. The second exception restricts the granting of an SBL if the applicant is a corporate officer (definition which includes board members) in a CBF holder or an entity which is affiliated with a CBF holder, thereby restricting the ability of board members in commercial television from being interest holders in a satellite multichannel television licensee (Article 11(a)(3) SBLReg).

§5. Restriction of Cooperation Agreements

514. In order to increase the competition in commercial broadcasts, the SATRL (Article 62a) prohibits franchisees from collaborating unless it is specifically allowed by the SAC. The SAC may set rules regarding cooperation among franchisees for the purpose of acquiring foreign programmes (Article 24(a)(11) SATRL). Permission has been given for the purposes of purchasing broadcasting rights for sports events and for the purchase and broadcast of a 'soap opera'/tele-novella series that is broadcasted daily.[269] The latter would be impossible without such a permission because weekdays are divided between the CBF holders.

515. On the other hand, Rule 41 SAFraB foresees predatory competition between the CBF holders and prohibits the CBF holder from acquiring an 'unreasonable amount' of programme broadcasting rights in order to prevent other CBF holders from obtaining these rights. The rule defines 'unreasonable amount' as an amount of programmes that in the opinion of the SATR Director exceeds the ability or the intention of the CBF holder top broadcast. The rule empowers the SATR to prevent the CBF holder from acquiring the excess rights or to order the cancellation of the acquisition *ex post facto.*

516. CRF holders are specifically allowed to cooperate in selling their advertisement time, subject to rules stipulating that the advertisement marketing corporation retained for this purpose by the CRF holders will not held by an advertising agency of any kind (Rule 12g SARaAD) and that the SATR will have the right to inspect the terms of the contract between the CRF holders and the marketing corporation (Rule 12k SARaAD).

517. In the production of local news, a CBL holder (or the independent news producer from which the regional news is acquired by the CBL holder) is prohibited from cooperating with a newspaper, weekly or monthly magazine (Rule 14(c)(4) BCL). According to the rule, the CSBC may authorize an exception provided that the cooperation is not with one of the two largest newspapers or two largest local newspapers chains (or interest holders in these media) and is not the entity in control of the CBL holder.

§6. Transparency Obligations

518. Transparency obligations are mostly directed towards supplying information to the regulatory authorities in order to enable the supervision of ownership restrictions.[270]

269. Karniel, *supra* n. 194, at 73.

270. The shares of HOT were traded in the Tel Aviv Stock Exchange until 2013, which means it was subject to corporate reporting obligations according to the Securities Law, 1968, but now it is a private corporation. YES is a subsidiary of a publicly traded corporation which means some of the

519. Applicants in SATR and CSBC tenders must supply any information required by the tender committee including the financial and equity structures and information concerning holders of more than 5% of the means of control in the applicant (Article 43 SATRL; Article 6(15) Communications Law).

520. The SAC's broad powers include the authority to require information from the broadcasters and it is obliged to publish an annual report on the broadcasters' compliance with their obligations under the SATRL, which may include references to issues of incompliance with ownership restrictions (Article 23(2)(b) SATRL.

521. Incompliance with a demand for information by the SAC or the tender committee could result in the limitation or cancellation of the broadcaster's franchise or license (Article 37(a)(3) SATRL).

522. The CSBC has a similar authority with regards to CBL holders, which it has the power to extend to SBL holders (Article 6(11)(a)(1) and 6(53) Communications Law). There is no specific obligation on the CSBC to publish an annual report to the public however, as an administrative unit of the MOC it is subject to the general FOIL obligations.

523. The Minister of Communications also has the authority to include reporting obligations as part of the conditions for granting a CBL or SBL license (Article 6(9) Communications).

524. In comparison, there are no media-related transparency obligations on newspapers in Israeli law.[271]

§7. Monitoring of Ownership and Pluralism

525. The ownership monitoring mechanism is very similar for commercial channels and for the multichannel platforms, but the normative level of the regulation varies. The commercial channels' monitoring mechanism is set in the SATRL whereas the mechanism for the CBL and SBL holders is stipulated in the license terms.

526. Any transfer of control in the ownership of a commercial channel operator as well as any transfer of more than 10% of the means of control or of the right to appoint at least one director requires the prior authorization of the SAC (Article 36(b) SATRL). Any transfer of 5% or more of the means of control in the commercial channel operator must be reported to the SAC (Article 36(d) SATRL).

financial data about it is available to the public. However, in both cases these reporting obligations concern information relevant to financial investors and not necessarily to media consumers.

271. An attempt to introduce such obligations in a bill failed in 2008. However, Maariv has floated its shares in the Tel Aviv Stock Exchange and therefore it was subject to reporting obligations according to the Securities Law, 1968. It is again a private company as of 2013.

527. The transfer, forfeiture or attachment of a CBL or any of the rights granted as part of the CBL is prohibited (Article 6(10) Communications Law), unless the terms of the CBL specifically derogated from this provision or if the Minister of Communications has given consent. An attachment of the CBL as collateral towards a legally registered bank is allowed, but the a realization of the collateral by the bank may only be done according to instructions given by the Minister of Communications and in a manner that shall not harm the broadcasts (Article 6(10)(3) Communications Law). The same applies to SBLs.

528. The license terms of the cable television provider stipulate that the CSBC must approve in advance any change in the control of a CBL holder, any change in more than 10% of the means of control, or any change that would result in a person becoming an interested party or a party with significant influence in the CBL holder. The license terms also stipulate that any other change in the ownership will be reported to the CSBC, although no prior authorization is required. The license terms of the satellite television provider, YES, stipulates that the Minister of Communications must give prior authorization to any change in the ownership of the SBL holder and that the CSBC will have an advisory role in the minister's decision. The reporting and prior authorization terms are also part of the license terms for special and designated channel licenses.

Part V. Supervision: Media Regulator

Chapter 1. Organization

529. There is no central broadcast media regulator in Israel. The regulatory powers are a dispersed patch-work of legislation, regulation and rules handed down by different regulators empowered through different statutory sources. Aside from the wasteful duplicity of regulatory resources, this structure creates potential and sometimes actual regulatory arbitrage due to the imposition of different rules to the same subject matter or due to the different implementation of identical rules by different regulators. On the other hand, this historical evolution can also be productive if the competition between the regulators turns out to yield improved regulatory mechanisms that are later adopted across the board.

530. The laws regulating commercial broadcast media are characterized by an attempt to outline the general intentions of the legislators in the law itself while giving the regulators the authority to implement policy through rules and regulations. Some rule-making authority is granted to the ministerial level and some is granted to the relevant council overseeing the regulatory authority. Although the line is sometimes blurred, the delineation strives to grant the ministerial level rule-making authority and decision powers in the licensing phase rather than during the oversight of the broadcasting, as well as restricting the authority of the ministerial level to decisions on relatively procedural and financial matters such as the license fees and the tender procedures rather than on matters of content. In comparison, the councils that are supposed to reflect a political, social and cultural balance are empowered to set the rules in more sensitive matters including the choice of broadcasters and the broadcasted content.

531. Commercial television and radio broadcasting is regulated by the SATR, which is a statutory corporation based and seated in Jerusalem (Article 3 and 3a SATRL). The SATR is governed by the SAC which is comprised of 15 public figures appointed by the government at the recommendation of the Minister of Communications after he has consulted with representative cultural, scientific and educational organizations and proposed a list of candidates reflecting the country's social diversity (Article 7 SATRL). The government also elects the chairperson of the SAC from the 15 members (Article 7(a) SATRL).

532. The SAC must convene at least once every two months with a quorum of a majority of its members (Article 17 and 17 SATRL). The SAC's term lasts four years and may be prolonged until a new SAC is appointed. A SAC member can be reappointed for only one additional consecutive term (Article 8 SATRL). SAC members must be Israeli citizens and may not be leading party activists, members of the Knesset, civil servants, employees of the SATR or of broadcasters or persons that may have any other potential conflict of interest with the SAC's authorities, bankrupt or convicted of a felony that involves public disgrace (Article 10 SATRL).

533. The SAC appoints the SATR Director (Article 25 SATRL), who is the SAC's executive arm in performing its tasks (Article 28 SATRL). The SATR Director is appointed for a term of five years that may be prolonged for a second term and with a majority of two thirds of the SAC, for a third term (Article 26 SATRL).

534. The SATR ombudsman, appointed by the Minister of Communications for a term of five years (Article 114 SATRL), is charged with investigating complaints filed by the general public against the broadcasters and against the SATR's performance in its capacity as a broadcast supervisor. The ombudsman submits an annual report to the Minister of Communications and may publish the report to the public (Article 124 SATRL), which is in fact customary.

535. Cable and satellite broadcasts are regulated by the CSBC. The government appoints the CSBC (Article 6(2) Communications Law) which consists of 13 members of whom six are government employees and 7 are public representatives. Three of the government's appointees are recommended by the Minister of Communications and the rest are each recommended by the ministers of culture, justice and finance. The other seven members are public representatives of whom two are recommended by the Local Authorities Center, two represent consumers in the opinion of the Minister of Communications, two represent artists and creators in the opinion of the Minister of Communications and two are recommended by the Minister of Culture to represent bodies in the fields of culture and education. The chairperson of the CSBC is one of the appointees recommended by the Minister of Communications.[272]

536. The members of the CSBC are generally prohibited from attending discussions when personal conflict of interests arises (Article 6(3) Communications Law).

537. The CSBC has an operative arm, the Administration for Regulating Broadcasts to the Public ('ARBP'), established by a government decision from 1997. The ARBP conducts the supervision, enforcement and regulation tasks of the CSBC, including the publication of tenders.[273]

---

272. The complex appointment procedure often means that the CSBC operates with less than thirteen members. For example, in 2010 the council had only ten members. See CSBC Annual Report 2010, at 1.
273. CSBC Annual Report 2010, 6.

538. The Broadcast Coordination Committee ('BCC') is a statutory committee comprised of five representatives, from the IBA, SATR, CSBC, ETV and a chairperson appointed by the government. The BCC acts as the coordinating body between the broadcast regulators and it is set up by Article 111 SATRL. The inclusion of the IBA and especially of the ETV in the committee is problematic as both are broadcasters and the ETV is subject to the regulation of the SATR and the CSBC in some of its broadcasts, thereby creating a potential conflict of interests.

539. In 2012 the Israeli government proposed a bill to unify the CSBC and the SATR into a single regulatory authority. According to the proposal, a new council will be established within the MOC with oversight powers over all types of commercial television and radio broadcasts that will be implemented by the oversight authority. The council will be independent from the government in its decisions. It will be comprised of 10 public representatives and chaired by a civil servant, all of whom will be appointed by the government in an appointment procedure which is similar to the procedure adopted in Amendment 27 IBA Law (discussed *supra*, in paragraphs 208–219). The appointment procedure will thus include checks and balances to guarantee the independence of the council members. The bill is still in an early legislation phase. However, the proposed bill has already received critical attention due to the fact that it proposes to draw the media supervisory authority into the government whereas currently at least the SATR is an external independent authority.

Chapter 2. Tasks

540. The SATR is tasked with granting television and radio broadcast franchises and licenses (Articles 33(a) and 33a SATRL) as well as maintaining and supervising the broadcasts with the purpose of (Article 5 SATRL):

– Promoting Hebrew Israeli creative production.
– Fostering the values of good citizenship, democracy and humanism.
– Expressing Jewish heritage and Zionist values.
– Expressing international culture and civilization.
– Holding Arabic broadcasts for the Arabic speaking population and for the purpose of promoting peace and understanding with the neighbouring countries.
– Giving a suitable representation to the cultural diversity of the different regions of the country, its different forms of settlement, and different views.
– Supplying reliable, fair and balanced information.
– Holding broadcasts in foreign languages for the benefit of new immigrants and tourists.
– Preventing illegal broadcasts and supervising the application of various laws regarding age classification of programmes and the prevention of unlawful advertisements and promos.

541. Although the SATR is charged with maintaining the broadcasts the law states that the financial cost of broadcasting shall be borne by the licensees (Article 6 SATRL).

542. The SAC executes the SATR's tasks, including conducting an annual examination of the licensee's compliance with its obligation under the SATRL, setting the SATR's budget, appointing the SATR representatives in the news corporation's board of directors, setting the broadcasters seasonal broadcasting schedules, determining radio franchise geographical zones, preparing reports to the Minister of Communications and taking any additional decisions required in order to fulfil its tasks (Article 23 SATRL).

543. The SAC has broad rule-making authority with regards to maintaining and supervising broadcasts including the types of broadcasts; criteria for requiring prior approval; broadcast hours and times; the scope, style, content and time of advertisements; local productions; broadcasts in Arabic and other languages; etc. (Article 24(a) SATRL).

544. The CSBC's powers include (Article 6(5) Communications Law):

(a) Setting policy and rules regarding:
   – the types of broadcasts, their topics, quality, content, scope, time, including the approval or cancellation of an entire channel for broadcasting;
   – encouraging community broadcasting;
   – encouraging original local productions;

  - oversight of the broadcasting by CBL holders including the CBL holders' obligations concerning protection of minors, subtitles and sign language, etc.;
  - exclusivity in broadcasting;
  - ethics and consumer protection;

(b) Publishing tenders for CBLs, acting as the deciding committee in these tenders and granting the CBLs.
(c) Setting rules regarding the programming charts of the CBL holders.
(d) Approving cooperation between CBL holders in broadcasting and programming.

545. The Minister of Communications oversees the CSBC and may require it in writing to fulfil its duties within a specified period of time if the minister believes the CSBC has not done so. If the CSBC has not responded, the minister has the authority to disperse the CSBC and act in its stead until a new council is appointed (Article 6(6) Communications Law).

546. The CSBC has the authority to conduct a tender or any other procedure for the purpose of granting CBLs and set the conditions and the provisions of the CBL (Article 6(8) Communications Law), unless the Minister of Communications sets rules regarding the terms of a cable broadcast license, which is in the authority of the minister as long as it is done with the consent of the CSBC (Article 6(9) Communications Law). The Minister of Communications is authorized to set rules regarding (Article 6(9) Communications Law):

- the process of granting a CBL and whether it should be tendered or not;
- the license fee and methods for its payment;
- collateral or guarantees that the CBL holder must provide as a condition for the granting of a CBL;
- prices that the CBL holder may charge from subscribers including a minimum or maximum subscription fee, which must be considered in light of the purpose of promoting competition in broadcast media;
- license terms limiting the transfer or acquisition of the means of control in the CBL or the CBL holder, appointment of officials therein, as well as the obligation of the CBL holder to keep a separate accounting system in order to enable the auditing of its activities;
- the professional know-how and experience available to the CBL holder and its financial ability;
- the region in which the CBL holder must provide its services;
- the length of the CBL term;
- obligations of the CBL holder towards its subscribers and towards other CBL holders.

547. Even if the Minister of Communications has not used the powers to set the abovementioned rules, the law grants the minister an authority to override the CSBC decisions for 'special reasons' and also to add technical requirements to the CBL (Article 6(8)(e) and (f) Communications Law).

548. The CSBC has the authority to determine the channel in which certain broadcasts will be provided (Article 6(21)1 Communications Law). The authority exists with respect to the Knesset channel (broadcasted on Channel 99) the changing of which requires also the consent of the chairperson of the Knesset, broadcasting by the IBA (Channels 11 and 33) the changing of which requires the consent of the Minister of Communications, and by the licensed broadcasters of the SATR (Channels 10 and 22) as well as designated cable channels.

549. Designated CBLs are granted by the CSBC after a tender process (Article 6(24)1 Communications Law) but the Minister of Communications is the regulator charged with setting the tender rules and – with the consent of the Minister of Finance – the royalties to be paid by the licensees (Article 6(24)1(h) Communications Law).

550. Designated cable channels are regulated by the CSBC. However, the Minister of Communications has the authority to decide after consulting with the CSBC and with the approval of the government and the relevant Knesset committee that a designated cable broadcaster shall be allowed to finance its broadcasts through the selling of advertisements (Article 6(24)(a1) Communications Law). Aside from this ministerial authority, Article 6(21)3 of the Communications Law includes an elaborate list of issues regarding which the CSBC is empowered to set rules governing the broadcasts of designated channel broadcasters, including limitations on the transfer of the designated CBL in order to secure multiplicity of broadcasters, language quotas for designated channels in specific languages, separation between advertisements and other content, a minimum 20% local production requirement, etc.

551. The Minister of Communications sets the license fees and royalties paid by CBL holders (Article 6(36) Communications Law).

552. In a 1998 amendment Chapter B2 was added to the Communications Law, regulating satellite broadcasting. The regulatory regime is similar to the regime that applies to CBL holders and the obligations of CBL holders apply, *mutatis mutandis*, to the SBL holders. The primary difference between the regimes is that in Chapter B2 of the Communications Law the SBL is granted by the Minister of Communications rather than the CSBC in the case of CBL and therefore the minister is a far more dominant figure in the process of granting the SBL as compared to the CBL.

553. The CSBC has the authority to set rules imposing obligations that apply to general CBL holders also on SBL holders (Article 6(52) Communications Law). Article 6(57) of the Communications Law extends to SBL holders the CSBC's powers to regulate and set policy as elaborated in chapter B1 of the law with respect to CBL holders. This includes the CSBC's powers to set policy and rules regarding the diversity and the content of broadcasts, the production of local programmes and local news, the production of joint channels with other SBL holders, amendments to SBL terms, curtailing the transfer of an SBL, cancellation or restriction of an

SBL, intervention in the broadcasts for emergency state announcements by the government, prohibition on advertisements, prohibition of broadcasts containing political propaganda or racism or sexual content, and guaranteeing that the license fees and royalties will be directed initially to cover the costs of the CSBC's operations. As with the regulation of cable television, where the CSBC has not acted to set policy or rules according to its authority the Minister of Communications may step in and act in its stead (Article 6(57) in conjunction with 6(38)(b) Communications Law).

554. The Minister of Communications after consulting with the Minister of Finance is empowered to set the license fees and royalties for an SBL (Article 6(56) Communications Law).[274]

555. The tasks of the BCC as the overarching regulatory coordination committee is to limit the acquisition of foreign programmes, to prevent the broadcasting of identical or similar programmes by the various broadcasters including programmes already produced, and any other coordination issues as charged by the government (Article 112 SATRL).

274. There are no royalties as of 2013 and the license fee if paid only once at the issuance of the SBL.

Chapter 3. Sanctioning Powers

556. The regulatory authorities can be said to have four types of sanctions at their disposal: criminal sanctions for severe violations; administrative monetary sanctions for less severe violations; administrative taking of advertisement broadcast time also implemented for less severe violations; and the taking or limiting of a license or a franchise which is an administrative sanction with somewhat harsher implications.

557. Criminal sanctions in media legislation require the filing of a complaint to the police and are therefore imposed only after a lengthy criminal process which is mostly outside the control of the regulatory authorities, whereas administrative sanctions may be imposed by the various regulators themselves.

558. The SATRL criminalizes the following activities:[275]

- Broadcasting without a franchise or a license is punishable by up to three years in prison or a fine of 4.7 million NIS (Article 90 SATRL).
- Advertising, providing an advertisement or paying for an advertisement in a radio station that is not legally licensed or franchised is punishable by up to one year in prison or a fine of 2.35 million NIS (Article 90a SATRL).
- An intentional destruction of broadcasting equipment or prevention of broadcasts is punishable by up to five years in prison (Article 91 SATRL).
- If the SAC decides to hold confidential discussions, then breaching the obligation to maintain confidentiality is a criminal offence punishable by up to one year in prison (Article 93 SATRL).
- Broadcasting legally prohibited broadcasts exposes the broadcaster to a criminal fine whereas the relevant employee breaching the law is exposed to up to one year in prison (Article 95 SATRL).

559. With respect to cable and satellite broadcasting, Article 6(37) Communications Law lists criminal sanctions for incompliance with the law which apply to CBL and SBL holders, and include *inter alia*:

- Broadcasting prohibited content in violation of Article 6(25) Communications Law is a criminal offence punishable by up to three years in prison or a fine of approximately 9 million NIS.
- Preventing or interrupting cable broadcasting is a criminal offence punishable by up to three years in prison.
- Interrupting the legitimate construction, operation or fixing of a cable broadcasting centre is punishable by a fine.
- A court may order the seizure of equipment in the event that a reasonable suspicion is shown that such equipment is used in order to conduct unlicensed broadcasting.

275. The sanctions apply to a broadcaster or the organs of the broadcaster in the event that the broadcaster is a corporation (Art. 98 SATRL).

- Assisting unlicensed broadcasting is punishable by up to six months in prison or a maximum fine of approximately 1 million NIS. Assistance includes technical support, financial support, participation in production, supplying advertisements or broadcasts or news, etc.

560. Considering the need to react effectively and swiftly to incompliance in broadcasts, administrative sanctions are a far more useful regulatory stick as compared to criminal proceedings.

561. For the commercial channels, the administrative sanctioning regime is prescribed in the SATR (Taking of Broadcast Time) Rules 2007 ('The SATak Rules'),[276] which defines a 'breaching broadcast' as any broadcast contrary to SATR Rules or franchise terms (Rule 1 SATak). The implementation of the sanction regime is vested with the SATR Director who has the authority to inform the CBF holder that a breach has been found. The CBF holder may object in writing within seven days (Rule 2 SATak).

562. The SATR administrative sanction regime is based on the taking of broadcast time from the breaching broadcaster. The SATak Rules are relatively tough in the sense that they define that the length of a breach will be the entire length of a breaching programme or a breaching advertisement unless the breaching part of a programme can be separated completely from the rest of the programme (Rule 3(a) SATak). The SATR Director may inflict a sanction of taking advertisement time or any other broadcasting time, as deemed fit (Rule 4 SATak).

563. The SATak Rules contains an internal appeal process which is designed to be relatively speedy. The CBF holder may apply to the SATR Director for a review of the sanction (Rule 5 SATak), and most decisions may also be appealed before an appeal committee comprised of three members of the SAC (Rule 5a SATak). As the SAC is an administrative regulatory authority the sanctioned CRF holder may eventually petition the administrative court to set the sanction aside.

564. The SATR may use the taken broadcast time immediately or aggregate it for its own broadcasts, during which the CBF holder will not be allowed to broadcast advertisements (Rule 9 SATak).

565. It should be noted that the rules also authorize the SATR Director to intervene immediately, in real time, and stop a broadcast which is legally prohibited, on top of the authority to sanction the CBF holder by taking away broadcast time for the said breach (Rule 8 SATak). We do not know of an occasion in which this authority has been implemented in such a manner. However, in 2013 the SATR obliged one CBF holder to refrain from broadcasting a whole season of morning lifestyle magazine after the SATR Director found that it violated the prohibition against product placement.

276. Promulgated in accordance with the power of the SATR to take broadcast time in Art. 49 SATRL.

566. Additionally, the CBF terms empower the SATR to inflict administrative monetary sanctions on the CBF holders for breaching their obligations.[277]

567. The Communications Law includes an administrative monetary sanctions regime which allows the general director of the MOC to impose a monetary sanction on a CBL or SBL holder when there exists reasonable evidence of incompliance with rules or instructions set forth by the Minister of Communications whereas in matters that are regulated by the CSBC, the authority to impose the sanction lies with the chairperson of the CSBC (Article 37b1 Communications Law).

568. With respect to designated channels that are permitted to broadcast advertisements, in case of incompliance with CSBC's rules, the CSBC is empowered to sanction a designated channel broadcaster by deducting one minute of commercial time for every minute of incompliance with the CSBC's rules or the broadcasting of prohibited broadcasts such as racial incitement or pornography (Article 6(34)2 Communications Law).

569. The power to revoke, restrict or curtail a CBF or a commercial broadcast license is vested with the SATR according to Article 37(a) SATRL which stipulates that the SATR shall be empowered to do so (after allowing the broadcaster the opportunity to object) if the broadcaster:

- Violated the SATRL or rules or regulations thereof which is sufficiently severe to justify the sanction.
- Violated Articles 36 (transfer of ownership), 46 (relating to prohibited broadcasts such incitement to racism) or failed to transfer funds to the SATR for the erection of digital transmission stations.
- Violated disclosure obligations at the tender stage or afterwards.
- Violated a material condition of the franchise or the license.
- No longer fulfils the conditions that were required in order to apply for the franchise or the license.
- Did not start broadcasting or stopped broadcasting for an unreasonable period of time.
- Requested to nullify its license or franchise.
- Should have its license or franchise revoked for reasons of public good, in the opinion of two thirds of the members of the SAC.

570. The power to revoke or limit a CBL or SBL is vested with the CSBC after allowing the CBL holder a prior hearing (Article 6(11) Communications Law). The CBL may be revoked or limited in the following instances[278]:

277. In HCJ 5872/07 *The Israeli Film and Television Producers Association v. The SATR* (2010) the court denied the CRF holders' assertion that the SATR may not impose monetary sanction and pointed out that the SATR is also empowered to forfeit financial guarantees in that context.
278. The CSBC's authority is extended to SBL holders (Art. 6(52) Communications Law).

- The CBL holder did not provide required information or provided false information to the Minister of Communications, the CSBC or the tender committee.
- The CBL holder failed to abide by the provisions of the relevant chapter (Chapter B1) of the Communications Law or its pursuant regulations or rules.
- The CBL holder breached a material provision of the CBL.
- The CBL holder breached an immaterial provision of the CBL but has not corrected the breach after being informed of the obligation to correct it by the Minister of Communications or the CSBC.
- The CBL holder did not start its broadcasting during a reasonable period of time or stopped broadcasting for an unreasonable period of time.
- One or more of the conditions qualifying a CBL holder ceased to exist.
- The CBL holder died, was declared legally incapable or bankrupt and if the CBL holder is a corporation it was appointed a receiver or given a dissolution order, or voluntarily dissolved itself.
- The CBL holder requested the cancellation of the CBL.

571. The Minister of Communications has the power to regulate or give orders with regards to guaranteeing continued broadcasting in the event that a CBL is revoked or limited, including the appointment of a trustee to take over the management of the CBL. In fact, the license of an already broadcasting channel has never been revoked. The only cases in which licenses have been revoked occurred after designated channels failed to launch. This occurred twice in 2004. The license granted to cable news channel licensee '*Hadshot Israel*' (Israel News) was revoked after the channel failed to launch its broadcasts two years after the license had been granted. Similarly, the license granted to the Israel History Channel was revoked that year six months after it had been granted.

Selected Bibliography

§1. ENGLISH

I. Books and Articles

Avrahami, Eli & First, Anat. 'Can a Regulator Change Representation of Minority Groups and Fair Reflection of Cultural Diversity in National Media Programs? Lessons From Israel', *Journal of Broadcasting & Electronic Media* 54 (2010): 136.

Ben-Zvi, Abraham. 'The Limits of Israel's Democracy in the Shadow of Security'. *Taiwan Journal of Democracy* 1 (2005): 1–23.

Birnhack, Michael & Elkin-Koren, Niva. 'Does Law Matter Online? Empirical Evidence on Privacy Law Compliance'. *Mich. Telecomm. Tech. L Rev.* 17 (2011): 337.

Budde, Paul.*Middle East – Telecoms, Mobile & Broadband in the Mediterranean & Levant Countries* (2008).

Carmi, Guy E. '"Dignitizing" Free Speech in Israel: The Impact of the Constitutional Revolution on Free Speech Protection'. *McGill Law Journal* 57 (2012).

Caspi, Dan. 'Israel: Media System'. *The International Encyclopedia of Communication* (2008).

Cohen-Almagor, Raphael. 'The Press Council'. *Israel Affairs* 11 (2005): 445.

Cohen-Almagor, Raphael. 'Regulating Hate and Racial Speech in Israel'. *Cardozo J. of Int'l. & Comp. L.* 17 (2009): 405.

Gilboa, Eytan. 'The Evolution of Israeli Media'. *Middle East Review of International Affairs* 12 (2008): 88.

Jamal, Amal. *The Arab Public Sphere in Israel: Media Space and Cultural Resistance* (2009).

Karniel, Yuval. 'Defamation on the Internet - A New Approach to Libel in Cyberspace'. *Journal of International Media & Entertainment Law* 2 (2009): 215.

Karniel, Yuval & Lavie-Dinur, Amit. '2006 Elections in Israel: Marking the End of an Era for the Controlled Televised Election Campaign Broadcast'. *Journal Media and Communication Studies* 2 (2010): 29.

Karniel, Yuval & Lavie-Dinur, Amit. 'Entertainment and Stereotype: Representation of the Palestinian Arab Citizens of Israel in Reality Shows on Israeli Television'. *Journal of Intercultural Communication Research* 40 (2011): 65.

Katz, Yaron. 'The "Other Media" – Alternative Communications in Israel'. *International Journal of Cultural Studies* 10 (2007): 383.

Katz, Yaron. 'Protecting Local Culture in a Global Environment: The Case of Israel's Broadcast Media'. *International Journal of Communication* 3 (2009): 332.

Limor, Yehiel & Gable, Ines. 'Five Versions of One Code of Ethics: The Case Study of the Israel Broadcasting Authority'. *Journal of Mass Media Ethics: Exploring Questions of Media Morality* 17 (2002): 136.

Limor, Yehiel. 'Journalism and Moonlighting: An International Comparison of 242 Codes of Ethics', *Journal of Mass Media* 21 (2006): 265.

Meyers, Oren. 'Israeli Journalism During the State's Formative Era: Between Ideological Affiliation and Professional Consciousness'. *Journalism History* 31 (2005): 88.

Nossek, Hillel & Limor, Yehiel. 'Fifty Years in a "Marriage Of Convenience": News Media and Military Censorship in Israel'. *Communication Law & Policy* 26 (2001): 1.

Nossek, Hillel. 'The Israeli Paradox: The Military Censorship as a Protector of the Freedom of the Press'. *Research in Social Problems and Public Policy* 103 (2011).

Peled, Roy & Rabin, Yoram. 'The Constitutional Right to Information'. *Colum. Hum. Rts. L. Rev.* 42 (2011): 357.

Schejter, Amit M. 'The Fairness Doctrine Is Dead and Living in Israel'. *Fed. Comm. L. J.* 51 (1999): 281.

Schejter, Amit M. 'The People Shall Dwell Alone: The Effect of Transfrontier Broadcasting on Freedom of Speech and Information in Israel'. *N.C.J. Int'l L. & Com. Reg.* 31 (2005): 337.

Schejter, Amit M. 'The Stranger That Dwelleth with You Shall Be unto You as One Born among You – Israeli Media Law and the Cultural Rights of the "Palestinian-Israeli" Minority'. *Middle East Journal of Culture & Communication* 1 (2008): 156.

Schejter, Amit M. *Muting Israeli Democracy* (2009).

Schejter, Amit M. & Yemini, Moran. 'Eyes Have They, But They See Not': Israeli Election Laws, Freedom of Expression and the Need for Transparent Speech'. 14 *Comm. L. & Pol'y* (2009): 411.

Shamir, Jacob. 'Israeli Elite Journalists: Views on Freedom and Responsibility'. *Journalism & Mass Communication Quarterly* 65 (1988): 589.

Shetreet, Shimon (ed.). *Free Speech and National Security* (1991).

Zandberg, Eyal. 'The Right to Tell the (Right) Story: Journalism, Authority and Memory'. *Media, Culture & Society* 32 (2010): 5.

Zandberg, Eyal & Neiger, Motti. 'Between the Nation and the Profession: Journalists as Members of Contradicting Communities'. *Media, Culture & Society* 27 (2005): 131.

II. Electronic Sources

Banisar, David. *Freedom of Information Around the World* (2006). www.civicus.org/new/media/global_survey2006.pdf.

Fries, Todd Harris. *The Law of Defamation in Israel - A Comparative Study*. http://toddharrisfries.weebly.com/uploads/5/1/9/9/5199097/the_law_of_defamation_in_israel_-_a_comparative_study.pdf.

Gentile, Carlo. *Media Landscape* (2010). www.ejc.net/media_landscape/article/israel/.

Gidron, Tamar. *Publication of Private Information: An Examination of the Right to Privacy from a Comparative Perspective* (2009). http://papers.ssrn.com/sol3/papers.cfm?abstract_id=1422525.

Lehman, E. & Limor, Y. *The 'Right to Reply' in Journalistic Ethics: The Case Study of the Ruling by the Israel Press Council*, Paper presented at the annual meeting of the International Communication Association, Dresden International Congress Centre, Dresden, Germany Online. 2009-05-25 (2009). http://citation.allacademic.com/meta/p_mla_apa_research_citation/0/9/0/9/6/pages 90962/p90962-1.php.

Limor, Yehiel. *The Printed Media: Israel's Newspapers* (2010). www.mfa.gov.il/MFA/Facts%20About%20Israel/Culture/The%20Printed%20Media-%20Israel-s%20Newspapers.

Rabina, Debbie L. *Access to Government Information in Israel: Stages in the Continuing Development of a National Information Policy, in* 66th IFLA Council and General Conference. http://archive.ifla.org/IV/ifla66/papers/018-160e.html.

Widlanski, Michael. *The Media in Israel* (2009). www.jewishvirtuallibrary.org/jsource/isdf/text/widlanski.html.

§2. Hebrew

I. Books and Articles

Arbel, Yonatan & Schwartz Altshuler, Tehilla. *Information Wants to Be Free: Implementing the Freedom of Information Act in Israel*. (2008): 23–47.

Altschuler, Tehilla Schwartz (ed.). *Online Newspapers in Israel* (2007).

Arian, Asher, Ben-Nun, Pazit, Barnea, Shlomit & Tsfati, Yariv. *The Media and Israeli Democracy: A Variety of Vantage Points Auditing Israeli Democracy* (2005).

Barak, Aharon. 'Freedom of Expression and its Limits'. *HaPraklit* 40 (1991): 5.

Barak, Daphne. 'Freedom of Access to the Media: A Balance of Interests within the Right to Freedom of Expression'. *Iyunei Mishpat* 12 (1987): 183.

Birnhack, Michael. *Private Space: The Right to Privacy between Law and Technology* (2010).

Birnhack Michael (ed.). *Be Quiet, Someone is Speaking!* (2012).

Dill, Sigalit & Natanzon, Orli. *Freedom of expression in the Media: Defamation Law – Case Law and Commentary* (2005).

Ezrahi, Yaron, Ben-Shachar, Omri & Lael, Rachel. *Reform in the Public Broadcasting and ways to cope with the Dangers Lurking for the Public Broadcasting in the Israeli Democracy* (1997).

Ezrahi, Yaron, Goshen, Zohar & Comaneshther, Hanny. *Multi-Channel Television in Israel: The Public Aspect* (2001).

Selected Bibliography

Ezrahi,Yaron, Goshen, Zohar & Leshem Shmuel. *Cross Ownership: Control and Competition in the Israeli Media - Economic and Legal Aspects and the Impact on the Israeli Democracy* (2003).

Ghanayim, Khalid, Kremnitzer, Mordechai & Shnoor, Boaz. *Libel Law: De Lege Lata and de Lege Ferenda* (2005).

Hammer, Yoav. 'Local Culture, Minority Cultures and the Law: Regulation of Television and Radio Content in Israel'. *Mishpat Umimshal* 14 (2012): 149.

Karniel, Yuval. *Commercial Media Law* (2003).

Negbi, Moshe. *Freedom of the Journalist and Freedom of the Press - Media Law and Ethics* (2011).

Pessach, Guy. 'Broadcasting Rights'. *Hamishpat* 10 (2005): 131.

Ronen, David. *Censorship Law: The Media, Freedom of Expression and National Security* (2011).

Rubinstein, Amnon and Medina, Barak. *The Constitutional Law of the State of Israel* (5th Ed., 1998).

Rubinstein, Elyakim. 'On Freedom of Expression and the Policy of the Prosecution in Incitement to Violence Offences'. *HaPraklit* 44 (1998): 5.

Segev, Reem. *Freedom of Expression: Justifications and Restrictions* (2008).

Shenhar, Ori. *The Law of Defamation* (1997).

Tal, Yizhar & Ivri-Omer, Dina. *Regulation of Electronic Services in Israel: The Need to Establish a Communications Authority* (2009).

Sommer, Hillel, Adar, Dan & Aliman, Amit. *The constitutional Right to Freedom of Information* (2005).

Zilberschatz, Yafa. 'On the Freedom of Commercial Speech'. *Mishpat Umimshal* 3 (2005): 509.

Index

The numbers refers to the paragraph numbers

Index

www.ingramcontent.com/pod-product-compliance
Lightning Source LLC
Chambersburg PA
CBHW071339230926
51846CB00002B/393
9789041151797